Negative Space

PRAEGER FILM BOOKS

Advisory Editor: Annette Michelson

NEGATIVE SPACE

Manny Farber on the Movies

PRAEGER PUBLISHERS
New York · Washington

Grateful acknowledgment is made for permission to reprint the following articles. Original titles, where different from those used in this volume, are given in parenthesis.

"The Gimp" ("Movies Aren't Movies Anymore"), "Underground Films," "The Decline of the Actor" ("The Fading Movie Star") : reprinted from *Commentary* by permission; copyright © 1952, 1957, 1963, by the American Jewish Committee.

"White Elephant Art vs. Termite Art": reprinted from *Film Culture* magazine with permission.

"Preston Sturges: Success in the Movies": reprinted from *City Lights*, 1954, with permission.

"Rain in the Face, Dry Gulch, and Squalling Mouth," "Day of the Lesteroid," "The Cold That Came into *The Spy*," "Pish-Tush": reprinted from *Cavalier* magazine with permission.

"Short and Happy": reprinted by permission of *The New Republic*, © 1951, Harrison-Blaine, of New Jersey, Inc.

"Nearer My Agee to Thee": reprinted from the *New Leader* with permission.

"Blame the Audience": © Commonweal Publishing Co., Inc.

"*Home of the Brave*," a section of "Parade Floats" ("*The Quiet Man*"), "*The Third Man*," "*Detective Story*," "*In the Street*," "John Huston," "Val Lewton," "Frank Capra," " 'Best Films' of 1951," "Ugly Spotting," "Fight Films": reprinted from *The Nation*, 1949, 1950, 1951, 1952, with permission.

"Hard-Sell Cinema": reprinted from *Perspectives*, 1957.

The following appeared as untitled film reviews in *Artforum*: "The Subverters" (Dec. 1966), New York Film Festival essays (Nov. 1967; Nov. 1968; Dec. 1968; Nov. 1969), "Cartooned Hip Acting" (Dec. 1967), "*How I Won the War*" (Jan. 1968), "Experimental Films" (Feb. 1968), "One-to-One" (March 1968), "*La Chinoise*" (Summer 1968), "*Belle de Jour*" (Summer 1968), "Carbonated Dyspepsia" (Sept. 1968), "Jean-Luc Godard" (Oct. 1968), "Canadian Underground," (Jan. 1969), "*Shame*," (Feb. 1969), "Howard Hawks" (April 1969), the second section of "Parade Floats" (May 1969), "Luis Buñuel" (Summer 1969), "Samuel Fuller," (Sept. 1969), "Don Seigel" (Dec. 1969), "Michael Snow" (Jan. 1970) : reprinted from *Artforum* with permission.

BOOKS THAT MATTER

Published in the United States of America in 1971
by Praeger Publishers, Inc.
111 Fourth Avenue, New York, N.Y. 10003

© 1971 by Manny Farber

Library of Congress Catalog Card Number: 72–101659

Printed in the United States of America

This book is dedicated to the New Yorker Theater,
where the movie sometimes equals the grace and style of
the theater's staff: Dan, José, Frank, and Dan's mother-in-law.

This particular path of criticism is strewn with victims of my deadline miseries. Those who have bled most profusely over the years deserve more than this tepid recognition. From the present, going back in time, I am extremely grateful to an army: Patricia Patterson, Gregory Ford, his mother, Donald Phelps (night and day), Duncan Shepherd, Phil Leider, John Hochmann, Marjorie Farber, Marsha Picker, Jerry Tallmer, Virginia Admiral, Margaret Marshall, Janet Richards, Betty Huling, and, for special assistance, Pauline Kael, Annette Michelson, and the Guggenheim Foundation.

CONTENTS

Negative Space

INTRODUCTION

Space is the most dramatic stylistic entity—from Giotto to Noland, from *Intolerance* to *Weekend*. How an artist deploys his space, seldom discussed in film criticism but already a tiresome word of the moment in other art, is anathema to newspaper editors, who believe readers die like flies at the sight of esthetic terminology.

If there were a textbook on film space, it would read: "There are several types of movie space, the three most important being: (1) the field of the screen, (2) the psychological space of the actor, and (3) the area of experience and geography that the film covers." Bresson deals in shallow composition as predictable as a monk's tonsure, whereas Godard is a stunning de Stijlist using cutout figures of American flag colors asymmetrically placed against a flat white background. The frame of *The Wild Bunch* is a window into deep, wide, rolling, Baroque space; almost every shot is a long horizontal crowded with garrulous animality.

Jeanne Moreau, always a resentful wailing wall, works in a large space, which becomes empty as she devastates it with scorn. Ida Lupino, an unforgettable drifter in a likable antique, *High Sierra* (1941), works close and guardedly to the camera, her early existentialist-heroine role held to size: she's very unglorious, has her place, and, retracting into herself, steals scenes from Bogart at his most touching. Whereas Moreau is a sensibility ember burning from beginning to movie's end—there's no specific woman inside all the emotion—and Lupino is a specific woman in a cliché pushed-around-gal role, Laurence Olivier's Archie Rice is a specific man as well as a flamboyant type. In the *Entertainer* role, which is part burlesque and part pathos, he works from small nuances of exchange with his daughter to broad gestures, while brazening his way through cheap, humiliating skirmishes with his creditors.

One curious fact about 1969 acting—Jane Fonda's jugular wisecracker silencing everybody in *They Shoot Horses, Don't They?*, Michel Bouquet's meek-murderous husband trying to hold his domestic status quo in *La Femme Infidèle*, a gentle

3

Black Girl performance that goes from glee to silent misery and is very much like sleepwalking—is that it inhabits a much smaller space than the ballroom-museum-golf-course that Katherine Hepburn treats as her oyster in *Bringing up Baby*. The attitude is all different from Hepburn's egotistical-bitchy "Oh, Davids!" Both Audran (*Infidèle*) and Jane Fonda appear to own every inch of a small principality that extends about six inches to any side of their bodies, and anything else on the horizon is uncontrollable, unattainable, and therefore hardly concerns them. Where Roz Russell in *His Girl Friday* and Hepburn are swashbucklers running everyone in sight, particularly men, Audran's skillful niggling act of undulating sensuality or Fonda's stubborn life-loathing is very inside, grudging, thoughtful, always faced toward the situation—nothing escapes their suspicious cool observance. It is heroic acting, but it is also enclosed, inclement, and battle ready.

Since the days when Lauren Bacall could sweep into a totally new locale and lay claim to a shamus's sleazy office, a world in which so much can be psychically analyzed and criticized through the new complex stare technique has practically shrunk to nothing in terms of the territory in which the actor can physically prove and/or be himself. In pre-1960's acting, a Bogart could swing in indeterminate space: his selfless hurt dignity overpowered, practically ran kingdoms set up quickly, half-authentically, across the U.S., in *High Sierra*. The solid thing about Trintignant in Rohmer's *Chez Maud* is that he's incapacitated, on guard, defensive, in a sexy divorcée's threatening living room. Delphine Seyrig, an elegant blonde wife of a shoe-store owner in *Stolen Kisses*, enforces this same restricted psychology. Guarded, knowing, exact estimations are going on all the time: she's very aware where she's at, a middle-aged beauty unable to sustain a shoe-clerk's dream of her for more than an afternoon. She knows exactly how much she can commit herself.

Because it's the uniting style plus the basic look of a film, the third kind of space controls everything else—acting, pace, costume. In *La Femme Infidèle*, Chabrol's completely controlled horizontal moves—arch and languorous, picking up an insurance exec's paralyzed existence of posh domesticity—set the tone, almost blueprint the way actors eat, like a paper cutout family, the distanced politeness of their talk. *Virginia Woolf*, an American marriage of 1960, seen for all its vicious, despairing, negating features, is middle-aged academe flagellating in a big, hollow, theatrical space. The George-Martha shenanigans, hokey and virulent, are designed, grand-opera-style, as though the curtain were going up or down on every declamation. *In a Lonely Place*, a 1950 Nick Ray, is a Hollywood scene at its most lackluster, toned down, limpid, with Ray's keynote strangeness: a sprawling, unbent composition with somewhat dwarfed characters, each going his own way. A conventional studio movie but very nice: Ray stages everything, in scenes heavily involved with rules of behavior, like a bridge game amongst good friends, no apparent sweat. A sad piece of puff pastry, Demy's *Model Shop* (1969) comes together in a lazy open space: overblown, no proportions, skittering, indulgent. The scene is an absolutely transient one—drive-in bank, rock and roll group, J. C. Penney houses—that saunters lackadaisically in the most formless imagery. *The Round Up* (1966), a stark overhead lighting from beginning to end, geometric shadows, hard peasant faces, stiff coats, bit sculpture hats, is a movie of hieratic stylized movement in a Kafka space that is mostly sinister flatness and bald verticals. Sometimes there is violent action, but Jancso's fascinating, but too insistent, style is based on a taut balance between a harsh, stark imagery and a desolate pessimism. In all the movies mentioned here, the space is most absolutely controlled, given over to rigidly patterned male groups.

The emphasis being given to space by today's leading directors forces a look backward at what has been done in movie space. In *What Price Glory?* (1926), space is used innocently for illustrational purposes, which is not to say that it isn't used well. Raoul Walsh's film is still an air-filled, lyrical masterpiece: the haphazard, unprecious careers of two blustery rivals who swagger around trench and village exquisitely scaled in human terms to the frame of the screen, suggesting, in their unhesitating grace, the sweet-tough-earthy feeling that is a Walsh trademark. This is a very early example of Walsh's special aptitude, getting people from place to place gracefully, giving an enchantment to bistro or barracks through repetitions in which the engineering slightly alters each trip, jump-cutting his movie into and out of events with unabashed shorthand and beautiful detail.

Whereas Walsh bends atmosphere, changes camera, singles out changes in viewpoint to give a deeper reaction to specific places, *The Big Sleep* (1948) ignores all the conventions of a gangster film to feast on meaningless business and witty asides. Walsh keeps re-establishing the same cabin retreat; Hawks, in another spatial gem, gives the spectator *just enough* to make the scene work. One of the fine moments in 1940's film is no longer than a blink: Bogart, as he crosses the street from one bookstore to another, looks up at a sign. There is as much charm here as Walsh manages with fifteen different positioning setups between Lupino and Arthur Kennedy in a motel cabin. All the unbelievable events in *The Big Sleep* are tied together by miserable time jumps, but, within each skit, there is a logic of space, a great idea of personality, gesture, where each person is. Bogart's sticking shirt and brain-twisting in front of a princely colonel, which seems to have present-tense quality, is typically out of touch with other events and probably dropped into its slot from a facetious memory of Faulkner.

Touch of Evil (1958) is about many things: murder, gang rape (an American blonde marries a Mexican attorney, and all her fears about Mexicans come true), a diabolic sheriff, and a dozen other repellent figures. Basically it's a movie about terrorizing, an evil-smelling good movie in which the wildly Baroque terror and menace is another world from Hawks-Walsh: an aggressive-dynamic-robust-excessive-silly universe with Welles's career-long theme (the corruption of the not-so-innocent Everyman through wealth and power) and his inevitable efforts with space —to make it prismatic and a quagmire at the same time. Welles's storm tunnel has always the sense of a black prankster in control of the melodrama, using a low-angle camera, quack types as repulsive as Fellini's, and high-contrast night light to create a dank, shadowy, nightmare space.

Basically the best movie of Welles's cruddy middle peak period—when he created more designed, less-dependent-on-Hollywood films (*Arkadin, Lady from Shanghai*)—*Touch of Evil* is

a sexual allegory, the haves and have-nots, in which the dis-
orienting space is worked for character rather than geography.
An amazing film, the endless bits of excruciating black humor are
mostly involved with illogical space and movement, pointing up
some case of impotence or occasionally its opposite. A young
Mexican lawyer jumps around jack-rabbit fashion while a toad-
like sheriff floats away in grease; a whacky episode has the lawyer
stuffing an elevator with old colleagues while he zips up the stairs
(''Well, Vargas, you're pretty light on your feet''). The funniest
scenes, spatially, revolve around a great comic grotesque played
by Dennis Weaver, a motel night man messed up with tics who is
last seen clinging to a leafless tree, and, before that, doing wood-
pecker spastic effects at the sight and thought of Janet Leigh on a
motel bed.

His allegorical space is a mixture of tricks, disorientation,
falling apart, grotesque portraits. A deaf-mute grocery clerk
squints in the foreground, while Charlton Heston, on the phone,
embarrassed over his wife's eroticism from a motel bed, tries
to suggest nonchalance to the store owner. A five-minute street
panorama develops logically behind the credits, without one cut,
just to arrive at a spectacular reverse zoom away from a bombed
Cadillac. Just before the car goes up in fire, the car's blonde
has given a customs agent one of those black speeches that dis-
locate themselves from the image: ''I've got this ticking noise
in my head.''

Those who blew their cool in the 1960's were shipwrecked on
spatial problems, among other things. So much is possible or
acceptable in photography-acting-writing now that films expand
with flashy camera work, jazzy heat flutters, syrupy folk music, different projection speeds, and a laxity about the final form
that any scene takes. *The Gypsy Moths; Goodbye, Columbus;
The Arrangement; The Swimmer; The Graduate; Pretty Poison*
are caked with glamour mechanisms.

Winning and Polonsky's *Willie Boy* seem the perfect examples; the former an auto-racing film with no action, but inflated
with slow motion, slight and oblique acting, a leaky savvy about
marital dalliance, and the latter a racial Western with affected
photography and ambiguous motivation. Though there is smug-

ness, neither film comes to a head, because of the vague, approximate way in which events are shown, the confusion about being spatially sophisticated.

Polonsky's invective against the crushing of the Paiutes, a disappointing but hardly loathsome movie, loses itself behind the unwieldiness of the very wide scenes. There's a fiesta going on at Willie's reservation, and the point of any shot is gracefully ignored while a lyrical snowstorm of camera shots occurs. In a scene of big heads and upper torsos, an interesting crowd of Indians are involved in something interesting, but what is seen is tinted coloring and Willie, a heavy jerky wave moving through a crowd of shoulders and hats. Seen between two of the sententiously parted shoulders is Willie's Lola, an ambiguous solitary gardenia in an otherwise maidenless tribe. The movie implies no Indians can act: Katharine Ross is the only Paiute maid, and the only actual Indians are bit players.

A film cannot exist outside of its spatial form. Everything in a good movie is of a piece: Joe Calleia, scared out of his wits, is a grey little bureaucrat fitted perfectly into *Touch of Evil* with the sinister lighting and tilted scenes in which he's found, buglike at the end of hallways and rooms. Godard doesn't start a project until it is very defined in its use of space: *La Chinoise* is an indoor picture with primary colors to look like Maoist posters and stiltlike, declamatory actors to go with a didactic message. Space seems so dramatic and variable in *Weekend* (1968); this exciting shake-up movie is made up in progressive segments, each one having a different stylistic format, from the fixed camera close-up of a comic-porno episode ("... and then she sat in a saucer of milk ...") through the very Hawkslike eye-level dollying past a bumper-to-bumper tie-up on the highway, to the Hudson River pastoralism at the end, when Godard clinches his idea of a degenerate, cannibalistic society and a formless, falling-apart culture. At least half the moviemakers are oblivious to the space excitement that is front-center in *Weekend*; the other half are flying off in all directions.

It's very exciting to see the stylistic unity that goes into *Weekend* or *Fellini Satyricon*, where a stubborn artist is totally committed to bringing an idea together with an image. After a whole year of varied films, it's pertinent that *Weekend* seems to increase in resonance. These hopped-up nuts wandering in an Everglades, drumming along the Mohawk, something about *Light in August*, a funny section where Anne Wiazemsky is just sitting in grass, thumb in mouth, reading a book. Compared to the podium-locked image of *They Shoot Horses, Weekend* is a rambling mystery not unlike the long, knotted tail swirling under an old dime-store kite.

What does one get from the vast sprawl of film reviewed in this book? That the spatial threads seamlessly knit together for the illustrative naturalism that serviced Keaton's *Navigator* through *Red River* simply broke apart. When the 1960's directors became fascinated with the formal excitements that could be gotten through manipulation of space, each film became a singleminded excavation in a particular type of space. Pasolini, in *Teorema*, places the figure as though it were sculpture in deep space. His movie becomes an ecstatic, mystical, hortatory use of mid-anatomy: Terence Stamp, languid silence and superior smile, his crotch exposed in tight, spiffy jeans, exuding compassion for all the flipping-out individuals around him. From *Breathless* through *Teorema*, the path is strewn with singularized vocabulary. *L'Avventura* is like a long serpentine through desolate environments: the human figure isolated, posing in a vast, anonymous, sinister space. Godard's career, a movie-by-movie exploration of one image or another, always involves a philosophical proposition matched by a pictorial concept, i.e., an unraveled bleak image serves as a metaphor for the brutalizing, rag-tag conditions of war.

Most of what follows involves a struggle to remain faithful to the transitory, multisuggestive complication of a movie image and/or negative space. Negative space, the command of experience which an artist can set resonating within a film, is a sense of terrain created partly by the audience's imagination and partly by camera-actors-director: in *Alexander Nevsky*: the feeling of endless, glacial landscape formed by glimpses of frozen flatness expanded by the emotional interplay of huge-seeming people. Negative space assumes the director testing himself as an intelligence against what appears on screen, so that there is a murmur of poetic action enlarging the terrain of the film, giving the scene an extra-objective breadth. It has to do with flux, movement, and air; always the sense of an artist knowing where he's at: a movie filled with negative space is always a textural work throbbing with acuity.

Criticism can subjugate the bestiality of the screen image by breaking it down into arbitrary but easily managed elements—acting, story logic, reasonableness, the identifiable touches of a director—that bring the movie within the doctoring talents of the critic. Suggesting where a film went wrong and how it could have had the logic of an old-style novel or theater piece seems a pedantic occupation compared to the activity in modern film, which suggests a thousand Dick Cantino accordionists in frenetic action, heaving and hawling, contracting and expanding. Because the space in film has been wildly and ingenuously singularized into cool (*Judex*), charted (*Rio Grande*), schematized (*Pickpocket*), jagged (*M*), or graceful (Satyajit Ray's *Two Daughters*), it doesn't seem right that the areas for criticism should be given over so completely to measuring.

Most of what I liked is in the termite area. The important trait of termite-fungus-centipede art is an ambulatory creation which is an act both of observing and being in the world, a journeying in which the artist seems to be ingesting both the material of his art and the outside world through a horizontal coverage. The Senegalese *Black Girl* is a series of spiritual odysseys: through a kitchen; a ceremonial procedure before the bathtub suicide; a small boy, holding an African mask over his face, following his sister's employer across Dakar; in which the imagination of Ousmane Sembene appears to be covering all the ground that his experience can encompass. *La Femme Infidèle* is often antitermite in its backward idolatry of the Hitchcock murder plot and old-movie formulas for showing cuckoldry, lustfulness, the way a sheet-wrapped body sinks in pod-covered water. Aside from its central murder-cops plotting, the movie is quite different when the material gets into straight business-living and the acting, Chabrol's strong suit in this film, becomes mobile, whether anyone's moving or not, charged with watchfulness, frankness, purity. The measured flow that Chabrol has perfected—a world of forms observed, acts performed without flubs or awkwardness—is hypnotic, suggesting the tension of an embarrassed subordinate saying yes-sir-no-sir, getting his drama through the pasty, worried heaviness of an unblinking face.

It is not likely that any esthetic system can enclose all the art ever made—fetishistic, religious, decorative, children's, absurdist, primitive. Why even invent two such categories: white elephant and termite, one tied to the realm of celebrity and affluence and the other burrowing into the nether world of privacy? The primary reason for the two categories is that all the directors I like—Fuller's *art brut* styling; Chuck Jones's *Roadrunners;* the inclement charm Godard gets with drizzly weather, the Paris outskirts, and three nuts scurrying around the same overcast *Band of Outsiders* terrain—are in the termite range, and no one speaks about them for the qualities I like.

UNDERGROUND FILMS 1957

The saddest thing in current films is watching the long-neglected action directors fade away as the less talented De Sicas and Zinnemanns continue to fascinate the critics. Because they played an anti-art role in Hollywood, the true masters of the male action film—such soldier-cowboy-gangster directors as Raoul Walsh, Howard Hawks, William Wellman, William Keighley, the early, pre-*Stagecoach* John Ford, Anthony Mann—have turned out a huge amount of unprized, second-gear celluloid. Their neglect becomes more painful to behold now that the action directors are in decline, many of them having abandoned the dry, economic, life-worn movie style that made their observations of the American he-man so rewarding. Americans seem to have a special aptitude for allowing History to bury the toughest, most authentic native talents. The same tide that has swept away Otis Ferguson, Walker Evans, Val Lewton, Clarence Williams, and J. R. Williams into near oblivion is now in the process of burying a group that kept an endless flow of interesting roughneck film passing through the theaters from the depression onward. The tragedy of these film-makers lies in their having been consigned to a Sargasso Sea of unmentioned talent by film reviewers whose sole concern is not continuous flow of quality but the momentary novelties of the particular film they are reviewing.

Howard Hawks is the key figure in the male action film because he shows a maximum speed, inner life, and view, with the least amount of flat foot. His best films, which have the swallowed-up intricacy of a good soft-shoe dance, are *Scarface, Only Angels Have Wings, His Girl Friday,* and *The Big Sleep.* Raoul Walsh's films are melancholy masterpieces of flexibility and detailing inside a lower-middle-class locale. Walsh's victories, which make use of tense, broken-field journeys and nostalgic background detail, include *They Drive by Night, White Heat,* and *Roaring Twenties.* In any Bill Wellman operation, there are at least four directors—a sentimentalist, deep thinker, hooey vaudevillian, and an expedient short-cut artist whose special love is for mulish toughs expressing themselves in drop-kicking heads and somber standing around. Wellman is at his best in stiff, vulgar, low-pulp material. In that setup, he has a low-budget ingenuity, which creates flashes of ferocious brassiness, an authentic practical-joke violence (as in the frenzied inadequacy of Ben Blue in *Roxie Hart*), and a brainless hell-raising. Anthony Mann's inhumanity to man, in which cold mortal intentness is the trademark effect, can be studied best in *The Tall Target, Winchester 73, Border Incident,* and *Railroaded.* The films of this tin-can de Sade have a Germanic rigor, caterpillar intimacy, and an original dictionary of ways in which to punish the human body. Mann has done interesting work with scissors, a cigarette lighter, and steam, but his most bizarre effect takes place in a taxidermist's shop. By intricate manipulation of athletes' bodies, Mann tries to ram the eyes of his combatants on the horns of a stuffed deer stuck on the wall.

The film directors mentioned above did their best work in the late 1940's, when it was possible to be a factory of unpretentious picture-making without frightening the front office. During the same period and later, less prolific directors also appear in the uncompromising action film. Of these, the most important is John Farrow, an urbane vaudevillean whose forte, in films like *The Big Clock* and *His Kind of Woman,* is putting a fine motoring system beneath the veering slapstick of his eccentric characterizations. Though he has tangled with such heavyweights as Book of the Month and Hemingway, Zoltan Korda is an authentic hard-grain cheapster telling his stories through unscrubbed action, masculine characterization, and violent explorations inside a fascinating locale. Korda's best films—*Sahara, Counterattack, Cry the Beloved Country*—are strangely active films in which terrain, jobs, and people get curiously interwoven in a ravening tactility. William Keighley, in *G-Men* and *Each Dawn I Die,* is the least sentimental director of gangster careers. After the bloated philosophical safe-crackers in Huston's *Asphalt Jungle,* the smallish cops and robbers in Keighley's work seem life-size. Keighley's handling is so right in emphasis, timing, and shrewdness that there is no feeling of the director breathing, gasping, snoring over the film.

The tight-lipped creators whose films are mentioned above comprise the most interesting group to appear in American culture since the various groupings that made the 1920's an explosive era in jazz, literature, silent films. Hawks and his group are perfect examples of the anonymous artist, who is seemingly afraid of the polishing, hypocrisy, bragging, fake educating that goes on in serious art. To go at his most expedient gait, the Hawks type must take a withdrawn, almost hidden stance in the industry. Thus, his films seem to come from the most neutral, humdrum, monotonous corner of the movie lot. The fascinating thing about these veiled operators is that they are able to spring the leanest, shrewdest, sprightliest notes from material that looks like junk, and from a creative position that, on the surface, seems totally uncommitted and disinterested. With striking photography, a good ear for natural dialogue, an eye for realistic detail, a skilled inside-action approach to composition, and the most politic hand in the movie field, the action directors have done a forbidding stenography on the hardboiled American handyman as he progresses through the years.

It is not too remarkable that the underground films, with their twelve-year-old's adventure-story plot and endless palpitating movement, have lost out in the film system. Their dismissal has been caused by the construction of solid confidence built by daily and weekly reviewers. Operating with this wall, the critic can pick and discard without the slightest worry about looking silly. His choice of best salami is a picture backed by studio build-up, agreement amongst his colleagues, a layout in *Life* mag (which makes it officially reasonable for an American award), and a list of ingredients that anyone's unsophisticated aunt in Oakland can spot as comprising a distinguished film. This prize picture, which has philosophical undertones, panfried domestic sights, risqué crevices, sporty actors and actresses, circuslike gymnastics, a bit of tragedy like the main fall at Niagara, has every reason to be successful. It has been made for that purpose. Thus, the year's winner is a perfect film made up solely of holes and evasions, covered up by all types of padding and plush. The cavity-filling varies from one prize work to another, from *High Noon* (cross-eyed artistic views of a clock, silhouettes against a vaulting sky, legend-toned walking, a big song), through *From Here to Eternity* (Sinatra's private scene-chewing, pretty trumpeting, tense shots in the dark and at twilight, necking near the water, a threatening hand with a broken bottle) to next year's winner, which will probably be a huge ball of cotton candy containing either Audrey Hepburn's cavernous grin and stiff behind or more of Zinnemann's glacéed picture-making. In terms of imaginative photography, honest acting, and insight into American life, there is no comparison between an average underground triumph (*Phenix City Story*) and the trivia that causes a critical salaam across the land. The trouble is that no one asks the critics' alliance to look straight backward at its "choices," for example, a horse-drawn truckload of liberal schmaltz called *The Best Years of Our Lives*. These ridiculously maltreated films sustain their place in the halls of fame simply because they bear the label of ART in every inch of their reelage. Praising these solemn goiters has produced a climate in which the underground picture-maker, with his modest entry and soft-shoe approach, can barely survive.

However, any day now, Americans may realize that scrambling after the obvious in art is a losing game. The sharpest work of the last thirty years is to be found by studying the most unlikely, self-destroying, uncompromising, roundabout artists. When the day comes for praising infamous men of art, some great talent will be shown in true light: people like Weldon Kees, the rangy Margie Israel, James Agee, Isaac Rosenfeld, Otis Ferguson, Val Lewton, a dozen comic-strip geniuses like the creator of "Harold Teen", and finally a half-dozen directors such as the master of the ambulance, speedboat, flying-saucer movie: Howard Hawks.

The films of the Hawks-Wellman group are *underground* for more reasons than the fact that the director hides out in subsurface reaches of his work. The hard-bitten action film finds its natural home in caves: the murky, congested theaters, looking like glorified tattoo parlors on the outside and located near bus terminals in big cities. These theaters roll action films in what, at first, seems like a nightmarish atmosphere of shabby transience, prints that seem overgrown with jungle moss, sound tracks infected with hiccups. The spectator watches two or three action films go by and leaves feeling as though he were a pirate discharged from a giant sponge.

The cutthroat atmosphere in the itch house is reproduced in

the movies shown there. Hawks's *The Big Sleep* not only has a slightly gaseous, subsurface, Baghdadish background, but its gangster action is engineered with a suave, cutting efficacy. Walsh's *Roaring Twenties* is a jangling barrelhouse film, which starts with a top gun bouncing downhill, and, at the end, he is seen slowly pushing his way through a lot of Campbell's scotch broth. Wellman's favorite scene is a group of hard-visaged ball bearings standing around—for no damned reason and with no indication of how long or for what reason they have been standing. His worst pictures are made up simply of this moody, wooden standing around. All that saves the films are the little flurries of bulletlike acting that give the men an inner look of credible orneriness and somewhat stupid mulishness. Mann likes to stretch his victims in crucifix poses against the wall or ground and then to peer intently at their demise with an icy surgeon's eye. Just as the harrowing machine is about to run over the wetback on a moonlit night, the camera catches him sprawled out in a harrowing image. At heart, the best action films are slicing journeys into the lower depths of American life: dregs, outcasts, lonely hard wanderers caught in a buzzsaw of niggardly, intricate, devious movement.

The projects of the underground directors are neither experimental, liberal, slick, spectacular, low-budget, epical, improving, or flagrantly commercial like Sam Katzman two-bitters. They are faceless movies, taken from a type of half-polished trash writing, that seem like a mixture of Burt L. Standish, Max Brand, and Raymond Chandler. Tight, cliché-ridden melodramas about stock musclemen. A stool pigeon gurgling with scissors in his back; a fat, nasal-voiced gang leader; escaped convicts; power-mad ranch owners with vengeful siblings; a mean gun with an Oedipus complex and migraine headaches; a crooked gambler trading guns to the redskins; exhausted GI's; an incompetent kid hoodlum hiding out in an East Side building; a sickly-elegant Italian barber in a plot to kill Lincoln; an underpaid shamus signing up to stop the blackmailing of a tough millionaire's depraved thumb-sucking daughter.

The action directors accept the role of hack so that they can involve themselves with expedience and tough-guy insight in all types of action: barnstorming, driving, bulldogging. The im-

portant thing is not so much the banal-seeming journeys to nowhere that make up the stories, but the tunneling that goes on
inside the classic Western-gangster incidents and stock hood-
lum-dogface-cowboy types. For instance, Wellman's lean, elliptical talents for creating brassy cheapsters and making gloved
references to death, patriotism, masturbation, suggest that he
uses private runways to the truth, while more famous directors
take a slow, embalming surface route.

The virtues of action films expand as the pictures take on the
outer appearance of junk jewelry. The underground's greatest
mishaps have occurred in art-infected projects where there is
unlimited cash, studio freedom, an expansive story, message,
heart, and a lot of prestige to be gained. Their flattest, most
sentimental works are incidentally the only ones that have at-
tained the almond-paste-flavored eminence of the Museum of
Modern Art's film library, i.e., *GI Joe, Public Enemy*. Both
Hawks and Wellman, who made these overweighted mistakes,
are like basketball's corner man: their best shooting is done
from the deepest, worst angle. With material that is hopelessly
worn out and childish (*Only Angels Have Wings*), the underground director becomes beautifully graphic and modestly human in his flexible detailing. When the material is like drab
concrete, these directors become great on-the-spot inventors, using their curiously niggling, reaming style for adding background detail (Walsh); suave grace (Hawks); crawling,
mechanized tension (Mann); veiled gravity (Wellman); svelte
semicaricature (John Farrow); modern Gothic vehemence
(Phil Karlson); and dark, modish vaudeville (Robert Aldrich).

In the films of these hard-edged directors can be found the
unheralded ripple of physical experience, the tiny morbidly life-
worn detail which the visitor to a strange city finds springing
out at every step. The Hawks film is as good on the mellifluous
grace of the impudent American hard rock as can be found in
any art work; the Mann films use American objects and terrain
—guns, cliffs, boulders, an 1865 locomotive, telephone wires—
with more cruel intimacy than any other film-maker; the Wellman film is the only clear shot at the mean, brassy, clawlike
soul of the lone American wolf that has been taken in films. In
other words, these actioneers—Mann and Hawks and Keighley

and, in recent times, Aldrich and Karlson—go completely underground before proving themselves more honest and subtle
than the water buffaloes of film art: George Stevens, Billy
Wilder, Vittorio De Sica, Georges Clouzot. (Clouzot's most
successful work, *Wages of Fear,* is a wholesale steal of the mean
physicality and acrid highway inventions in such Walsh-Well-
man films as *They Drive by Night.* Also, the latter film is a more
flexible, adroitly ad-libbed, worked-in creation than Clouzot's
eclectic money-maker.)

Unfortunately, the action directors suffer from presentation
problems. Their work is now seen repeatedly on the blurred,
chopped, worn, darkened, commercial-ridden movie programs on
TV. Even in the impossible conditions of the "Late Show,"
where the lighting is four shades too dark and the porthole-
shaped screen defeats the movie's action, the deep skill of Hawks
and his tribe shows itself. Time has dated and thinned out the
story excitement, but the ability to capture the exact homely-
manly character of forgotten locales and misanthropic figures is
still in the pictures along with pictorial compositions (Ford's
Last of the Mohicans) that occasionally seem as lovely as anything that came out of the camera box of Billy Bitzer and
Matthew Brady. The conditions in the outcast theaters—the
Lyric on Times Square, the Liberty on Market Street, the Victory on Chestnut—are not as bad as TV, but bad enough. The
screen image is often out of plumb, the house lights are half left
on during the picture, the broken seats are only a minor annoyance in the unpredictable terrain. Yet, these action-film homes
are the places to study Hawks, Wellman, Mann, as well as their
near and distant cousins.

The underground directors have been saving the American
male on the screen for three decades without receiving the slightest credit from critics and prize committees. The hard, exact
defining of male action, completely lacking in acting fat, is a
common item *only* in underground films. The cream on the top
of a *Framed* or *Appointment with Danger* (directed by two first
cousins of the Hawks-Walsh strain) is the eye-flicking action
that shows the American body—arms, elbows, legs, mouths, the
tension profile line—being used expediently, with grace and the
suggestion of jolting hardness. Otherwise, the Hollywood talkie

seems to have been invented to give an embarrassingly phony impression of the virile action man. The performance is always fattened either by coyness (early Robert Taylor), unction (Anthony Quinn), histrionic conceit (Gene Kelly), liberal knowingness (Brando), angelic stylishness (Mel Ferrer), oily hamming (José Ferrer), Mother's Boy passivity (Rock Hudson), or languor (Montgomery Clift). Unless the actor lands in the hands of an underground director, he causes a candy-coated effect that is misery for any spectator who likes a bit of male truth in films.

After a steady diet of undergrounders, the spectator realizes that these are the only films that show the tension of an individual intelligence posing itself against the possibilities of monotony, bathos, or sheer cliché. Though the action film is filled with heroism or its absence, the real hero is the small detail which has arisen from a stormy competition between lively color and credibility. The hardness of these films arises from the esthetic give-and-go with banality. Thus, the philosophical idea in underground films seems to be that nothing is easy in life or the making of films. Jobs are difficult, even the act of watching a humdrum bookstore scene from across the street has to be done with care and modesty to evade the type of butter-slicing glibness that rots the Zinnemann films. In the Walsh film, a gangster walks through a saloon with so much tight-roped ad-libbing and muscularity that he seems to be walking backward through the situation. Hawks's achievement of moderate toughness in *Red River*, using Clift's delicate languor and Wayne's claylike acting, is remarkable. As usual, he steers Clift through a series of cornball fetishes (like the Barney Google Ozark hat and the trick handling of same) and graceful, semicollegiate business: stances and kneelings and snake-quick gunmanship. The beauty of the job is the way the cliché business is kneeded, strained against without breaking the naturalistic surface. One feels that this is the first and last hard, clamped-down, imaginative job Clift does in Hollywood—his one nonmush performance. Afterward, he goes to work for Zinnemann, Stevens, Hitchcock.

The small buried attempt to pierce the banal pulp of underground stories with fanciful grace notes is one of the important feats of the underground director. Usually, the piercing consists in renovating a cheap rusty trick that has been slumbering in the "thriller" director's handbook—pushing a "color" effect against the most resistant type of unshowy, hard-bitten direction. A mean butterball flicks a gunman's ear with a cigarette lighter. A night-frozen cowboy shudders over a swig of whisky. A gorilla gang leader makes a cannonaded exit from a barber chair. All these bits of congestion are like the lines of a hand to a good gun movie; they are the tracings of difficulty that make the films seem uniquely hard and formful. In each case, the director is taking a great chance with clichés and forcing them into a hard natural shape.

People don't notice the absence of this hard combat with low, commonplace ideas in the Zinnemann and Huston epics, wherein the action is a game in which the stars take part with confidence and glee as though nothing can stop them. They roll in parts of drug addicts, tortured sheriffs; success depending on how much sentimental bloop and artistic japery can be packed in without encountering the demands of a natural act or character. Looking back on a Sinatra film, one has the feeling of a private whirligig performance in the center of a frame rather than a picture. On the other hand, a Cagney performance under the hands of a Keighley is ingrained in a tight, malignant story. One remembers it as a sinewy, life-marred exactness that is as quietly laid down as the smaller jobs played by the Barton MacLanes and Frankie Darros.

A constant attendance at the Lyric-Pix-Victory theaters soon impresses the spectator with the coverage of locales in action films. The average gun film travels like a shamus who knows his city and likes his private knowledges. Instead of the picture-postcard sights, the underground film finds the most idiosyncratic spot of a city and then locates the niceties within the large nicety. The California Street hill in San Francisco (*Woman in Hiding*)with its old-style mansions played in perfect night photography against a deadened domestic bitching. A YMCA scene that emphasizes the wonderful fat-waisted, middle-aged physicality of people putting on tennis shoes and playing handball (*Appointment with Danger*). The terrorizing of a dowdy middle-aged, frog-faced woman (*Born to Kill*) that starts in a decrepit hotel and ends in a bumbling, screeching, crawling murder at midnight on the shore. For his big shock effect, director Robert Wise (a sometime member of the underground) uses the angle going down to the water to create a middle-class mediocrity that out-horrors anything Graham Greene attempted in his early books on small-time gunsels.

Another fine thing about the coverage is its topographic grimness, the fact that the terrain looks worked over. From Walsh's *What Price Glory?* to Mann's *Men in War,* the terrain is special in that it is used, kicked, grappled, worried, sweated up, burrowed into, stomped on. The land is marched across in dark, threading lines at twilight, or the effect is reversed with foot soldiers in white parkas (*Fixed Bayonets*) curving along a snowed-in battleground as they watch troops moving back—in either case, the cliché effect is worked credibly inward until it creates a haunting note like the army diagonals in *Birth of a Nation.* Rooms are boxed, crossed, opened up as they are in few other films. The spectator gets to know these rooms as well as his own hand. Years after seeing the film, he remembers the way a dulled waitress sat on the edge of a hotel bed, the weird elongated adobe in which ranch hands congregate before a Chisholm Trail drive. The rooms in big-shot directors' films look curiously bulbous, as though inflated with hot air and turned toward the audience, like the high school operetta of the 1920's.

Of all these poet-builders, Wellman is the most interesting, particularly with Hopper-type scenery. It is a matter of drawing store fronts, heavy bedroom boudoirs, the heisting of a lonely service station, with light, furious strokes. Also, in mixing jolting vulgarity (Mae Clarke's face being smashed with a grapefruit) with a space composition dance in which the scene seems to be constructed before your eyes. It may be a minor achievement, but, when Wellman finishes with a service station or the wooden stairs in front of an ancient saloon, there is no reason for any movie realist to handle the subject again. The scene is kept light, textural, and as though it is being built from the outside in. There is no sentiment of the type that spreads lugubrious shadows (Kazan), builds tensions of perspective (Huston), or inflates with golden sunlight and finicky hot air (Stevens).

Easily the best part of underground films are the excavations of exciting-familiar scenery. The opening up of a scene is more concerted in these films than in other Hollywood efforts, but the most important thing is that the opening is done by road-mapped strategies that play movement against space in a cunning way, building the environment and event before your eyes. In every underground film, these vigorous ramifications within a sharply seen terrain are the big attraction, the main tent. No one does this anatomization of action and scene better than Hawks, who probably invented it—at least, the smooth version —in such 1930's gunblasts as *The Crowd Roars*. The control of Hawks's strategies is so ingenious that, when a person kneels or walks down the hallway, the movement seems to click into a pre-determined slot. It is an uncanny accomplishment that carries the spectator across the very ground of a giant ranch, into rooms and out again, over to the wall to look at some faded fight pictures on a hotel wall—as though he were in the grip of a spectacular, mobile "eye." When Hawks landscapes action—the cutting between light tower and storm-caught plane in *Ceiling Zero*, the vegetalizing in *The Thing*, the shamus sweating in a greenhouse in *The Big Sleep*—the feeling is of a clever human tunneling just under the surface of terrain. It is as though the film has a life of its own that goes on beneath the story action.

However, there have been many great examples of such vein-ing by human interactions over a wide plane. One of the special shockers, in *Each Dawn I Die*, has to do with the scissoring of a stooly during the movie shown at the penitentiary. This Keigh-ley-Cagney effort is a wonder of excitement as it moves in great leaps from screen to the rear of a crowded auditorium: crossing contrasts of movement in three points of the hall, all of it done in a sinking gloom. One of the more ironic crisscrossings has to do with the coughings of the stuck victim played against the screen image of zooming airplanes over the Pacific.

In the great virtuoso films, there is something vaguely re-sembling this underground maneuvering, only it goes on above the story. Egocentric padding that builds a great bonfire of pyrotechnics over a gapingly empty film. The perfect example is a pumped-up fist fight that almost closes the three-hour *Giant* film. This ballroom shuffle between a reforming rancher and a Mexican-hating luncheonette owner is an entertaining creation in spectacular tumbling, swinging, back arching, bend-ing. However, the endless masturbatory "building" of excitement—beautiful haymakers, room-covering falls, thunderous sounds—is more than slightly silly. Even if the room were valid, which it isn't (a studio-built chromium horror plopped too close to the edge of a lonely highway), the room goes unexplored because of the jumbled timing. The excess that is so noticeable in Stevens's brawl is absent in the least serious undergrounder, which attains most of its crisp, angular character from the modesty of a director working skillfully far within the earthworks of the story.

Underground films have almost ceased to be a part of the movie scene. The founders of the action film have gone into awkward, big-scaled productions involving pyramid-building, a passenger plane in trouble over the Pacific, and postcard Westerns with Jimmy Stewart and his harassed Adam's apple approach to gutty acting. The last drainings of the underground film show a tendency toward moving from the plain guttural approach of *Steel Helmet* to a Germanically splashed type of film. Of these newcomers, Robert Aldrich is certainly the most exciting—a lurid, psychiatric stormer who gets an overflow of vitality and sheer love for movie-making into the film. This enthusiasm is the rarest item in a dried, decayed-lemon type of movie period. Aldrich makes viciously anti-Something movies —*Attack* stomps on Southern rascalism and the officer sect in war, *The Big Knife* impales the Zanuck-Goldwyn big shot in Hollywood. The Aldrich films are filled with exciting characterizations—by Lee Marvin, Rod Steiger, Jack Palance—of highly psyched-up, marred, and bothered men. Phil Karlson has done some surprising modern Gothic treatments of the Brinks hold-up (*Kansas City Confidential*) and the vice-ridden Southern town (*The Phenix City Story*). His movies are remarkable for their endless outlay of scary cheapness in detailing the modern underworld. Also, Karlson's work has a chilling documentary exactness and an exciting shot-scattering belligerence.

There is no longer a literate audience for the masculine picture-making that Hawks and Wellman exploited, as there was in the 1930's. In those exciting movie years, a smart audience waited around each week for the next Hawks, Preston Sturges, or Ford film—shoe-stringers that were far to the side of the expensive Hollywood film. That underground audience, with its expert voice in Otis Ferguson and its ability to choose between perceptive trash and the Thalberg pepsin-flavored sloshing with Tracy and Gable, has now oozed away. It seems ridiculous, but the Fergusonite went into fast decline during the mid-1940's when the movie market was flooded with fake underground films —plushy thrillers with neo-Chandler scripts and a romantic style that seemed to pour the gore, histrionics, decor out of a giant catsup bottle. The nadir of these films: an item called *Singapore* with Fred MacMurray and Ava Gardner.

The straw that finally breaks the back of the underground film tradition is the dilettante behavior of intellectuals on the subject of oaters. Esthetes and upper bohemians now favor horse operas almost as wildly as they like the cute, little-guy worshipings of DeSica and the pedantic, interpretive reading of Alec Guinness. This fad for Western films shows itself in the inevitable little-magazine review, which finds an affinity between the subject matter of cowboy films and the inner esthetics of Cinemah. The Hawks-Wellman tradition, which is basically a subterranean delight that looks like a cheap penny candy on the outside, hasn't a chance of reviving when intellectuals enthuse in equal amounts over Westerns by Ford, Nunnally Johnson, J. Sturges, Stevens, Delmer Daves. In Ferguson's day, the intellectual could differentiate between a stolid genre painter (Ford), a long-winded cuteness expert with a rotogravure movie scene (Johnson), a scene-painter with a notions-counter eye and a primly naïve manner with sun-hardened bruisers (John Sturges), and a *Boys Life* nature lover who intelligently half-prettifies adolescents and backwoods primitives (Daves). Today, the audience for Westerns and gangster careers is a sickeningly frivolous one that does little more than play the garbage collector or make a night court of films. With this high-brow audience that loves banality and pomp more than the tourists at Radio City Music Hall, there is little reason to expect any stray director to try for a hidden meager-looking work that is directly against the serious art grain.

HOWARD
HAWKS 1969

Scarface (1932) is a passionate, strong, archaic photographic miracle: the rise and fall of an ignorant, blustery, pathetically childish punk (Paul Muni) in an avalanche of rich, dark-dark images. The people, Italian gangsters and their tough, wise-cracking girls, are quite beautiful, as varied and shapely as those who parade through Piero's religious paintings. Few movies are better at nailing down singularity in a body or face, the effect of a strong outline cutting out impossibly singular shapes. Boris Karloff: long stove-pipe legs, large-boned and gaunt, an obsessive, wild face; Ann Dvorak: striking out blindly with the thinnest, sharpest elbows, shoving aside anyone who tries to keep her from the sex and excitement of a dance hall. Besides the sulphurous, extreme lighting and so many feverish, doomed types, like Osgood Perkins as Johnny Lovo, top hood on the South Side until his greedier right-hand man Tony Camonte takes over, the image seems unique because of its moody energy: it is a movie of quick-moving actions, inner tension, and more angularity per inch of screen than any street film in history.

Crisp and starched where *Scarface* is dark and moody, *His Girl Friday* (1940) is one of the fastest of all movies, from line to line and gag to gag. Besides the dynamic, highly assertive pace, this *Front Page* remake with Rosalind Russell playing Pat O'Brien's role is a tour de force of choreographed action: bravado posturings with body, lucid Cubistic composing with natty lapels and hat brims, as well as a very stylized discourse of short replies based on the idea of topping, outmaneuvering the other person with wit, cynicism, and verbal bravado. A line is never allowed to reverberate but is quickly attached to another, funnier line in a very underrated comedy that champions the sardonic and quick-witted over the plodding, sober citizens.

The thing you remember most about Cary Grant's sexy, short-hop Lindbergh in *Only Angels Have Wings* (1939), a rather charming, maudlin Camp item, is his costume, which belongs in a Colombian Coffee TV commercial: razor-creased trousers that bulge out with as much yardage as a caliph's bloomers and are belted just slightly under his armpits. Except for a deadpan, movie-stealing performance by Richard Barthelmess, this movie about a Zeta Beta Tau fraternity of fliers in a South American jungle is a ridiculous film of improbability and coincidence, the major one being that Bat McPheerson, the blackest name in aviation, the man who betrayed Thomas Mitchell's kid brother and married Grant's old flame, should show up years later broke and in need of a job in Barranca, where buddies Grant and Mitchell are busting up planes on the strangest stalactite mountains.

Red River (1948), as a comment on frontier courage, loyalty, and leadership, is a romantic, simple-minded mush, but an ingeniously lyrical film nonetheless. The story of the first trip from Texas to the Abilene stockyards is a feat of pragmatic engineering, working with weather, space, and physiognomy. The theme is how much misery and brutality can issue from a stubbornly obsessed bully (John Wayne, who barks his way through the film instead of moving), while carving an empire in the wilderness. Of the one-trait characters, Wayne is a sluggish mass being insensitive and cruel-minded on the front of the screen; Joanne Dru is a chattering joke, even more static than Wayne; but there is a small army of actors (Clift, John Ireland) keyed in lyrically with trees, cows, and ground.

The very singular compact names that beat like a tom-tom through the above films are as eccentric and Hollywoodish as the character who makes them. They're summing up names, they tie a knot around the whole personality, and suggest the kind of bravura signature that underlines itself. Jeff Carter, Tess Millay, Mathew Garth, Guino Rinaldo, Buck Kennelley, Johnny Lovo, Molly Malloy, Cherry Valance are dillies of names that indicate a Breughel type who creates a little world of his own, outfitted in every inch with picturesque hats, insensitive swagger, and good-natured snobberies.

Howard Hawks is a bravado specialist who always makes pictures about a Group. Fast dialogue, quirky costumes, the way a telephone is answered, everything is held together by his weird Mother Hen instinct. The whole population in *Scarface,* cavemen in quilted smoking jackets, are like the first animals struggling out of the slime and murk toward fresh air. *Only Angels,* a White Cargo melodrama that is often intricately silly, has a family unit living at the Dutchman's, a combination bar, restaurant, rooming house, and airport run by a benevolent Santa Claus (some airline: the planes take off right next to the kitchen, and some kitchen: a plane crashes, the wreck is cleared and the pilot buried in the time it takes them to cook a steak; and the chief control is a crazy mascot who lives with a pet donkey and serves as a lookout atop a buzzard-and-blizzard-infested mountain as sharp as a shark's tooth). The wonderfully dour reporters in *His Girl Friday* and the mawkish cowboys in *Red River* are also strangely pinned in place by the idea of people being linked together in tight therapeutic groups, the creations of a man who is as divorced from modern *angst* as Fats Waller and whose whole movie-making system seems a secret preoccupation with linking, a connections business involving people, plots, and eight-inch hat brims.

The Mother Hubbard spirit gives the film a kind of romance that is somewhat WASP-ish with a Gatsby elegance and cool. Both the girls in *Scarface,* like Zelda Fitzgerald, would fling themselves away over a Russ Columbo recording of "Poor Butterfly." Ann Dvorak, dancing with a big, bland-faced clod who is bewildered by all her passion and herky-jerky cat's meow stuff, is so close to *Tender Is the Night* in her aura of silly recklessness. The sophomoric fliers of Barranca, like Fitzgerald's expatriates in Paris, are ravished with each other's *soignée*: Bonnie, playing real jazzy "Peanuts" with a whole saloon jammed around her piano cheering her on, is an embarrassing square version of supersquare Chico Marx. The feeling of snobbery in any Hawks work is overpowering, whether it is a Great White Father (Grant) patronizing a devitalized native with a gift watch or the female Jimmy Breslin (Rosalind Russell) breezily typing a socko story. This romanticism, which wraps the fliers-reporters-cowhands in a patina of period mannerism and attitude, makes for a film that isn't dated so much as removed from reality, like the land of Tolkien's Hobbits.

It is interesting how many plots are interwoven into a scene. The whole last part of the *Front Page* remake is a fugue in fast humor, peculiar for the way each figure touches another in ricochets of wild absurdity. Molly Malloy, the killer's lady defender ("Ah come on fellahs, he didn't even touch me, I just gave him some tea, and he was shaking all over") jumps out the window and is forgotten; her boyfriend, who has been entombed forlornly inside a rolltop desk, is dragged to his cell, presumably to be hung the next morning; Hildy Johnson finally gets maneuvered back to the *Morning Star* by her arch-heel editor; the mayor and the sheriff are politically destroyed for trying to bribe a fat Baby Huey, who turns up with a reprieve for the convicted killer. Then there's Louie, a terrific heist artist who steals a mother-in-law and gets mangled by a police car which was driving in the wrong lane. People who talk reams about great film comedy never mention this version of Hecht's play with its one twist, an elegantly played, pragmatic girl, sharp and immediately aware of everything in the ace reporter's role. It is a prime example of Hawks's uncelebrated female touch: the light flouncy foot, the antipomposity about newspaper problems, and the Mother Hen way of setting up family relationships. The ingenuity of its pragmatic engineering is that every gesture (she picks up the phone, it's funny) contributes to the plot, is laugh-provoking, and adds up to a supply of intricately locked humor so large that there's hardly time to relish any one gag.

The films have a musical comedy hokeyness joined to a freedom, a mellifluous motion, which is summed up in the line "Wherever they roam, they'll be on my land," spoken as a couple of cows—the start of a mighty herd: the man's bull and the boy's cow—wander off into a nice, sparse landscape. But the deep quality in any Hawks film is the uncannily poetic way an action is unfolded. Sometimes this portrayal of motion is thrilling (the cattle going into Abilene), funny (Abner Biberman's harmless hood: "Everybody knows Louie"). gracefully dour (Karloff's enigmatic cockiness in a bowling alley, like a Muybridge photograph), or freakishly mannered (Karen Morley sizing up Scarface's new pad: "It's kinda gaudy, isn't it"), but it is always inventive, killingly expressive, and gets you in the gut. One blatantly colloquial effect is slammed against another. The last section of *Scarface* builds detail on detail into a forbidding whirlwind. As the incestuous duo shoots it out with the cops, slightly outnumbered eighty to one, the lighting is fabulous, Dvorak's clamoring reaches an unequaled frenzy ("I'm just like you, Tony, aren't I, I'm not afraid"), and there is an authentic sense of the primeval, life coming to smash the puny puffed-up egos.

Not many moviemakers have gone so deeply into personality-revealing motion, the geography of gesture, the building and milking of a signature trait for all its worth. Hawks's abandon with his pet area, human gesture, is usually staggering, for better or worse. Why should Cary Grant get away with so much Kabukilike exaggeration, popping his eyes, jutting out his elbows, roaring commands at breath-taking speed in a gymnasium of outrageous motion? Sometimes Hawks's human-interest detailing falls on its face: the beginning of a cattle drive with Wayne a tiny speck moving down a channel of earth, the Knute Rockne of Cattledom, and, then, those endless ghastly close-ups of every last cowboy, one after the other, giving his special version of a Yahoo.

Scarface, as vehement, vitriolic, and passionate a work as has been made about Prohibition, is a deadly grim gangster movie far better than *White Heat* or *Bonnie and Clyde,* a damp black neighbor to the black art in Walker Evans's subway shots or the Highway 90 photographic shot at dawn by Robert Frank. Nowhere near the tough-lipped mentality or hallucinatory energy of Hawks's only serious film, *His Girl Friday* is still better than a clever, arch, extremely funny newspaper film. It's hard to believe that anything in Chaplin or W. C. Fields has so many hard, workable gags, each one bumping the other in an endless interplay of high-spirited cynicism. But rating these close camaraderie films, teeming with picturesque fliers-punks-pundits and a boys' book noble humanism, in the Pantheon division of Art and giving them cosmic conceptions is to overweight them needlessly.

A director who's made at least twenty box-office gold mines since 1926 is going to repeat himself, but the fact is that Howard Hawks's films are as different as they're similar. In each action film, he's powerfully interested in the fraternal groups that he sets up, sticking to them with an undemonstrative camera that is always eye level and acute on intimate business, and using stories that have a straight-ahead motion and develop within a short time span. The point is that each picture has a widely different impact: from the sulphurous lighting and feverish style of *Scarface* to the ignorant blustering of John Wayne in a soft Western that doesn't have any pace at all. Within the devil-may-care silliness of his *Angels* picture, the difference in acting between Barthelmess (crafty and constipated), Thomas Mitchell (maudlin, weepy), and Jean Arthur (good grief!) is so violent as to suggest the handling of three directors.

Hawks, a born movie-manipulator who suggests a general moving little flag pins around on a battle map, is not very fussy about the pulp-story figures nor the fable-ized scenery into which he jams them. The opening shots of his Andes airline movie are supposed to "vividly create Barranca, the South American town" in and around which the "completely achieved masterpiece" is set. This operetta seaport, with boas of smoke hanging in swirly serpentines and pairs of extras crisscrossing through the fake mist, might be good for a Douglas, Arizona, high school production. In the next "vividly created" scene, Jean Arthur is being dim and blithe, snapping her fingers (the first of the block-headed swingers) in time with some fairly authentic calypso dancers who are being unbelievably passionate at ten in the morning. In such movies, where a broken-down Englishman or a drunken rubber planter is seated in the corner muttering "Only two more months and I get out of this godforsaken place," a Rhonda Fleming or Brian Keith (in something called *Jivaro*) is far classier than the dopy inner-tubes who so seriously act characters getting the mail through for seven straight days in Hawks's corny semicatastrophe.

Hawks gets exhilarating situations: the stampede in *Red River* is great, maybe because everyone shuts up during the panic. He can be very touching, as in Harry Carey Jr.'s death with four or five cowboys standing in straight-line silence in a strangely hollowed out terrain that suggests Gethsemane. Yet no artist is less suited to a discussion of profound themes than Hawks, whose attraction to strutting braggarts, boyishly cynical dialogue, and melodramatic fiction always rests on his poetic sense of action. It would be impossible to find anything profound in Rosalind Russell's Hildy, but there is a magic in the mobile unity of the woman: her very mannish pinstripe suits, the highly stylized way she plants a hand on her hip, and her projecting of the ultimate in sophisticated swagger, taking off her hat and coat and showing how a real reporter sets up shop. The genius of such action engineering is that Hawks is able to poeticize dialogue as well as faces and costume, making a 100 per cent ordinary line—Hildy's parting shot to Earl Williams in his death cell: ''Goodbye Earl and good luck''—seem to float in an air of poignant, voluptuous cynicism.

JOHN
HUSTON 1950

Hollywood's fair-haired boy, to the critics, is director John Huston; in terms of falling into the Hollywood mold, Huston is a smooth blend of iconoclast and sheep. If you look closely at his films, what appears to be a familiar story, face, grouping of actors, or tempo has, in each case, an obscure, outrageous, double-crossing unfamiliarity that is the product of an Eisenstein-lubricated brain. Huston has a personal reputation as a bad boy, a homely one (called "Double-Ugly" by friends, "monster" by enemies), who has been in every known trade, rugged or sedentary: Mexican army cavalryman, editor of the first pictorial weekly, expatriate painter, hobo, hunter, Greenwich Village actor, amateur lightweight champ of California. His films, which should be rich with this extraordinary experience, are rich with cut-and-dried homilies; expecting a mobile and desperate style, you find stasis manipulated with the surehandedness of a Raffles.

Though Huston deals with the gangster-detective-adventure thriller that the average fan knows like the palm of his hand, he is Message Mad, and mixes a savage story with puddin'-head righteousness. His characters are humorless and troubled and quite reasonably so, since Huston, like a Puritan judge, is forever calling on them to prove that they can soak up punishment, carry through harrowing tasks, withstand the ugliest taunts. Huston is a crazy man with death: he pockmarks a story with gratuitous deaths, fast deaths, and noisy ones and, in idle moments, has his characters play parlor games with gats. Though his movies are persistently concerned with grim interpersonal relationships viewed from an ethic-happy plane, half of each audience takes them for comedies. The directing underlines a single vice or virtue of each character so that his one-track actions become either boring or funny; it expands and slows figures until they are like oxen driven with a big moralistic whip.

Money—its possession, influence, manufacture, lack—is a star performer in Huston's moral fables and gilds his technique; his irony toward and preoccupation with money indicate a director who is a little bitter at being so rich—the two brief appearances Huston makes in his own films are quite appropriately as a bank teller and a rich, absent-minded American handing out gold pieces to a recurring panhandler. His movies will please a Russian audience: half the characters (Americans) are money mad, directly enriching themselves by counterfeiting, prospecting, blackmail, panhandling.

His style is so tony it should embarrass his threadbare subjects. The texture of a Panama hat is emphasized to the point where you feel Huston is trying to stamp its price tag on your retina. He creates a splendiferous effect out of the tiniest details—each hair of an eyelid—and the tunnel dug in a week by six proletarian heroes is the size of the Holland Tunnel.

Huston's technique differs on many counts from classic Hollywood practice, which, from Sennett to Wellman, has visualized stories by means of the unbroken action sequence, in which the primary image is the fluid landscape-shot where terrain and individual are blended together and the whole effect is scenic rather than portriature. Huston's art is stage presentation, based on oral expression and static composition: the scenery is curiously deadened, and the individual has an exaggerated vitality. His characters do everything the hard way—the mastication of a gum-chewing gangster resembles the leg-motion in bicycling. In the traditional film, life is viewed from a comfortable vantage point, one that is so unobtrusive that the audience is seldom conscious of the fact that a camera had anything to do with what is shown. In Huston's, you are constantly aware of a vitaminized photographer. Huston breaks a film up into a hundred disparate midget films: a character with a pin head in one incident is megacephalic in another; the first shot of a brawl shows a modest Tampico saloon, the second expands the saloon into a skating rink.

The Huston trademark consists of two unorthodox practices —the statically designed image (objects and figures locked into various pyramid designs) and the mobile handling of close three-figured shots. The Eisenstein of the Bogart thriller, he rigidly delimits the subject matter that goes into a frame, by chiaroscuro or by grouping his figures within the square of the screen so that there is hardly room for an actor to move an arm: given a small group in close quarters, around a bar, bonfire, table, he will hang on to the event for dear life and show you peculiarities of posture, expression, and anatomy that only the actor's doctor should know. The arty, competent Huston would probably seem to an old rough-and-ready silent-film director like a boy who graduated from Oxford at the age of eight, and painted the Sistine Chapel during his lunch hours.

Aside from its typical compressions and endless padding with perspiration, mad scenes, and talking, the chief fact about the tempoless, shapeless *We Were Strangers* is that Huston doesn't know where the movie's going or how long it's going to take to get there. Played largely in interiors and demanding lightness rather than philosophic noodling, his Cuban picture is divided between two huge white figures: Jennifer Jones, who wears a constant frown as though she has just swallowed John Garfield. Garfield acts as though he's just been swallowed.

The Asphalt Jungle, directed for MGM with a surface vivacity and tricky hucksterish flash that earlier Huston doesn't have, sums up a great deal about his work and adds a freakishness that isn't far from Camp. Almost all of his traits, the strange spastic feeling for time, lunging at what he feels is the heart of a scene and letting everything else go, the idea that authority is inherent in a few and totally absent in everyone else, a ticlike need for posh and elegance, are funneled into this film, which describes the planning, organization, specialization, and cooperation surrounding a million-dollar jewel heist. At best, it is a trade-journal report of the illegal acquisition of jewels, its most absorbing stretch being the painstaking breakdown of a professional robbery, recalling the engineering details of the mine operation in *Sierra Madre* in which huge men seem nailed in front of mountains, or the tunnel-digging in the Cuban film, the tunnel ending up slightly smaller than the ones entering Grand Central Station.

Apparently influenced by French 1930's films like *Port of Shadows,* with their operatic underworld portraits getting lost in the gray trashiness of back rooms, *Asphalt Jungle* is just as inventive as Huston's other job-oriented films in its selection: a top-flight safe-cracker wears a magician's coat honeycombed with the tools of his trade—monstrous crowbar for prying open a manhole cover, three-eighth-inch mortar chisel for separating bricks, lapel-anchored cord for safely suspending the bottle of nitro (no jostling, as any student knows), extra bits for his electric drill. Few directors project so well the special Robinson Crusoe effect of man confronted by a job whose problems must be dealt with, point by point, with the combination of personal ingenuity and scientific know-how characterizing the man of action. Two exquisite cinematic moments: the safe-cracker, one hand already engaged, removing the cork from the nitro bottle with his teeth; the sharp, clean thrust of the chisel as it slices through the wooden strut.

Throughout this footage, Huston catches the mechanic's absorption with the sound and feel of the tools of his trade as they overcome steam tunnel, door locks, electric-eye burglar alarm, strongbox. It is appropriate that the robbers dramatically subordinate themselves to their instruments and the job at hand, move with the patient deadpan *éclat* of a surgical team drilled by Stroheim.

Huston unfortunately betrays the documentary invention of the robbery by clumsy stratagems for making his gangsters something more than human. Borrowing *Battleground*'s racy technique of divulging character by idiosyncratic tabs, actors are distinguished unto extinction: as in a masquerade, red, yellow, blue harlequin costumes urge contrast while withholding identity. The safe-cracker (Anthony Caruso) worries over a wife and kids; the hunchbacked driver (James Whitmore) loves cats; the mean-faced murderer (Sterling Hayden) jabbers nostalgically about the horses on his father's farm; the mastermind (Sam Jaffe) leers at young girls in the flesh or sprawled on calendars. These traits are so arbitrary and unilluminating that Huston's effort to show the Criminal as Human Being deteriorates into humorless Damon Runyon. Like Runyon's gunsels, Huston's thugs terrorize shopkeepers by night, but morning returns them to their homes, gentle-faced and clean-shaven, again to defend the dispossessed (cats, etc.) from the citizenry who terrorize by day.

The citizenry of Huston's movies, like Robin Hood's opponents, are dreary, anemic souls who fail every crisis through constitutional deficit of the courage of which every gangster worth his salt has an abundance. When the hoodlum slowly bleeds to death through the last third of the movie as he tries to reach the old farm, Huston has the attending physician say admiringly, "Anyone else would be dead after bleeding that much!" Victims of hemophilia have bled for years without comparable eulogy. It is really this laboring of the outcast's courage that raises a point which seems to turn Huston's blood to water; isn't it *fear* of the citizenry's ordinary responsibilities that provokes the criminal to crime and makes him unequal to the citizen unless he is fortified by gun and gang? By his evasion of the criminal's central cowardice, Huston is unable to countenance the possibility of every gentleman being a murderer at heart, preferring instead every murderer being a gentleman at heart.

The consequence of his evasion is an endless piling up of mawkish footnotes on how the gangster passes his time between jobs. The safe-cracker's apartment ($20,000 per caper?) is standard Italian-tenement decor: narrow hallway, beaten-up four-poster bed, harassed mother with her arms protectively outstretched toward her weeping child. With equal banality, the hunchbacked driver, Whitmore, pitifully explains his deformity, "I didn't grow this, I was born with it," belying the whole previous impression of his being an eager, cheery, indomitable assassin. Sterling Hayden begins credibly enough as an unthinking, prideful brute, meeting every remark with uncomprehending surliness, yet, twenty-four hours later, he is so intoxicated by the mastermind's charm that he is willing to forgo his fee for the unsuccessful robbery, wishes Jaffee godspeed with the wistful comment "That little squarehead, I can't figure him."

While it is Huston's talent to untype the familiar character actor by blowing up a particular physical gesture, he seems also to incapacitate actors with anticipated, summarized characters. Hayden, mostly a curled lower lip and hick sullenness, is practically stapled to what must have been a one-line comment, "stoic but sentimental farmer," in the shooting script. Jean Hagen's stylized jerkiness as a debauched gangster's moll, while eye catching for a few seconds, incapacitates her in terms of credibility for the materialism asked of her at the end of the picture, when she tends the bleeding Hayden.

With the end of the movie, Huston's faults—working against his adventurous self by telegraphing punches: 90 per cent of *We Were Strangers,* everything but the gray bit player going mad, is taken care of in written compressions—combine with MGM's postcard elegance in a scene almost unequaled in vulgarity: on the ripe green meadow of his father's farm, Hayden breathes his last, while colts gently lick his face in bucolic farewell. The ending suggests that Huston may not have the simple underworld courage to withstand MGM's glossy impositions.

THE THIRD MAN 1950

The most depressing movie irony is that American longhairs—
raised on the nonliterary naturalism of Barthelmess, Fairbanks,
and movies like *The Crowd Roars,* along with the revolutionary
Griffith, Sennett, Keaton—continue to coddle and encourage
European directors in their burnt-out sentimentality and esthetic cowardice. Carol Reed's *The Third Man* (the short happy
life of Orson Welles, who, having killed or crazed half of Vienna
by black-marketing diluted penicillin, evades the police by playing dead) is one import in which the virtuosity is tied in with
some (not much) of Reed's *Odd Man Out* talent, the musically
sensitive ear for middle-brow talk, the fractional, almost surreptitious, revelation of character through gestures, quietness,
modulated voice. Though there is an unfortunate alliance here,
as in *Fallen Idol,* with Graham Greene's glib incapsulation of
people, and the feeling here that Reed is deserting intelligence
for a lyrical-romantic kick, the precocious use of space, perspective, types of acting (stylized, distorted, understated, emo-
tionalized) and random, seemingly irrelevant subject matter,
enlarges and deepens both the impression of a marred city and a
sweet, amoral villain (Welles), who seems most like a nearly
satiated baby at the breast. But it bears the usual foreign
trademarks (pretentious camera, motorless design, self-conscious
involvement with balloon-hawker, prostitute, porter, belly
dancer, tramp) overelaborated to the point of being a monster-
piece. It uses such tiresome symbol-images as a door that swings
with an irritating rhythm as though it had a will of its own; a
tilted camera that leaves you feeling you have seen the film from
a foetal position; fiendish composing in Vuillard's spotty style,
so that the screen crawls with patterns, textures, bulking shapes,
a figure becoming less important than the moving ladder of
shadow passing over it.

The Third Man's murky, familiar mood springs chiefly from
Greene's script, which proves again that he is an uncinematic
snob who has robbed the early Hitchcock of everything but his

genius. Living off tension maneuvers that Hitchcock wore out, Greene crosses each event with one bothersome nonentity (a Crisco-hipped porter, schmoo-faced child) tossed in without insight, so that the script crawls with annoying bugs. While a moony, honest American (Joe Cotten) unearths facts of Welles's death, Greene is up to his old trick of showing a city's lonely strays blown about the terrain by vague, evil forces. Greene's famous low sociology always suggests a square's condescension and ignorance. He sets Cotten up for quaint laughs by characterizing him as a pulp writer, having the educated snipe at him in unlikely fashion ("I never knew there were snake-charmers in Texas") and the uneducated drool over him; every allusion to Cotten's Westerns, from their titles to their format, proves that no one behind the movie ever read one. Greene's story, a string of odd-sized talky scenes with no flow within or between them, is like a wheelless freight train.

But Reed manages to turn the last half of this tired script into a moving experience of a three-dimensional world in which life is sad, running simply from habit, and ready to be swept away by street-cleaners. In Reed's early films (*The Stars Look Down, Kipps, Night Train*), sordid domesticity was scored in a poky, warm, unbiased way; in the daylight scenes of *Third Man,* his paterfamilias touch with actors is tied to a new depersonalizing use of space that leaves his characters rattling loose, like solitary, dismal nuts and bolts in vaulting landscapes. A beautiful finale—Welles's girl Valli, returning from his burial down a Hobbema avenue of stark trees—picks up the gray, forlorn dignity of a cold scene and doubles the effect by geometrically pinpointing the figure and moving her almost mechanically through space and finally into and around the camera. Reed has picked up a new toy-soldier treatment of conversations, where the juxtapositions and movements are articulated like watch cogs, each figure isolated and contrastingly manipulated till the movie adds up to a fractured, nervous vista of alienation in which people move disparately, constantly circling, turning away, and going off into their own lost world. But the movie's almost antique, enervated tone comes from endless distance shots with poetically caught atmosphere and terrain, glimpses of languid, lachrymose people sweeping or combing their hair, and that limp Reed manner with actors, which makes you feel you could push a finger straight through a head, and a sweater or a hat has as much warmth and curiosity as the person wearing it.

Always a soft director, Reed turns to chicken fat on night scenes, where his love of metallically shining cobblestones, lamps that can hit a face at eighty paces, and the mysterious glow at every corner turns the city into a stage set that even John Ford would have trouble outglamorizing. For instance, endless shots of Cotten and Welles sliding baseball-fashion in rubbled wastelands that look like Mount Everest touched up by an MGM art director. Both are seen only momentarily in these wastes because it is obvious that no human could make the descent without supplies. Reed is seldom convinced that anything artistic is being said unless the scene looks like a hock shop. Scenes are engulfed in teddy bears, old photographs, pills; a character isn't considered unless he is pinpointed in a panorama of baroque masonry, seen bird-fashion through bridge struts or rat-fashion through table legs; like most current art movies, Reed's are glued to majestic stairways.

The movie's verve comes from the abstract use of a jangling zither and from squirting Orson Welles into the plot piecemeal with a tricky, facetious eyedropper. The charm, documentary skill, and a playful cunning that fashioned this character make his Morse-code appearances almost as exciting visually as each new make-believe by Rembrandt in his self-portraits. The cunning is in those glimpses—somewhat too small shoes, a distant figure who is a bit too hard and resilient, a balloon man, not Welles but flamboyant enough to suggest his glycerine theatricality in other films—that seem so Wellesian, tell so much about him, yet just miss being Welles. Through camera tricks and through a nonmobile part custom-built for this actor (whose flabby body and love of the overpolished effect make any flow in his performance seem a product of the bloodiest rehearsing), Welles achieves in brief, wonderful moments the illusion of being somebody besides Welles. Two of these—some face-making in a doorway, a slick speech about the Borgias that ends with a flossy exit—rate with entertaining bits like Paul Kelly's in *Crossfire* and the time Bob Hope tried to hide behind a man taking a shower in a glass cubicle. Reed's nervous, hesitant film is actually held together by the wires of its exhilarating zither, which sounds like a trio and hits one's consciousness like a cloudburst of sewing needles. Raining aggressive notes around the characters, it chastises them for being so inactive and fragmentary and gives the film the unity and movement the story lacks.

DETECTIVE STORY 1951

Detective Story spends a day in a precinct squad room, making
it jump with hokum, "business," and the acrobatic mugging of
a horde of aggressive actors, all of whom have wonderfully sculp-
tured faces. Though the station house is realistically crummy—
as any New York set should be but almost never is—the cameraman, Lee Garmes, in an effort to instill some outdoor excitement
into an indoor stage play, has pumped it full of a curious gray
mist. Mist or no mist, the squad room is the most credible thing
you're going to see in this high-powered, entertaining piece of
histrionic schmaltz. Through the station door—which bangs
back and forth, back and forth, until, at last, exactly as anticipated, it bangs some poor cop in the behind—swarm riffraff, the
mulcted, mouthpieces, and minions of the law, each a walking
caricature in physiognomy and mannerism of certain familiar
Manhattan types.

Among this traffic is a string of recent Broadway exiles: Lee
Grant as a man-hungry shoplifter with a sinuously unfeminine
wriggle, a parrotlike head thrust, and some other not quite hilar-
ious tricks, which she moiders with her East Side dialect; Joseph
Wiseman, a degenerate cat-burglar who sweeps into the familiar
Jewish palms-up gesture as no man ever did before—yet he
seems to have genuine pool-hall cynicism and chilling scorn for
the "artists" with whom he is working; Michael Strong, Wiseman's dumb crony, who crosses the affectations of a slack-jawed
delinquent with those of a hep cat, doing this with a glib exaggeration that makes actor seem more confused than character.
While these evil-doers are booked and printed by grumbling
detectives, they are jumbled into a mass of lively movement
designed to make you laugh—sentimentally—at Bronx-Brook-
lyn-East Side deficiencies.

The central figure in the crew of suffering, sweating cops is
Kirk Douglas, a one-man army against crime who, in the course
of the day, third-degrees a lot of crooks, discovers his beloved
wife is not so immaculate, goes off his rocker, and dies walking

into the bullets of four-time loser Wiseman. Douglas's mad-dog style of acting is bound to make any character into a one-sided surface of loud-pedaled ugliness. In this instance, his stiff-lipped biting off of dialogue, his muscle-bound strut, his grotesque posturing complicate a character already cluttered with the snapping documentary facts that Sidney Kingsley has dredged from three years of research in New York precinct stations.

The casting of gymnastic-minded Douglas for the rigid, unmerciful cop's role is a puzzling one, since both Kingsley and the producer-director, Wyler, are trying, in a wrangling hit-or-miss manner, to give some understanding of the psychology of an authoritarian sadist. And yet it isn't puzzling at all when you remember (a) that Douglas is top box-office these days and (b) that he has been built by Hollywood, film by film, into the cine-symbol of the Hollow Man who flies high, blind, and arrogant above the rest of us until the poison vapors of our rotten society at least reach his innards and bring him, too, cringing, crumbling, squirming to earth. (Question: Is our society rotten because there are too many honest cops running around? Is it the honest cop, as a matter of fact, who has been blowing his brains out lately? Question: Could misanthropic film-makers peddle this nonsense without a Douglas—or, before him, a Widmark, or, before that, a Muni—to serve as chief huckster? I wonder.) The cop dreamed up for us by Douglas, Wyler, and Kingsley is developed no more than one inch below the surface. For no other reason than that he has been uncharitably tough and just, he suddenly starts screaming and doing silly things like wanting to cut out his brain, take it in his hand, and examine the "dirty pictures" put in it by his wife. (The emptied skull is one of Kingsley's many images of hollowness; others are bells, graves, ticking meters, and, gaudiest of all, the cop's stomach, in which, according to Douglas, there stands some "pore little guy"—that is to say, his criminal father—laughing and crying with scorn and pity.) What all this "meaningful" color adds up to is total confusion, even unto the hammy death scene when you are finally given to understand that Detective McLeod, if he had it all to do over again, would have gone about it more like one of Harry Gross's friends and less like Johnny Broderick.

The movie's big item is the crack-up of Douglas's marriage to

Eleanor Parker, a tremulous actress with a genius for finely shaded whimpering, bawling, tense-legged walking. Kingsley bears down on the emotions, words, and thoughts of these two as sadistically as his belligerent hero pursues the criminal abortionist, who, it turns out, once did a small favor for Mrs. McLeod. With stricken face and trembling lips, Douglas will mention that he's afraid to go home armed if his wife isn't there, while Parker, with her insidiously flexible lips, talks constantly of being unable to go to sleep without Douglas's arms around her. Then he learns the awful truth about her. There has never been anything, for theatrical agony, like the stricken faces, clenched hands, and agonized hate-poetry that ensue between the two.

Detective Story is far more absorbing than some equally lurid message melodramas (*A Place in the Sun, A Streetcar Named Desire*) now being touted for the Academy Award. But it plays the same hoax on its audience, transforming a sordid locale with full-color effects that seem so wrong one suspects a writer and director of selling out everything they know in order to dislodge the spectator's eyeballs—and reason.

IN THE
STREET 1952

Documenting life in the raw with a concealed camera has often been tried, in Hollywood and experimental films, but never with more success than in the Spanish Harlem documentary *In the Street,* shot entirely with a 16-millimeter sneak camera by Janice Loeb, Helen Levitt, and James Agee. One problem was finding a camera either small enough to be hidden or made in such a way that it could be focused directly on the scene without being held to the operator's eye. The Film Documents group used an old model Cine-Kodak, which records the action at a right angle to the operator who gazes into his scenefinder much as was done with the old-fashioned "Brownie." The people who wound up in this movie probably thought the camera-wielder was a stray citizen having trouble with the lock of a small black case that could contain anything from a piccolo to a tiny machine gun. For dramatic action, the film deals with one of the toughest slum areas extant: an uptown neighborhood where the adults look like badly repaired Humpty Dumpties who have lived a thousand years in some subway rest room and where the kids have a wild gypsy charm and evidently spend most of their day savagely spoofing the dress and manners of their elders. The movie, to be shown around the 16-millimeter circuit, has been beautifully edited (by Miss Levitt) into a somber study of the American figure, from childhood to old age, growing stiffer, uglier, and lonelier with the passage of years.

Let me say that changing one's identity and acting like a spy or a private eye are more a part of the American make-up than I'd ever imagined before seeing this picture. This not only holds for Levitt, Inc., who had to disguise their role of film-makers to get the naked truth, but also goes for the slum people who are being photographed. The film is mostly concerned with kids who are trying to lose themselves in fake adultness by wearing their parents' clothes and aping grown-ups' expressions; even the comparatively few adults (at a wartime bond rally) go in for disguises—Legionnaire uniforms, etc.—and seem afraid to be

45

themselves. The chief sensation is of people zestfully involved in making themselves ugly and surrealistic, as though everything Goya's lithographs indicated about the human race had come true. This mood is established right off in a wonderful shot of a Negro tot mashing her tongue and face out of shape against a windowpane. This private bit of face-making is followed by a shot of a fat man leaping up and down and chortling with glee at the sight of a neighborhood kid carrying another one on his shoulders, solemnly impersonating a new two-bodied grown-up. And this scene gives way to a macabre game of gypsy kids making like maniacs by clubbing each other with flour-filled stockings swiped from their mothers.

Every Hollywood Hitchcock-type director should study this picture if he wants to see really stealthy, queer-looking, odd-acting, foreboding people. Even the kids, whose antics make their elders look like a lost tribe of frozen zombies, act a bit like spies from the underground. Enigmatic and distrustful, a small boy watches the little colored girl (mentioned above) smear her features on the window; an older, smart-alecky one slyly bats a flour stocking against the back of a teenage princess—the Mary Pickford of the neighborhood—carefully watching her every move to see if she's getting erotically excited. It is this very watchfulness which makes one part of the picture so brilliant: these kids must jeweler's-eye everything, and, when the cameraman (Agee) reveals himself, the space in front of the camera fills up with every kid in the neighborhood staring at the now bared camera like one Huge Eye.

To see what these kids will be like when they grow up, all we have to do is look at the shots of their parents. The watchfulness of youth has now become a total preoccupation—an evil-faced pimp, a Grant Wood spinster, a blowsy Irish dame picking her teeth, are all forever staring at the world as though it were a dangerous, puzzling place filled with hidden traps. The great American outdoors, once a wide-open prairie for adventurers is here, in one shrunken pocket of New York City, a place of possible terror to people who spend their time looking at it with 100 per cent distrust.

VAL
LEWTON 1951

The death of Val (Vladimir) Lewton, Hollywood's top producer of B movies, occurred during the final voting on the year's outstanding film contributors. The proximity of these two events underlines the significant fact that Lewton's horror productions (*Death Ship, The Body Snatcher, Isle of the Dead*), which always conveyed a very visual, unorthodox artistry, were never recognized as "Oscar" worthy. On the other hand, in acclaiming people like Ferrer, Mankiewicz, and Holliday, the industry has indicated its esteem for bombshells who disorganize the proceedings on the screen with their flamboyant eccentricities and relegate the camera to the role of passive bit player.

Lewton always seemed a weirdly misplaced figure in Hollywood. He specialized in gentle, scholarly, well-wrought productions that were as modest in their effects as his estimate of himself. Said he: "Years ago I wrote novels for a living, and when RKO was looking for producers, someone told them I had written horrible novels. They misunderstood the word horrible for horror and I got the job." Having taken on the production of low-cost thrillers (budgeted under $500,000) about pretty girls who turn into man-eating cats or believe in zombies, Lewton started proving his odd idea, for a celluloid entertainer, that "a picture can never be too good for the public." This notion did not spring from a desire to turn out original, noncommercial films, for Lewton never possessed that kind of brilliance or ambition; it came instead from a pretty reasonable understanding of his own limitations. Unlike the majority of Hollywood craftsmen, he was so bad at supplying the kind of "punch" familiar to American films that the little mayhem he did manage was crude, poorly motivated, and as incredible as the Music Hall make-up on his Indians in *Apache Drums*—the last and least of his works. He also seemed to have a psychological fear of creating expensive effects, so that his stock in trade became the imparting of much of the story through such low-cost suggestions as frightening shadows. His talents were those of a mild bibliophile whose idea of "good" cinema had too much to do with using quotes from Shakespeare or Donne, bridging scenes with a rare folk song, capturing climate with a description of a West Indian dish, and, in the pensive sequences, making sure a bit player wore a period mouth instead of a modern lipsticky one. Lewton's efforts not infrequently suggested a minor approximation of *Jane Eyre.*

The critics who called Lewton the "Sultan of Shudders" and "Chill-master" missed the deliberate quality of his insipidly normal characters, who reminded one of the actors used in small-town movie ads for the local grocery or shoe store. Lewton and his script-writers collaborated on sincere, adult pulp stories, which gave sound bits of knowledge on subjects like zoanthropia or early English asylums while steering almost clear of formula horror.

The Curse of the Cat People, for instance, was simply for the overconscientious parent of a problem child. The film concerns a child (Ann Carter) who worries or antagonizes the people around her with her daydreaming; the more they caution and reprimand, the more she withdraws to the people of her fantasies for "friends." When she finds an old photograph of her father's deceased, psychopathic first wife (Simone Simon, the cat woman of an earlier film), she sees her as one of her imagined play-mates; the father fears his daughter has become mentally ill and is under a curse. His insistence that she stop daydreaming brings about the climax, and the film's conclusion is that he should have more trust and faith in his daughter and her visions. Innocuous plots such as these were fashioned with peculiar ingredients that gave them an air of genteel sensitivity and enchantment; there was the dry documenting of a bookworm, an almost delicate distrust of excitement, economical camera and sound effects, as well as fairy-tale titles and machinations. The chilling factor came from the perverse process of injecting tepid thrills with an eyedropper into a respectable story, a technique Lewton and his favorite scriptwriter, Donald Henderson Clarke, picked up during long careers writing sex shockers for drugstore book racks. While skittering daintily away from concrete evidences of cat women or brutality, they would concentrate with the fascination of a voyeur on unimportant bric-a-brac, reflections, domestic animals, so that the camera would take on the faintly unhealthy eye of a fetishist. The morbidity came from the obsessive preoccupation with which writers and cameramen brought out the voluptuous reality of things, such as a dangerously swinging ship's hook, which was inconspicuously knocking men overboard like tenpins.

Lewton's most accomplished maneuver was making the audience think much more about his material than it warranted. Some of his devices were the usual ones of hiding information, having his people murdered offstage, or cutting into a murderous moment in a gloomy barn with a shot of a horse whinnying. He, however, hid much more of his story than any other filmmaker, and forced his crew to create drama almost abstractly with symbolic sounds, textures, and the like, which made the audience hyperconscious of sensitive craftsmanship. He imperiled his characters in situations that didn't call for outsized melodrama and permitted the use of a journalistic camera—for example, a sailor trying to make himself heard over the din of a heavy chain that is burying him inside a ship's locker. He would use a spray-shot technique that usually consisted of oozing suggestive shadows across a wall, or watching the heroine's terror on a lonely walk, and then add a homey wind-up of the cat woman trying to clean her conscience in a bathtub decorated with cat paws. This shorthand method allowed Lewton to ditch the laughable aspects of improbable events and give the remaining bits of material the strange authenticity of a daguerrotype.

The Leopard Man is a cleaner and much less sentimental Lewton, sticking much more to the suspense element and misdirection, using some of his favorite images, people moving in a penitential, sleep-walking manner, episodes threaded together with a dramatic sound. This fairly early peak example of his talent is a nerve-twitching whodunit giving the creepy impression that human beings and "things" are interchangeable and almost synonymous and that both are pawns of a bizarre and terrible destiny. A lot of surrealists like Cocteau have tried for the same supernatural effects, but, while their scenes still seem like portraits in motion, Val Lewton's film shows a way to tell a story about people that isn't dominated by the activity, weight, size, and pace of the human figure. In one segment of the

film, a small frightened señorita walks beyond the edge of the
border town and then back again, while her feelings and imagination keep shifting with the camera into sagebrush, the darkness of an arroyo, crackling pebbles underfoot, and so on, until
you see her thick dark blood oozing under the front door of her
house. All the psychological effects—fear and so on—were transformed by Tourneur into nonhuman components of the picture as
the girl waited for some noncorporeal manifestation of nature,
culture, or history to gobble her up. But, more important in terms
of movie invention, Lewton's use of multiple focus (characters
are dropped or picked up as if by chance, while the movie goes
off on odd tacks trying to locate a sound or a suspicion) and his
lighter-than-air sense of pace created a terrifically plastic camera style. It put the camera eye on a curiously delicate wave
length that responds to scenery as quickly as the mind, and gets
inside of people instead of reacting only to surface qualities.
This film still seems to be one of Hollywood's original gems—
nothing impure in terms of cinema, nothing imitative about
its style, and little that misses fire through a lack of craft.

Unfortunately, his directors (he discovered Robson and Wise
in the cutting department) become so delirious about scenic
camera work that they used little imagination on the acting. But
the sterile performances were partly due to Lewton's unexciting
idea that characters should always be sweet, "like the people
who go to the movies"—a notion that slightly improved such
veteran creeps as Karloff, but stopped the more pedantic actors
(Kent Smith, Daniell) dead in their tracks. Lewton's distinction
always came from his sense of the soundly constructed novel;
his $200,000 jobs are so skillfully engineered in pace, action,
atmosphere that they have lost little of the haunting effect they
had when released years ago.

SHORT AND HAPPY 1943

Some of the best movies of the year are seven-minute cartoons called by names like *All This and Rabbit Stew* or *The Fighting 69th 1/2*, which come on as unheralded transitions in the double bill and feature the notorious Bugs Bunny, a rabbit that not only performs physical feats of a Paul Bunyan magnitude but is equally sharp with his mind. They come from Warner Brothers, are produced by Leon Schlesinger, made by Chuck Jones, Friz Freling, Bob McKimson, and called *Merrie Melodies*; ten of them are being reissued this fall still as *Merrie Melodies* but with the addition of a Blue Ribbon.

One reason for the brightness of *Merrie Melodies* and for their superiority over Disney's product is that Jones is out to make you laugh, bluntly, and, as it turns out, cold-bloodedly. This runs him against the grain of the several well-worked grooves down which the animated cartoon has traveled under the belief these grooves will never wear through. However, it no longer seems funny to see animals who talk and act like human beings, who do all sorts of ingenious tricks—most of them superhuman—who go through lives of the highest excitement and reward, but have no inner, or mental, life. The complex emotional life and three-dimensional nature of Jones-Mc-Kimson characters allow their makers to poke fun at everything in sight, or out of sight—especially if it is something familiar and well loved, like McKimson's *Hiawatha,* a kind person, or any bad actress's great moments. It is an illusion of most cartoon-makers that they must have a moral, or do good, if it means only killing the villain; Warner's crew isn't under this illusion. The masterpiece, *Inki and the Lion,* is also a masterpiece of amorality—so far the other side of goodness that it is a parody of *Bambi.* In this version of forest life, man is the likable spear-thrower, preyed on by animals, and the king of the forest is a supernatural horror called the Myna bird, who hates man and beast alike.

The artistic method in Warner cartoons is neither in Disney's top drawer (at his best) nor Popeye's bottom one, but, even so, it has gone off at a tangent lately that may open up new paths to the cartoon method. It is a change from the straight, insipid realism to a sophisticated shorthand, made up of flat, stylized, posterlike representations, using a sort of Persian color of fancy tones like dusty pink. It is a much simpler style of cartoon drawing, the animation is less profuse, the details fewer, and it allows for reaching the joke and accenting it much more quickly and directly: it also gets the form out of the impossible dilemma between realism and the wacky humor.

The goal in heroes is a comic figure with a temperament and behavior as peculiarly his own as those of a Chaplin or Fields, which goal is never achieved; but it leads to several rewards, like the Myna bird, who appears in the *Inki* (little African boy) series. The Myna bird is like a toucan, shaped like an acorn, coal black, who moves inscrutably in an atmosphere of overwhelming supernaturalism, to the tune of Mendelssohn's overture to *Fingal's Cave*. At the end of each musical phrase, he gives one prodigious, syncopated hop, thereafter moving forward indomitably. The Myna bird is inevitably followed by a passive three-year-old individual named Inki, who loves to throw spears, and by a lion (the lion is Jones's least successful creation—he looks like Robinson Crusoe). The famous Bugs Bunny is Avery-Jones one-animal advertisement of the moral that unadulterated torturing of your fellow men pays off.

Despite the various positions on humor (Tex Avery is a visual surrealist proving nothing is permanent, McKimson is a show-biz satirist with throw-away gags and celebrity spoofs, Friz Freling is the least contorting, while Jones's speciality, comic character, is unusual for the chopping up of motion and the surrealist imposition: a Robin Hood duck, whose flattened beak springs out with each repeated faux pas as a reminder of the importance of his primary ineptness), the Warner cartoonists are refreshing iconoclasts because they concentrate on so many other humor antecedents besides brutal mishaps, cultural punning, balletlike sadism. One of Jones's key inventions is the animal who is a totally invulnerable, can't-possibly-be-stopped adversary, a mysterious force like rain that is always surrounded by a hush that is a mixture of the awe, revelation, instinctive reverence of a soon-to-be-victim just before he is maneuvered off the cliff or into a distant puff of smoke miles away in the desert. Ridiculousness is behind every Jones gag, but it is labyrinthine in effect because of how much gentleness is mixed in along with an infinite response to one animal's brass, hunger, manipulative power, or blinding speed. Disney's boredom-encased drawing, Barbara's cat-mouse drag, and the smugly "mature" Hubley works are incapable of this Warner's lightness: that there should be no end in defining the human quality of hunger (an animal fated from birth to be a scrawny piece of meat trying to eat tin cans, blindly grabbing at flies in a hostile environment of doomful rocks) as long as the metaphorical elaboration is kept within lighter-than-air feats of quick, fractional wit. The never-stop, pushing-on insistence in Warner's cartoons is important: having eaten some Earthquake Pills from a little bottle, the effect on the victim's body is a tremor that has the insistence and unsolvable disaster of hiccups.

Because of the twenty-six-issues-per-year rate at which they are thought up, the *Merrie Melodies* are bound to vary greatly in quality. The surprising facts about them are that the good ones are masterpieces and the bad ones aren't a total loss. For instance, the poor *Rabbit Who Came to Dinner* (Freling) is given a tremendous lift when, in the midst of the inevitable and tedious chase of the rabbit by Elmer, the clock strikes twelve and Bugs breaks into one of his typical emotional upsets, roaring out *Auld Lang Syne*, kissing Elmer, flinging confetti in the age-old tradition of New Year's Eve—Elmer being as easily diverted in July as in any other month.

Jones-McKimson-Freling are in the Sennett tradition, which uses the whole sphere of man's emotion and behavior simply as a butt for humor, no matter what it leads to. The aim is purely and simply laughter. Schlesinger's men are rich and inventive humorists, and their smart-alecky freshness has turned what is meant to be an interval on the program into the moment when the whole audience brightens up.

BLAME THE AUDIENCE 1952

While Hollywood, after all, still makes the best *motion* films, its 1952 products make me want to give Los Angeles back to the Conquistadores. Bad films have piled up faster than they can be reviewed, and the good ones (*Don't Bother to Knock, Something to Live For, The Lusty Men, My Son John, The Turning Point, Clash by Night*) succeed only as pale reminders of a rougher era that pretty well ended with the 1930's. The people who yell murder at the whole Hollywood business will blame the current blight on censorship, the star system, regimentation, the cloak-and-suit types who run the industry, the dependence of script-writers on a small group of myths, TV, the hounding of the Un-American Activities Committee, and what I shall laughingly call montageless editing.

There is plenty of justification for trying to find what is causing this plague, and I point my thumb accusingly at the audience, the worst in history. The present crowd of movie-goers, particularly the long-haired and intellectual brethren, is a negative one, lacking a workable set of values or a sense of the basic character of the medium, so that it would surprise me if any honest talent in Hollywood had the heart to make good pictures for it.

Their taste for preciously styled, upper-case effects and brittle sophistication has encouraged Hollywood to turn out some of the most smartly tooled art works of the times—films like *Sunset Boulevard* and *The Bad and the Beautiful,* stunning mixtures of mannerism, smooth construction, and cleverly camouflaged hot air. While I find these royal creations pretty good entertainment, I keep telling myself that the audiences craving for costly illusion (overacting, overscoring, overlighting, overmoralizing) may produce total confusion in Hollywood. The industry is still turning out movies that are supposed to be moderately naturalistic, but it must grow puzzled by having to make plain simple facts appear as special and delectable as the audience demands. So what we have to deal with now is a spectator who has Tiffany-styled esthetics and tastes in craftsmanship, and whose idea of good movies is based on an assortment of swell attitudes.

If some stern yearner makes a movie full of bias for the underdog, or a clever actor crowds his role with affectations picked out of real life, or the script-writer sets up innumerable situations wherein the camera can ponder over clocks, discarded cigar bands, and assorted bric-a-brac, the audience responds as though it were in the climate of high art.

Faced with such an audience—half tory and half culture bug —Griffith, with his practical genius, or Sennett, with his uninhibited improvising talents, would probably have passed up moviemaking for something more virile and exciting.

The reason movies are bad lies is this audience's failure to appreciate, much less fight for, films like the unspectacular, unpolished "B," worked out by a few people with belief and skill in their art, who capture the unworked-over immediacy of life before it has been cooled by "Art." These artists are liberated from such burdens as having to recoup a large investment, or keeping a star's personality intact before the public; they can experiment with inventive new ideas instead of hewing to the old sure-fire box-office formula.

Such pictures are often made in "sleeper" conditions (sometimes even the studio hotshots didn't know they were being made), and depend, for their box-office success, on word-of-mouth approval instead of "colossal" ads. But since there is no longer an audience response to fresh filmic trends, this type of movie is being replaced, by most of the big Hollywood factories, with low budget jobs that emulate prodigious spectacles, foreign-film sentiments, or best-seller novels, until you can no longer tell the "B" from an "A".

In the past, when the audience made underground hits of modest "B" films, Val Lewton would take a group of young newcomers who delighted in being creative without being fashionably intellectual, put them to work on a pulp story of voodooists or grave robbers and they would turn $214,000 into warm charm and interesting technique that got seen because people, rather than press agents, built its reputation. After 1940, a Lewton, Preston Sturges, Sam Fuller, Alan Dwan, or Budd Boetticher finds his best stride in a culture-free atmosphere that allows a director to waste his and the audience's time, and then loses himself in the culture-conscious conditions of large-scale work.

The low budget appears to economize the mind of a director, forcing him into a nice balance between language and what is seen. Given more money and reputation actors, Sam Fuller's episodic, spastically slow and fast film would probably dissolve into mouthy arrogance where characters would be constantly defining and apologizing for the class separation that obsesses Fuller and burying in words the skepticism and energy which he locates in his 1949–52 low budgets. The structure that Fuller invented in *I Shot Jesse James* depends on close-ups of large faces and gestures, combustive characters in close face-to-face confrontations where they seem bewitched with each other but where each one is actually in a private, lightly witty rumination about the wondrous information that springs up from being professionals pursuing highly perfected skills. In *Steel Helmet,* the weight of too many explanations about race-class-position seems to leaden Fuller's work, drives him into a pretentious strain that is not apparent in the totally silent *Jesse James* opening.

Sturges's turning point occurs in *Hail the Conquering Hero,* when he begins patronizing, caricaturing his small towners with patriotic sentimentality. The Eddie Bracken hero—no energy, desiring isolation, trying to free himself of responsibility—is a depressing symbol suggesting the spiritual difficulties Sturges must have been under, trying to psych himself into doing culture-conscious work. The last good Sturges occurs in *Sullivan's Travels,* which is not low budget, but its best sections— the hobo material, rudimentary slapstick, an expensive cross-country bus trying to stay with a kid's homemade motor tank, Veronica Lake's alertness within leisure—are elemental "B" handling.

In 1943, William Castle, the director of the Monogram melodrama *When Strangers Marry,* could experiment with a couple of amateurs (Robert Mitchum and Kim Hunter), try out a then new Hollywood idea of shooting without studio lights in the sort of off-Broadway rented room where time seems to stand still for years and the only city sounds come through a postage stamp opening on the air well. The movie was a hit with perceptive moviegoers, made a fair profit, and prepared audiences for two new stars and some of the uninvented-looking cinema later made famous in *Open City*. All this was possible because Castle wasn't driven to cater to cliché tastes.

Once, intellectual moviegoers performed their function as press-agents for movies that came from the Hollywood underground. But, somewhere along the line, the audience got on the wrong track. The greatest contributing cause was that their tastes had been nurtured by a kind of snobbism on the part of most of the leading film reviewers. Critics hold an eminent position, which permits control of movie practice in one period by what they discerned, concealed, praised, or kicked around in the preceding semester of moviemaking. I suggest that the best way to improve the audiences' notion of good movies would be for these critics to stop leading them to believe there is a new "classic" to be discovered every three weeks among vast-scaled "prestige" productions. And, when they spot a good "B," to stop writing as though they'd found a "freak" product.

"BEST FILMS" OF 1951 1952

Let Stevens or Kazan win their Oscars; *The Nation's* Emanuel —a life-size drip-celluloid statue of Kirk Douglas, ranting and disintegrating in the vengeful throes of death—goes to the man or men responsible for each of the following unheralded productions of 1951.

Little Big Horn. A low-budget western, directed by Charles Marquis Warren, starring John Ireland and Lloyd Bridges. This tough-minded, unconventional, persuasive look-in on a Seventh Cavalry patrol riding inexorably through hostile territory to warn Custer about the trap Sitting Bull had set for him, was almost as good in its unpolished handling of the regular-army soldier as James Jones's big novel. For once, the men appear as individuals, rather than types—grousing, ornery, uprooted, complicated individuals, riding off to glory against their will and better judgment; working together as a team (for all their individualism) in a genuinely loose, efficient, unfriendly American style. The only naturalistic photography of the year; perhaps the best acting of the year in Ireland's graceful, somber portrait of a warm-hearted but completely disillusioned lieutenant, who may or may not have philandered with his captain's wife.

Fixed Bayonets. Sam Fuller's jagged, suspenseful, off-beat variant of the Mauldin cartoon, expanded into a full-length Korean battle movie without benefit of the usual newsreel clips. Funny, morbid—the best war film since *Bataan.* I wouldn't mind seeing it seven times.

His Kind of Woman. Good coarse romantic-adventure nonsense, exploiting the expressive dead-pans of Robert Mitchum and Jane Russell, a young man and a young woman who would probably enjoy doing in real life what they have to do here for RKO. Vincent Price is superb in his one right role—that of a ham actor thrown suddenly into a situation calling for high melodramatic courage. Russell's petulant, toneless rendition of "Five Little Miles from San Berdoo" is high art of a sort.

The Thing. Howard Hawks's science-fiction quickie directed by Christian Nyby; fast, crisp, and cheap, without any progressive-minded gospel-reading about neighborliness in the atomic age; good airplane take-offs and landings; wonderful shock effects (the plants that cry for human blood as human babies cry for milk); Kenneth Tobey's fine, unpolished performance as a nice, clean, lecherous American air-force officer; well-cast story, as raw and ferocious as Hawks's *Scarface,* about a battle of wits near the North Pole between a screaming banshee of a vegetable and an air-force crew that jabbers away as sharply and sporadically as Jimmy Cagney moves.

The Prowler. A tabloid melodrama of sex and avarice in suburbia, out of Cain by Joe Losey, featuring almost perfect acting by Evelyn Keyes as a hot, dumb, average American babe who, finding the attentions of her disc-jockey husband beginning to pall, takes up with an amoral rookie cop (nicely hammed up by Van Heflin). Sociologically sharp on stray and hitherto untouched items like motels, athletic nostalgia, the impact of *nouveau riche* furnishings on an ambitious ne'er-do-well, the potentially explosive boredom of the childless, uneducated, well-to-do housewife with too much time on her hands.

The People Against O'Hara. An adroit, scholarly example of sound story-telling that every Message Boy should be made to study as an example of how good you can get when you neither slant nor oversimplify. Also highly enjoyable for its concern about a "static" subject—the legal profession as such —and the complete authority with which it handles soft-pedaled insights into things like the structure and routine of law offices; the politics of conviviality between cops, DA's, judges, attorneys; the influence of bar associations; the solemn manner of memorializing the wrench caused by the death of a colleague; the painful "homework" of committing to memory the endless ramifications of your case, as well as the words you are going to feed the jury in the morning.

The Day the Earth Stood Still. Science-fiction again, this time with ideals; a buoyant, imaginative filtering around in Washington, D.C., upon the arrival of a high-minded interplanetary federalist from Mars, or somewhere; matter-of-fact statements about white-collar shabby gentility in boarding houses, offices, and the like; imaginative interpretation of a rocket ship and its robot crew; good fun, for a minute, when the visitor turns off all the electricity in the world; Pat Neal good, as usual, as a young mother who believes in progressive education.

The Man Who Cheated Himself. A lightweight, O'Henry-type story about a cop who hoists himself on his own petard; heavyweight acting by Jane Wyatt and Lee J. Cobb; as a consequence, the only film this year to take a moderate, morally fair stand on moderately suave and immoral Americans, aged about forty. An effortlessly paced story, impressionistically coated with San Francisco's oatmeal-gray atmosphere; at the end, it wanders into an abandoned fort or prison and shows Hitchcock and Carol Reed how to sidestep hokum in a corny architectural monstrosity. Cobb packs more psychological truths about joyless American promiscuity into one ironic stare, one drag on a cigarette, or one uninterested kiss than all the Mankiewicz heroes put together.

Background to Danger. Tough, perceptive commercial job glorifying the P-men (Post-Office sleuths), set in an authentically desolate wasteland around Gary, Indiana, crawling with pessimistic mail-robbers who act as though they'd seen too many movies like *Asphalt Jungle.* Tight plotting, good casting, and sinuously droopy acting by Jan Sterling, as an easily had broad who only really gets excited about—and understands—waxed bop. Interesting for Morgan-Webb bit playing, such sidelights as the semi-demi-hemiquaver of romantic attachment between the head P-man and a beautiful nun.

And, for want of further space, six-inch Emanuels to the following also rans: *The Tall Target, Against the Gun, No Highway in the Sky, Happiest Days of Your Life, Rawhide,* Skelton's *Excuse My Dust, The Enforcer, Force of Arms, The Wooden Horse, Night Into Morning, Payment on Demand, Cry Danger,* and a Chuck Jones animated cartoon—the name escapes me—about a crass, earnest, herky-jerky dog that knocks its brains out trying to win a job in a Pisa pizza joint.

UGLY SPOTTING
1950

Hollywood has spawned, since 1946, a series of ugly melodramas featuring a cruel esthetic, desperate craftsmanship, and a pessimistic outlook. These supertabloid, geeklike films (*The Set-up, Act of Violence, Asphalt Jungle, No Way Out*) are revolutionary attempts at turning life inside out to find the specks of horrible oddity that make puzzling, faintly marred kaleidoscopes of a street, face, or gesture. Whatever the cause of these depressing films—the television menace, the loss of 24 million customers since the mid-1940's—it has produced striking changes in film technique. Writers overpack dialogue with hackneyed bitterness, actors perfect a quietly neurotic style, while directors—by flattening the screen, discarding framed and centered action, and looming the importance of actors—have made the movie come out and hit the audience with an almost personal savagery. The few recent films unmarked by the new technique seem naïve and obsolete.

The new scripts are tortured by the "big" statement. *All About Eve* (story of the bright lights, dim wits, and dark schemes of Broadway) hardly gets inside theater because most of the movie is coming out of somebody's mouth. The actors are burdened with impossible dialogue abounding in clichés: "Wherever there's magic and make-believe and an audience—there's theater"; timely words: "We are the original displaced personalities"; and forced cleverness that turns each stock character into the echo of an eclectic writer. The new trick is to build character and plot with loaded dialogue, using hep talk that has discolored cheap fiction for years. In *The Breaking Point,* the environment is a "jungle," the hero a morose skipper "with only guts to peddle," who decides after a near fatal gun battle that "a man alone hasn't got a chance." His spouse comes through with, "You're more man than anyone I ever knew."

The stories, parading success-seekers through a jackpot of frustration, are unique in that they pick on outcasts with relentless cruelty that decimates the actor as much as the character. As a colored intern moves through the *No Way Out* blizzard of anti-Negro curses, everything about him is aggressively spiked so that a malignant force seems to be hacking at him. When the cruel estheticians really click on these sadistic epics, foreboding death lurks over every scene. Cameramen dismember the human body, accenting oddities like Darnell's toothpick legs or Pat Neal's sprawling mouth, to make them inanimate; faces are made up to suggest death masks, expanded to an unearthly size, spotlighted in dark, unknown vacuums; metaphorical direction twists a chimp's burial (*Sunset Boulevard*) into an uncanny experience by finding a resemblance between monkey and owner. Under the guise of sympathy, these brutally efficient artists are sneaky torturers of the defeated or deranged character.

Directors like Wilder and Mankiewicz mechanically recreate the unharnessed energy and surprise of great silent films with an elegantly controlled use of the inexplicable. In the jitter-bugging scene of *Asphalt Jungle*, Huston delicately undresses the minds of four characters and gauchely creates a sensuous, writhing screen, though his notion of jive is so odiously surrealistic it recalls Russian propaganda against the United States. The first glimpse of the faded star in *Sunset*, using Bonnard's suede touch on Charles Addams's portraiture (a witch surveying her real estate through shutters and dark spectacles) is lightning characterization with a poetic tang. Brando, in *The Men*, commands a GI troop into battle like a slow, doped traffic cop wagging cars through an intersection, but his affected pantomine electrifies the screen with the hallucinatory terror of an early painting by di Chirico. Movies have seldom if ever been as subtle as these scenes, or as depressing in the use of outrageous elements to expedite ambiguous craftsmanship.

To understand the motives behind the highly charged, dissonant acting employed today, one has to go back to the time-wasting, passive performance of an early talkie. No matter how ingenious the actor—Harlow, Garbo, Lee Tracy—effectiveness and depth were dissipated by the uninterrupted perusal of a character geared to a definite "type" and acted with mannerisms that were always so rhythmically and harmoniously related that the effect was of watching a highly attenuated ballet.

Directors today have docked the old notion of unremittingly consistent, riverlike performances, and present what amounts to a confusion of "bits," the actor seen only intermittently in garish touches that are highly charged with meaning and character, but not actually melted into one clear recognizable person. Darnell's honestly ugly characterization of a depressed slattern is fed piecemeal into *No Way Out,* which moves her toward and away from malevolence, confuses her "color," and even confounds her body. Her job—like the recent ones of Nancy Olson, John MacIntyre, Hayden—shouldn't be called a "performance," because it is more like a collage of personality, which varies drastically in every way to create the greatest explosion and "illumination" in each moment.

FIGHT
FILMS
1949

Thanks to Rocky Graziano's infamous fame, and the box-office killing of *Body and Soul*, the studios have been turning out fight films as fast as they could steal each other's material: though tightly humorless and supersaturated with worn-out morality, they remain pure fantasy in so far as capturing the pulse of the beak-busting trade is concerned. You go to this type of movie expecting to see plenty of good prize-fighting and the atmosphere that surrounds the trade. You come out on the street feeling like a sucker, having been frustrated by a jittery cameraman who is always in the wrong place, double-crossed by editing that switches you continually away from the fight, tricked by actors who couldn't fight their way out of a subway rush. These actors, with bodies attuned by years of acting to comfortable, easy, relaxed movement, foolishly try to ape a trade they may have studied for a month, instead of relying on their own imaginations to convey boxing technique. Occasionally an aggressive actor turns up, like Cagney or Mickey Rooney, who loves to act and move in his own way, which results in a style as unique and worth watching as the technique of the average pug.

The scenarios seem to have been written by a gossip columnist —they concentrate on spanking the hero for the un-Christian way he breaks training by smoking, the mean treatment he accords his friends, and, most of all, his crude, ugly approach to women. He goes with disreputable females, mistreats his mother and the girl back home waiting for him; but the fact of the matter is that he, more than any other movie hero, is swamped by a prize collection of boring, freakish women. While the gangster, cowboy, ballplayer are lauded, the boxer is never presented as anything but a bad nickel.

The romanticism of the script is quite restrained, compared to the peculiar business that goes on in the ring. Whereas real fighters actually hit each other about one-sixth of the time, the fearless "phenoms" of the cinema are hitting every second— and never anywhere but flush on the chin or in the stomach; in spite of this, the hero is usually looking around the audience for someone he knows. Hatred can propel a fighter who looks like a spent, squashed herring to heights that always surprise his opponent. There are no decisions, fights are never stopped, there are plenty of fouls, which the hero is above recognizing even when a blow tears his knee half off; it seems incredible that in-fighters, counterpunchers, "cuties" are never characterized —only one type is presented, a creaking version of the mauling club-fighter.

The two latest fight films, *Champion* and *The Set-up*, return to the movie-for-movie's-sake technique of pre-1935 B films, but they are dehumanized by an effort at newsreel realism and a compulsion to grind away at a message. Attempting to describe the sadism of the ring, the directors exaggerate the savagery inherent in prize fighting, dragging in enough peripheral mayhem to scare the officers of Buchenwald. The basic quality of these scripts seems to be a pure imaginative delight in the mangling of the human body: tired fighters inhale with the frightful expression that leaves one with the feeling the air is filled with needles rather than oxygen, while, outside the arena, people are thrown from trains, smacked by canes, bricks, and blackjacks—in *The Set-up* this builds into the overwhelming impression of a nightmare. What results is a double distortion —the effect of oversmearing brutality and the lust for ultra-realism—which strangles the actual movement. The action, mimicking reality, moves too fast to convey its meaning through the medium of the camera; unless realistic pace is transformed into the slower rhythm that movies can handle, it tends to jumble action. The hard, crassly clear photography of *Champion*, which aims at spotlighting reality, actually produces a metallic stage set, while the bitter moral realism which *The Set-up* aims at produces another type of overstatement which has the flavor of lurid melodrama.

Champion is hung on the weariest formula in boxing films— the success story. In the original Ring Lardner version, success is only a minor strain in a theme devoted to depicting a morosely malevolent pug; the movie reverses emphasis so that the hero (Kirk Douglas) exhibits above all things a flagrantly lucky, talented, bewitching adaptation of Hollywood's pet ideal that all amoral, egocentric behavior possesses an endurable charm and fascination. Douglas, as a windmill of activity on the screen, portrays a hard, quartzlike, malevolent show-off, yet maintains a smooth inner serenity. The movie's voltage is chiefly a tinny, quick wit displayed through the virtuosity of Douglas's performance and the director's strained vague realism. In an unbearably moving death scene, in which the hero throws himself over the moon of emotion, and the camera spills an oatmealish atmosphere around him, the style is a cross between Hawks and Euripides, and the visual details are magnificent. Except for this cinematic episode, *Champion* pivots on a vaudevilleish technique, which consists of strategizing scenes to the last detail before the actors go before the camera, thus saving the time and money that go into excessive reshooting. They rely on the self-sufficiency of their characters for movement rather than on expensive movement from locale to locale. Actors appear, as in no other film, loaded with material and perfectly trained. The result is a new esthetic in which every effect is the $64 one, perfectly executed and dehumanized.

The Set-up—its fighters aren't champions but the derelicts, beginners, old men who fight four-rounders in arenas that have more trash on the floor than seats—is a rhetorical Robert Wise film, overstating the malice in ordinary people (repeated near close-ups of a blind fight fan yelling "go for his eyes"), but often good in the intermediate nonbrutal scenes in a penny arcade and a cheap hotel room. Alan Baxter is good in a bad all-black fight-fixing role; whatever strength comes second-hand from the unity of a 1920's poem on which the film is based; but Wise's direction (not nearly as quietly authenticated as his *Curse of the Cat People* and *Body Snatcher* for Lewton) schizophrenically moves from hyperbole to its opposite, from the tabloid geekery of the arena crowd to a standout shot of a soured ring wife throwing her torn-up ticket off a bewitching bridge into the smoke of a passing train. The movie's honesty comes from the ruminating, suspicious performance of Robert

Ryan, a prelim fighter one punch away from punch-drunk, and the same distanced performance of his wife, Audrey Totter. A lot of intelligent in-fighting acting technique seeps in around the edges of what seems a static approach: don't act, move a muscle, or smile.

HOME OF THE
BRAVE 1949

In the static atmosphere of Hollywood film production, the appearance of Screen Plays Corporation, a peppery little band of young esthetes as hard and profit-minded as Du Pont, should cause more upheaval than any incident since the Santa Barbara earthquake. Hollywood has never experienced anything as brainy and volatile as this ant-hill organization, which has managed not only to shake the foundations of the elephant studios but to leave them standing still in their own race for the fattest loot. The curious aspect of this new company is that it blends the creative artist's imagination with the Sammy Glick talent for peeling cash off of nothing. Its aim seems to be to kill two birds by turning out a five-cent *Gone with the Wind* and introducing technique and ideas that are a few levels above the IQ of the average moviegoer, according to the superstitions prevailing in the industry. But Screen Plays is not the Prince on the White Charger, for, underneath, as is seen in its new movie, *Home of the Brave,* beats the heart of a huckster, a heart that has grown its tissues in the theatrical atmosphere of middle-brow and sentimental Broadway.

The irrelevantly titled *Home of the Brave* is a war film which starts with some good shattering shots depicting the brutality and destruction of battle but suddenly changes into idle, muddy psychiatric double-talk and a tepid display of the Negro problem. A Negro GI named Moss (James Edwards) returns from a dangerous mission traumatized and half-paralyzed; in this weakened condition, he is put under the care of a noisy psychiatrist (Jeff Corey) with the face of a manic hawk and a bellicose, exasperated attitude that should complete the ruin of Moss but instead puts him on his feet in a couple of days and gives him a lot of difficult thoughts to play around with for the rest of his life. After all this psychotherapy, Moss is told he suffers from discrimination chiefly because he is too sensitive. This gets a big laugh, particularly from Negroes in the audience who doubtless think of all the jobs they didn't get because of their oversensitivity.

The script-writer (Carl Foreman) plants some bold dashes of prejudice but never grounds the movie in the street-level type of incident that would illustrate the Negro situation in all its bulging ugliness. The bite has been taken out of the problem by constructing the black GI as a thoroughly passive creature who is ceaselessly tormented by his enemy, continually soothed by friends, who plays a meek guinea pig for the psychiatrist but scarcely makes an impression on anyone else; he is so suavely mute that this pioneering movie about antiblack prejudice unreels itself oblivious of the fact that the whole film does not contain a black (Moss is actually the man who wasn't there). James Edwards plays him as a bland, unmarked, self-possessed, and graceful character, very little different from the other players, although he is supposed to have been a long-standing victim of their conscious and unconscious prejudice. The character in the original play by Arthur Laurents was a Jew, and, in making the change, the producers simply lost sight of the fact that the black has suffered from a different, more violent kind of prejudice here; Moss appears to have neither offered nor suffered any kind of violence.

Home of the Brave is infused with a sophisticated technique that turns an essentially thin and artificial script into a clattering, virile movie with deeply affecting moments. The sophistication appears everywhere: instead of seeing the Jap sniper fall, as in any other war movie, all that you see in this movie is a broccoli jungle, accompanied by a slithering sound and a mild clonk to inform you that the sniper is done for. The script is so basically theatrical that it has to be acted almost entirely from seated or reclining positions, but the director works more variations on those two positions than can be found in a Turkish bath. The actors talk as though they were trying to drill the words into one another's skulls; this savage portentousness not only forces your interest but is alarming in that the soldiers are usually surrounded by Japs and every word can obviously be heard in Tokyo. The actors are never balanced within the picture frame; often a head is half cut by the top of the screen or, for no reason, some secondary figure will walk straight through a shot, knocking out your view of the principal figures, but giving an effect of careless spontaneity to a scene that is actually no more active than the inside of a can of sardines. This energetic technique has several limitations: the repetition of close eye-level shots practically puts the actors in your lap, but, after a few reels, I would have liked a long shot of all of them on top of a mountain; the cameramen are so enamored of shadows in outdoor scenes that the actors often seem afflicted by leprosy. Dimitri Tiomkin's background music only comes on in crises, adding extra heartthrobs where the action is as swollen with emotion as a Faulkner river.

Well-played and punchy, *Home of the Brave* is not quite clever or ingenious enough to conceal its profit-minded, inept treatment of important issues.

THE GIMP
1952

Somebody once told me, no doubt inaccurately, that lady golfers in the Victorian era used a certain gimmick that went by the name of "Gimp." It was a cord running from hem of skirt to waistband; when preparing to hit the ball, you flicked it with your little finger and up came the hem. Thus suddenly, for a brief instant, it revealed Kro-Flite, high-button shoes, and greensward, but left everything else carefully concealed behind yards of eyeleted cambric. Something like this device has now been developed in Hollywood. Whenever the modern film-maker feels that his movie has taken too conventional a direction and is neglecting "art," he need only jerk the Gimp-string, and—behold!—curious and exotic but "psychic" images are flashed before the audience, pepping things up at the crucial moment, making you think such thoughts as "The Hero has a mother complex," or "He slapped that girl out of ambivalent rage at his father image, which, he says, he carries around in his stomach," or "He chomps angrily on unlit cigarettes to show he comes from a Puritan environment and has a will of iron."

Over the past couple of years, one movie after another has been filled with low-key photography, shallow perspectives, screwy pantomime, ominously timed action, hollow-sounding voices. All this pseudo-undershot stuff, swiped from any and every "highbrow" work of films, painting, literature, has gone into ultraserious movies that express enough discontent with capitalist society to please any progressive. In these beautifully controlled Freud-Marx epics, the only things that really move are the tricks and symbols designed to make you think, "God, this is sensitive!"

Somehow the nature of this new mannerist flicker has been misinterpreted by critics, by the good ones as well as the merely earnest publicists. With their preconceptions, their ennui, and their formularized responses to stimuli, the critics go their complacent (or disgruntled) ways, finding movies better (or worse) than ever, but never noticing that movies *aren't* movies

any more. Not so long ago, the movies, whatever their oversim-
plifications and distortions, still rested on the assumption that
their function was to present some intelligible, structured image
of reality—on the simplest level, to tell a story and to entertain,
but, more generally, to extend the spectator's meaningful experience, to offer him a window on the real world. What are
they now?

Well, icebergs of a sort, one-tenth image, action, plot, nine-
tenths submerged popular "insights" à la Freud or Jung, Marx
or Lerner, Sartre or Saroyan, Frost, Dewey, Auden, Mann, or
whomever else the producer's been reading; or they are Dali
paintings, surrealist fun-houses with endless doors leading the
spectator to inward "awareness" and self-consciousness, and
far away from a simple ninety-cent seat in a simple mansion of
leisure-time art and entertainment, or they are expressionistic
shotguns peppering the brain of that deplored "escapist" with
millions of equally important yet completely unrelated pellets
of message—messages about the human personality and its
relations to politics, anthropology, furniture, success, Mom,
etc., etc. The trick consists in taking things that don't belong
together, charging them up with hidden meanings, and then
uniting them in an uneasy juxtaposition that is bound to shock
the spectator into a lubricated state of mind where he is forced
to think seriously about the phony implications of what he is
seeing.

Most readers will remember the calculated moment in *Sunset
Boulevard*—the kept man in the fashionable men's shop,
ashamed of buying the vicuña coat with the ex-star's money. Up
to a certain point, this scene was unfolded in a straight narrative line, and then Director Billy Wilder pulled his Gimp-string.
The camera moved in for a very close close-up, the atmosphere
became molecular and as though diseased—and there was a sleek
clerk whispering to the slightly ill gigolo: "After all, if the
lady is paying. . . ." Thus Wilder registered spiritual sickness
and business-world corruption in an ad-libbed shot that had all
the freshness of an old tire-patch, consisting as it did, under the
circumstances, of naïve moral gibberish that no adult in his
right mind would mouth. This indirect shot, with its leaden
overpantomiming going back to and beyond Theda Bara, offers

a classic example of what the Gimp can do for a director, helping him avoid monotony (by switching from storytelling to
symbolic "pseudoaction"), explaining hidden content, and en-
suring his position in movies as a brave, intransigent artist.

One of the most confusing films of all time, *People Will Talk,*
dealt with an unflaggingly urbane gynecologist, a liberal-minded
doctor, who cured patients with friendliness, played with electric trains, scoffed at ration programs and packaged food, and
generally behaved like a Lubitsch portrait of an enlightened
college professor. One scene showed him making vague epi-
grams and looking down his nose at overconscientious note-
takers in an anatomy class. Obviously all this suavity needed
some excitement, and so Director Mankiewicz jerked his string
and provided the well-analyzed doctor with a weird trick that
you'll never see again in a movie. The doctor undrapes the
corpse on the slab before him, and—surprise!—you are looking
at a naked brunette, not only the most ravishing person in the
movie but the whitest and least dead-looking. While the doctor
talks on about heartless people and gracefully does things with
the corpse's Godivalike tresses, the audience is so shocked by the
beauty and lifelikeness of the corpse that it starts thinking all
sorts of things about how society nags the individual, even unto
death. (Visually, in the best Gimp tradition, this scene was
bewitching for its pure unusualness; Gary Grant's classy erotic
playing with the dead girl evokes a compound of evil, new kinds
of sex, and terrific grace.)

The Gimp is the technique, in effect, of enhancing the ordinary with a different dimension, sensational and yet seemingly
credible. Camera set-ups, bits of business, lines ("They don't
make faces like that any more") are contrived into saying too
much. Every moment of a movie is provided with comment
about American society. "Original" characters are sought, the
amount of illogical and implausible material is increased, to
such a point that movies which try to be semidocumentary actually seem stranger than the Tarzan–Dracula–King Kong
fantasy.

We are getting such characters as the abortionist in *Detective
Story,* a close-mouthed Dutchman dressed like a low-paid
respectable clerk from an early Sinclair Lewis story about

department-store life in the Midwest. To make him look as though he has emerged from the bowels of common life in America, he is given a pinched, deathly pallor and a sickly personality that hardly allows him to breathe, much less talk. The apparent intention was to set up a significantly ordinary, true-to-life, entirely evil, grass-roots American; the result was a surrealistic creature who seemed ready at any moment to throw up. Thanks to the canny acting of George Macready, possibly Hollywood's most impressive character actor, this sour figure provided the film with its only good moments.

Two recent pictures have made especially adroit and unrelenting use of the Gimp. In *A Place in the Sun*, Director George Stevens, not content with letting a climax of violence follow naturally upon an inevitable train of events, treats us constantly to macabre darkenings of the landscape, metronome-timed hootings of a loon, and about six other sensational effects reeking with recondite significance. The story is about a not-quite-bright social climber, and Stevens so buries him in symbols of money, dominance, and sex that every last member of the audience must become involved with the vague meanings of the boy's daydreams. Wherever he walks, there is sex or wealth—usually both together—written out so big that no one can miss it: billboards that out-Petty Petty, languid and sophisticated aristocrats, a Gus Kahn love lyric coming from a midget radio. And of course his dingy furnished room in a depressed urban area must have a window facing on a huge neon factory sign standing for wealth and achievement.

In one protracted example of contrivance, a luscious babe in a Cadillac flashes by the boy as he hitchhikes on some spacious highway, and then comes a broken-down truck chugging straight out of *The Grapes of Wrath* to pick up the disappointed hiker. Immediately, the audience was saying to itself one or all of these things: "This is about the unfair distribution of wealth in the United States," or "His spirit is crying out for joy, ease, and love," or "He has a complex about being raised in a poor, harsh, confined neighborhood." Whenever any particularly delectable symbol crossed the boy's line of vision, he would freeze up with yearning, refusing to act, not answering questions for minutes on end, his wispy shoulders almost but not quite jerking, and occasionally one dead word straying out of his twisted mouth. There were eccentric scenes in which the boy met up with a deputy cop and a suspicious boatman, who—with the help of acting that was probably coached by Emily Brontë, and camera angles that gave the actors height and took away width—looked like ominous scoundrels from the Dark Ages and showed you Society intimidating the Outcast, American Justice breaking the Common Man on the wheel.

Symbols are a dime a dozen in Hollywood's storehouse, and Stevens bought up the stock: police sirens, train whistles, double shots of a boy's face and a remembered kiss, the lame leg of the sadistic district attorney (which makes him more formidable), a shadow going over a face to indicate an evil thought. Such things may seem to come from real life, but actually they are the products of medieval imaginations capable of grasping glaring features of contemporary life only in cliché terms. These creators have entrenched themselves within a vicious circle of decay: having helped to create and foster the world of lurid wealth, romantic love, and Big City glamour, they now express despair and chaos by exaggerating the same corny symbols they originally invented.

It has always been obvious that the movie camera not only reflects reality but interprets it. This fact used to imply the deepening and enrichment of an intelligible structure of plot and character. What is happening now is the complete disappearance of reality in the fog of interpretation: the underground "meaning" of every shot displaces the actual content, and the moviegoer is confronted with a whole crowd of undefined symbolic "meanings" floating entirely free. Shove the camera up against the pimple on an actor's face, and you automatically produce an image of immense importance: it will mean *something*—no matter if you don't know exactly what, and no matter if you have made it impossible to tell your story. Just as comedians now manufacture their humor out of immense card indexes of gags, so directors dip into their mental gag file of disconnected bits of social significance, amateur psychiatry, and visual shock effects.

In *A Streetcar Named Desire*, Elia Kazan pulls the Gimp-string so mercilessly that you never have one plain character or situation, but vast bundles of the most complicated sociological phenomena. For example, the hero, a sharp-witted Polish mechanic, conveys heavy passion by stuttering the first syllables of his sentences and mumbling the rest as though through a mouthful of mashed potatoes, a device that naturally forces the spectator to sociological speculation; disgusted with the fact that the hero has apparently been raised in a pigpen, the spectator is impelled to think about the relation of environment to individual development. Tennessee Williams's hero is getting ahead in his work, is a loving husband, makes "those colored lights" with his sexual genius, and is possessed of a delicate moral sensitivity. But all these bourgeois attributes have to be matched with their opposites for the sake of excitement, and so Kazan pulls his string and you see the Polack slobbering, licking his paws, howling like a troglodyte, hitting his wife so hard that he sends her to the maternity hospital, playing poker like an ape-man, exuding an atmosphere of wild screams, rape, crashing china, and drunkenness. And to make sure every two-year-old will understand how bad life is in this Grimm's fairy-tale hovel, Kazan hammers his point home with continual sinister lights, dancing shadows, gaseous oozings.

With its freakish acting, nightmare sets, and dreamy pace, *Streetcar* may seem like traditional, Hollywood poeticism, but looked at more closely, it becomes very different from movies of the past, and in the same odd, calculated way as *A Place in the Sun, People Will Talk,* etc. For one thing, the drama is played completely in the foreground. There is nothing new about shallow perspectives, figures gazing into mirrors with the camera smack up against the surface, or low intimate views that expand facial features and pry into skin-pores, weaves of cloth, and sweaty undershirts. But there is something new in having the whole movie thrown at you in shallow dimension. Under this arrangement, with the actor and spectator practically nose to nose, any extreme movement in space would lead to utter visual chaos, so the characters, camera, and story are kept at a standstill, with the action affecting only minor details, e.g., Stanley's back-scratching or his wife's lusty projection with eye and lips. On the screen, these grimly controlled gestures appear huge, florid, eccentric, and somewhat sinister. Again, there is nothing new about shooting into incandescent lights and nebulous darks, but there is something new in having every shot snotted up with silvery foam, black smoke, and flaky patterns to convey decay and squalor. Never before has there been such a use of darkness in masses as we find in the new films (at least not since the Russians, who probably didn't have any lights). All this to jazz up a pseudodrama in which nothing really happens on the screen except dialogue in which you see two faces talking, then a close-up of the right speaker asking, then a close-up of the left speaker answering, then back to the two, etc. The spectator is aware that a story is being told, but mostly he feels caught in the middle of a psychological wrestling match.

Though there has never been so massive a concentration on technique, the fact is these films actually fail to exploit the resources of the medium in any real sense. Kazan, Stevens, and their colleagues have been shrinking films down to an almost babyish level in situation and grouping. With slumbrous camera movement, slow choreographies of action, sustained close-ups of enigmatic faces surrounded by areas of gloom, and drifting dialogue that seemed to come out of the walls, Stevens in *A Place in the Sun* had time only to unreel in grandiose terms a kiss, a seduction, and a drowning that would have taken him all of five minutes to examine with the straight story-telling technique he used in *Penny Serenade* and *Alice Adams,* both of which he made in the 1930's. *Streetcar,* for dramatic action, shows one big character—a neurotic Southern girl on the last lap to the mental ward—in one main situation: talk, talk, talk with an uninhibited couple in a two-room apartment. *The African Queen* was shot entirely in the Belgian Congo, but the characters do almost nothing that couldn't have been done on one studio set with the aid of some library shots.

Movies have seldom, if ever, been so physically overbearing in their effect. The scenarios are set up so that the story can be told with a small cast, little movement, and few settings. The camera fastens itself on the actors with such obsessive closeness that every moment becomes of overwhelming importance and threatens to disclose some terrifying psychic or emotional fact. The effect becomes even stronger and more curious when the actors occasionally move across the room and this all-revealing eye just barely moves to keep them in focus—as in *Something to Live For,* when a worried advertising ace paces his office, while the camera seems to move back and forth no more than a fraction of an inch. One has the feeling that nothing is any longer of importance except a magnification of face, gesture, and dress, and that these can tell you all you need to know about life in our time.

All this seems to have started in an exciting, if hammy, 1941 picture called *Citizen Kane.* This grim mixture of suspense thriller and tabloid obituary, in which most of the surface facts paralleled events in the career of William Randolph Hearst, combined the thunderous theatrical trickery of Orson Welles with a reckless use of darkish photography and funny angles by a top cameraman named Gregg Toland. Toland threw into the film every device ever written into the accomplished cameraman's handbook—everything from undercranking (to make the people in "newsreel" clips jerk and scuttle) to crane-shots, two-shots, floor-shots, and his favorite perspective shot in which figures widely spaced and moving far off down long rooms were kept as clearly in focus as the figure closest to the audience. This stuff helped make an exciting film, though marred by obvious items of shopworn inspiration: camera angles that had been thoroughly exploited by experimental films, and the platitudinous characterization of Kane as a lonely man who wanted love from the world but didn't get it because he had no love of his own to give. This unpeeling of a tycoon was clearly the most iconoclastic stroke in major studio production since the days when D. W. Griffith and his cameraman, Billy Bitzer, were freeing movies from imitation of the stage. Orson Welles's bold jumbling of techniques from theater, radio, and film led inevitably to a shock-happy work that anticipated everything that has since become fashionable in American films.

Oddly enough, this film, which had the biggest cultural build-up before release since Eisenstein's Mexican film, made little impression at the time on Hollywood's veterans. Only in the 1950's did the ghost of *Citizen Kane* start haunting every A picture out of Hollywood. Before the advent of Orson Welles, the most important thing in motion-picture technique had been the story, the devising, spacing, and arranging of shots into a plot line that moved easily from one thing to another. Welles, more concerned with exhibiting his impudent showmanship and his deep thought about graft, trusts, yellow journalism, love, hate, and the like, fractured his story all along the line, until his film became an endless chain of stop effects. At every instant, the customer was encouraged to pause over some Kublai Khan setting, some portentously lit floor-shot of an actor, or some symbol (the falling-snow toy, the bird screaming in escape), and think in the terms of what it had to tell about a publisher's immoral pursuit of love-power-respect. The plot was simple enough: a famous man said something ("Rosebud") just before dying in his castle on a mountain, and "March of Time" sent out an inquiring reporter to make a story out of it. Eventually we did get the answer, not through the flashbacked memories of those interviewed—Kane's oldest friend, his newspaper manager, the girl, the butler in the castle—but in a final nerve-tingling shot, privy to the director and audience, of the "Rosebud" sled of Kane's lost, barren childhood. The story was presented in such complicated ways and made so portentous with the shadows of meaning cast off by a hundred symbols that you could read almost anything into it, including what Welles had put there. There were certain dramatic high points like the rough-cut in the "March of Time" projection room, the kid outside the window in the legacy scene, and the lurid presentation of an electioneering stage. But in between these was a great deal of talk, much less action, and almost no story.

Welles bequeathed to Hollywood, which had grown fat and famous on hurtling action films, a movie that broke up into a succession of fragments, each one popping with aggressive technique and loud, biased slanting of the materials of actual life. He told his story backward—which was nothing new—and slowed it even more by breaking it into four situations that didn't flow together but settled stiffly and ambiguously into a sort of parallel construction. He also complicated and immobilized each shot with mismated shock effects that had never been seen before in Hollywood. For example, the ominous figure of Kane was shown in the dark alongside a clearly lit pseudo-Grecian statue and a vast undone jigsaw puzzle that the cameraman had cleverly shot so that it seemed strewn over a marble floor. The spectator had trouble arranging these disparate items into a convincing visual whole, but his brain was mobilized into all sorts of ruminations about avarice, monomania, and other compulsions. Even the devices for moving the story along were complicating and interrupting: again and again, you went from the first part of a sentence spoken at one time and place to the last part of the same sentence spoken years later; this made one less conscious of time passing than of a director stopping time to play a trick on reality.

Welles also showed the Hollywood craftsmen how to inject trite philosophy, "liberalism," psychoanalysis, etc., into the very mechanics of moviemaking, so that what the spectator saw on the screen was not only a fat, contrived actor screaming down a staircase, but also some exotically rendered editorializing contributed by everyone from the actor to the set designer. The movie opened and closed on the iron fence around Kane's castle. In between this repetition, which spelled out the loneliness and baronial character of a tycoon, were similarly meaningful images: Kane in his castle among the boxed accumulations of his collecting; hopeful and innocent Kane gesticulating in front of a huge electioneering poster that showed him as a sinister demagogue. And always, practically on top of the cameraman, his unreal figure suggesting a blownup cue ball adorned with the facial features of Fu Manchu, with nothing inside him but a Freudian memory giggling around in the fumes cast off by Welles's ideas about how an American big shot goes wrong.

The hidden meanings and the segmented narration were the two most obvious innovations of this film. Toland's camera provided the third, and it was anything but what you'd expect from a film that was advertised as using an unbound camera. Toland's chief contribution was a shallow concept of movie space. His camera loved crane-shots and floor-shots, but contracted the three dimensional aspect by making distant figures as clear to the spectator as those in the foreground. To accomplish this, Toland had to arrange his actors in widely spaced, parallel arrays across the screen. He also had to immobilize them and cut them off from the natural obscurations of scenery and atmosphere. His powerful lens did the rest. The spectator was faced with an image that exaggerated the importance of the figures it showed to a point where the deep space between them seemed to have been negated. The chief visual effect was the microscopically viewed countenance, one into which you could read almost anything. Almost as important was the static grouping of figures, amounting to a reversal of everything Hollywood had previously perfected in the creation of fluid groupings in unbounded space.

Citizen Kane and its Gimp-effects were generally laughed off by high-brows in Hollywood and elsewhere. Their opinion of the film was that it was too obviously theatrical and exhibitionistic to be linked to the main journalistic path of cinema. But one had the feeling, during the war years, that, as Hollywood turned out dozens of progressively more realistic action films—Western, war, detective—it was more than a little concerned with what Welles had done in the symbolic enriching of a movie through florid mannerisms. For Hollywood directors and actors couldn't forget that *Citizen Kane* was crazily three-dimensional in the manner of a psychoanalytic hour and that it did start you thinking at every moment of ambiguous drives hidden inside each character. *Citizen Kane* seems to have festered in Hollywood's unconscious until after the Wylers and Hustons returned from their government film chores; then it broke out in full force.

In the acclaimed films of the early postwar years (*The Lost Weekend, The Best Years of Our Lives, The Treasure of the Sierra Madre, Champion*), one began to see Welles's theatrical innovations effectively incorporated into certain films that otherwise tried to look like untouched records of reality. There still had to be a long training in what is known as "semidocumentary" technique (movies shot in real streets with nonstudio make-up, natural lighting, spontaneous pantomime) before Hollywood could link Welles's florid symbolism with enough of the appearance or actuality to make it appear moderately reasonable. But by now the lesson has been learned, and the ghost of *Citizen Kane* stalks a monstrous-looking screen. The entire physical structure of movies has been slowed down and simplified and brought closer to the front plane of the screen so that eccentric effects can be deeply felt. Hollywood has in effect developed a new medium which plays odd tricks with space and human behavior in order to project a content of popular "insights" beneath a meager surface.

Thus has a revolution taken place in Hollywood, probably unbeknownst to the very men—directors, actors, and critics—who have led it. If the significance of the New Movie is understood, it may well be that Hollywood will never be able to go home again. Any attempt to resurrect the old flowing naturalistic film that unfolds logically and takes place in "reasonable" space seems doomed to look as old-fashioned as the hoop skirt. For better or worse, we seem stuck with an absurdly controlled, highly mannered, overambitious creation that feeds on everything in modern art and swallows it so that what you see is not actually on the screen but is partly in your own mind, partly on the screen, and partly behind it. You have to read these pictures in a completely different way from the one you've been accustomed to. They are no longer literally stories or motion pictures, but a succession of static hieroglyphs in which overtones of meaning have replaced, in interest as well as in intent, the old concern with narrative, character, and action for their own sakes. These films must be seen, not literally, but as X-rays of the pluralistic modern mind. But the popular ideas deliberately half-buried in them have the hard, crude ring of Stone Age tools, though most of them come out of psychoanalysis and the Popular Front morality plays of the depression. The most ambitious of the current film-makers got their higher, and highest, education in the New York of the latter 1930's and have never lost the obsessive need to "improve" the world through art. They are by now too sophisticated and weary really to believe that this will work, but the hangover of conscience, regret, guilt, and frustration still produces in their movies the new Worried Look. They have lost the spirit and convictions of the radical 1930's, but the characteristic feelings of these years remain expressed vaguely in a bleak, humorless, free-floating, and essentially pointless misanthropy—social significance gone sour. There may be nothing wrong with misanthropy as a working viewpoint, but when, as in *A Place in the Sun*, it takes its conception of workers, tycoons, and debutantes from a world of ideas fantastically unrelated to current American experience, it is merely a negative sentimentality. The emotional impact of a technique committed to elegant, controlled, mis-mated power effects is as modern as ammoniated toothpaste; but the popular ideas to which this technique is wedded seem almost as dated and provincial as those in *Damaged Goods* or *A Fool There Was.*

NEARER MY AGEE TO THEE 1958

James Agee was the most intriguing star-gazer in the middle-brow era of Hollywood films, a virtuoso who capped a strange company of stars on people's lips and set up a hailstorm of ideas for other critics to use. Of all the ham-on-wry critics who wrote for big little magazines, Agee had the prose and ad-libability to handle the business-craft from all sides. He gave any number of unsung creators their only "deep" coverage; certain key images like "gentleman director" (in the case of Howard Hawks) spotlighted a peculiarly mellifluous soft-shoe type.

While his Tol'able Jim classic, *Let Us Now Praise Famous Men,* disclosed that he was an unorthodox, unsure left-fielder, Agee was able to build skyscrapers in art out of cross-purposes and clay. Even at his worst, in reviews where he was nice, thoughtful, and guilty until he seemed an "intellectual" hatched in Mack Sennett's brain, Agee was a fine antidote to the paralyzing plot-sociologists who hit the jackpot during the 1940's. His great contribution was a constant emphasis on the individuals operating in what is wrongly supposed a "mass art" that assembly-lines the personal out of existence.

The writers who flowered in 1939–47 movie columns of liberal middle-class journals had the same kind of reader-employer freedom that encouraged good sportswriters in the 1920's—i.e., they served an undemanding audience that welcomed style and knew hardly anything about the inside of movies. Agee wrote reasonable exaggerations, beautifully articulated, about dull plodding treacle that stretched from Jean Simmons to Ingrid Bergman. (Olivia de Havilland, he once wrote, "has for a long time been one of the prettiest women in movies; lately she has not only become prettier than ever but has started to act as well. I don't see evidence of any remarkable talent, but her playing is thoughtful, quiet, detailed, and well sustained, and since it is founded, as some more talented playing is not, in an unusually healthful-seeming and likable temperament, it is an undivided pleasure to see.'')

Thus, Agee built a Jim-dandy fan club almost the equal of Dylan Thomas's. Given this terrain of Ageephiles (Auden's rave about Agee in a *Nation* fan letter included the proud ''I do not care for movies and I rarely see them''), it was predictable that Agee's contradictory, often unlikable genius would be distorted, simplified, and dulled by an ever-growing hero worship.

Even where he modified and showboated until the reader had the Jim-jams, Agee's style was exciting in its pea-soup density. As in his beloved films (*Treasure of the Sierra Madre,* Olivier's work), his criticism had an excessive richness that came from a fine writing ear as well as cautious hesitancy, ganglia, guilt. The sentences are swamps that are filled with a suspicious number of right-sounding insights. Actually, Agee's appreciations stick pretty close to what the middle-brow wants to hear, as when he accused Mel Tormé of being out of a jar, and raptured about the unequaled ''poetry'' of Huston's Mexicans (who were closer to a bottle—spirits of hammonia—than Tormé). His three-dimensional use of ''I'' constructions, which seldom aroused the reader to its essential immodesty, was buttressed by a moralism that hawked the theater looking for the ''sellout'' in art. The Hollywood technicians were put through a purgatory: a new angle—the artist's soul—was added to movie criticism, as Agee, borrowing words from God, decided whether the latest Hollywood sexpot, in *Blanche of the Evergreens,* was truthful, human, selfless, decent, noble, pure, honorable, really good, or simply deceitful, a cheat, unclean, and without love or dignity.

As he shellacked the reader with culture, Agee had one infallibly charming tool in his kit: an aristocratic gashouse humor that made use of several art centuries, a fantastic recall of stray coupons—like old song lyrics and the favorite thing people were saying in February, 1917—and a way of playing leapfrog with clichés, making them sparkle like pennies lost in a Bendix. The funniest passage Agee wrote had to do with a fairly deadpan description of a movie discussion in a *Time* elevator, humor coming from his capacity to capture an elevator's sociology in the fewest words. But more often he indicated great comic timing, winding up the top-heavy *Lost Weekend* review with one flashing line: "I undershtand that liquor interesh: innerish: intereshtsh are rather worried about thish film. Thash tough."

Agee built slow reviews with his pet multiplications: "It is unusually hard, tense, cruel, intelligent, and straightforward. But I see nothing in it that is new, sharply individual, or strongly creative." The humor, which came strictly in spots, acted as an oasis: "Otherwise, the picture deserves, like four or five other movies, to walk alone, tinkle a little bell, and cry 'Unclean, unclean.' "

At least half of the growing Agee legend—that he had a great camera eye, writing equipment, and love for moviemakers—is fantasy. Agee's visual recall, so apparent in *tour de force* pieces on Sennett's gang that hit like a cold shower of visual needles, is always wedded to a blindness to chic artiness. His humanity has a curious way of leveling performers with flattery, and overcompeting with directors by flooding their works with a consuming sensibility. His journalistic manner in the smaller *Time* reviews is flawless, but, unfortunately, Agee's reputation is based on heavier writing which has a sensitively tinctured glibness (as in this pontifical stretch: "In these long close-ups, as in much else that he does, Dreyer goes against most of the 'rules' that are laid down, even by good people, for making genuine and good motion pictures. In a sense I have to admit that he is far out at the edge rather than close to the center of all that I think might be most productive and original. But there is only one rule for movies that I finally care about. . . .")

Agee's *Time* stint added up to a sharp, funny encyclopedia on the film industry during the 1940's. Though he occasionally lapsed into salesmanship through brilliantly subtle swami glamour (*Henry V,* the Ingrid Bergman cover story), Agee would be wisely remembered for quick biographies and reviews, particularly about such happy garbage as June Haver musicals and an early beatnik satire *Salome Where She Danced,* where his taste didn't have to outrun a superabundant writing talent. But this is the writing that has been shrugged out of *Agee On Film* by too shrewd editing that is conscious of the art-minded and carriage trade. Other evidences of the book shortchanging Agee's richness: (1) no sign of those extended journeys on Luce limb for a box-office hero, and (2) no evidence of his conflicting reviews on the same picture for the power (*Time*) and the glory (*The Nation*).

Suffering from happy-plexis and booming emphasis, Agee's deep-dish criticism in *The Nation* was motivated by a need to bridge Hollywood with the highest mounts of art. Like Gilbert Seldes, he had a dozen ways to move films into the museum. For instance, Agee was a master of critics' patter, the numbers racket, and the false bracket. He used other critics' enthusiasms: ("Winsten and McCarten think it is one of the best ever made. I don't care quite that much for it, but. . . ."), expanded petty courage into infinity (Wilder's courage in making *The Lost Weekend*), and maneuvered in a pinch with the one-eyed emphasis. "June Allyson, who seems incapable of a superficial performance" is a typical Agee periscope of an actress's one trait, a minor sincerity, at the expense of an immobile, rangeless cuteness.

If Agee had struggled more with the actual material of the popular nonartist, it is inconceivable that he could have missed the vapidity of so much "good" film art. With his incurious response to super-present-tense material in films, he could praise the stuffed-shirt timing in Olivier's "Crispin's Day" speech or the academic woodchopper's emphasis on that leer in *Sunset Boulevard*. A great segment of fine Hollywood work isn't interested in Big Art, but in making a contemporaneous "point" that, by the nature of its momentary truth, dies almost the moment the movie is released.

In certain abrupt *Nation* reviews (Kazan's anonymous realism in *Boomerang*, Ford's smoglike *They Were Expendable*), there is a mild struggling with the awareness that the movie is talking not about art but of the necessity of placing itself in a likable position with the furthest advances in currency—whether that contemporaneity has to do with nonchalance (*Good News*), a manner of shorthand phrasing (early parts of *The Ox-Bow Incident*), or a way of looking at "hip" folk (*The Big Sleep*). Agee was a brick wall against pretense in small movies, but, on Big Scale work, where the Boulevard is made of

National Velvet and the Limelight's as stunning as the Sierra Madre, Agee's reviews suggested a busy day at Muscle Beach: flexing words, bulging rumps of talent, pyramidal displays of filming cunning.

Agee is perhaps as bewitching as his bandwagon believes, if his whole complexity of traits is admitted in the record. Seldom has more personality walked through American criticism with such slyly cloaked overpossessive manners. The present Hollywood film, in which a mishmash knowledge of faintly old modern art is presented in show-biz language, owes part of its inauthentic soul to a fine critic, who even felt obliged to place pictures he disliked in a company with "all the good writing of this century, the films of Pudovkin and Pabst, and some of the music of Brahms."

PRESTON STURGES:

Success in the
Movies; Written with
W. S. Poster

1954

By all odds, the most outstanding example of a successful director with a flamboyant unkillable personality to emerge in
Hollywood during the last two decades has been that of Preston
Sturges, who flashed into the cinema capital in 1939, wrote, produced, and directed an unprecedented series of hits and now
seems to be leaping into relative obscurity. Hollywood destiny
has caught up with Sturges in a left-handed fashion; most
whiz-bang directors of the Sturges type remain successes while
their individuality wanes. Sturges seems to have been so riddled
by the complexities, conflicts, and opposed ambitions that came
together to enrich his early work that he could not be forced
into a mold. Instead of succumbing to successful conformity,
Sturges has all but ceased to operate in the high-powered, smash-
hit manner expected of him.

It is a peculiarly ironic fate, because Sturges is the last person in the world it is possible to think of as a failure. Skeptical
and cynical, Sturges, whose hobbies include running restaurants
and marketing profitable Rube Goldberg inventions, has never
publicly acknowledged any other goal but success. He believes it
is as easily and quickly achieved in America, particularly by persons of his own demoniac energy, mercurial brain, and gim-
mick-a-minute intensiveness. During the time it takes the average
American to figure out how to save $3 on his income tax, Sturges
is liable to have invented "a vibrationless Diesel engine," a
"home exerciser," the "first nonsmear lipstick," opened up a
new-style eatery, written a Broadway musical, given one of his
discouraged actors his special lecture on happiness, and figured
out a new way to increase his own superhuman productiveness
and efficiency.

In fact, Sturges can best be understood as an extreme embodiment of the American success dream, an expression of it as a pure idea in his person, an instance of it in his career, and its generalizer in his films. In Sturges, the concept of success operates with purity, clogging the ideology of ambition so that it becomes an esthetic credo, backfiring on itself, baffling critics, and creeping in as a point of view in pictures which are supposed to have none. The image of success stalks every Sturges movie like an unlaid ghost, coloring the plots and supplying the fillip to his funniest scenes. His madly confused lovers, idealists, and outraged fathers appear to neglect it, but it invariably turns up dumping pots of money on their unsuspecting heads or snatching away million-dollar prizes. Even in a picture like *The Miracle of Morgan's Creek,* which deals with small-town, humble people, it is inevitable that bouncing Betty Hutton should end up with sextuplets and become a national institution. The very names of Sturges's best-known movies seem to evoke a hashish-eater's vision of beatific American splendor: *The Great McGinty, The Power and the Glory, The Miracle of Morgan's Creek, Hail the Conquering Hero, The Great Moment, Christmas in July* reveal the facets of a single preoccupation.

Nearly everyone who has written about Sturges expresses great admiration for his intelligence and talent, total confusion about his pictures, and an absolute certainty that Sturges should be almost anything but what he nakedly and palpably is—an inventive American who believes that good picture-making consists in grinding out ten thousand feet of undiluted, chaos-producing energy. It is not too difficult to perceive that even Sturges's most appreciative critics were fundamentally unsympathetic toward him. Throughout his career, in one way or another, Sturges has been pilloried for refusing to conform to the fixed prescriptions for artists. Thus, according to René Clair, "Preston is like a man from the Italian Renaissance: he wants to do everything at once. If he could slow down, he would be great; he has an enormous gift, and he should be one of our leading creators. I wish he would be a little more selfish and worry about his reputation."

What Clair is suggesting is that Sturges would be considerably improved if he annihilated himself. Similarly, Siegfried Kracauer has scolded him for not being the consistent, socially-minded satirist of the rich, defender of the poor, and portrayer of the evils of modern life which he regards as the qualifying characteristics of all moviemakers admissible to his private pantheon. The more popular critics have condemned Sturges for not liking America enough; the advanced critics for liking it too much. He has also been accused of espousing a snob point of view and sentimentally favoring the common man.

Essentially Sturges, probably the most spectacular manipulator of sheer humor since Mark Twain, is a very modern artist or entertainer, difficult to classify because of the intense effort he has made to keep his work outside conventional categories. The high-muzzle velocity of his films is due to the anarchic energy generated as they constantly shake themselves free of attitudes that threaten to slow them down. Sturges's pictures maintain this freedom from ideology through his sophisticated assumption of the role of the ruthless showman deliberately rejecting all notions of esthetic weight and responsibility. It is most easy to explain Sturges's highly self-conscious philosophy of the hack as a kind of cynical morality functioning in reverse. Since there is so much self-inflation, false piety, and artiness in the arts, it was, he probably felt, less morally confusing to jumble slapstick and genuine humor, the original and the derivative together, and express oneself through the audacity and skill by which they are combined. It is also probable that he found the consistency of serious art, its demand that everything be resolved in terms of a logic of a single mood, repugnant to his temperament and false to life.

"There is nothing like a deep-dish movie to drive you out in the open," a Sturges character remarks, and, besides being a typical Sturges line, the sentence tells you a great deal about his moviemaking. His resourcefulness, intelligence, Barnum-and-Bailey showmanship and dislike of fixed purposes often make the typical Sturges movie seem like a uniquely irritating pastiche. A story that opens with what appears to be a bitingly satirical exposition of American life is apt to end in a jelly of cheap sentiment. In *Hail the Conquering Hero,* for example, Eddie Bracken plays an earnest, small-town boy trying to follow in the footsteps of his dead father, a World War I hero. Discharged because of hay fever, Bracken is picked up by six

Marines who talk him into posing as a Guadalcanal veteran and returning home as a hero to please his mother. The pretense snowballs, the town goes wild, and Bracken's antics become more complicated and tormenting with every scene. After he has been pushed into running for Mayor, he breaks down and confesses the hoax. Instead of tarring and feathering him, the townspeople melt with admiration for his candor and courage.

This ending has been attacked by critics who claim that it reveals Sturges compromising his beliefs and dulling the edge of his satire. "At his beginning," Mr. Kracauer writes, referring to *The Great McGinty,* "Sturges insisted that honesty does not pay. Now he wants us to believe that the world yields to candor." Such criticism is about as relevant as it would be to say that Cubists were primarily interested in showing all sides of a bottle at once. To begin with, it should be obvious to anyone who has seen two Sturges pictures that he does not give a tinker's dam whether the world does or does not yield to candor. Indeed his pictures at no time evince the slightest interest on his part as to the truth or falsity of his direct representation of society. His neat, contrived plots are unimportant per se and developed chiefly to provide him with the kind of movements and appearances he wants, with crowds of queer, animated individuals, with juxtapositions of unusual actions and faces. These are then organized, as items are in any art which does not boil down to mere sociology, to evoke *feelings* about society and life which cannot be reduced to doctrine or judged by flea-hopping from the work of art to society in the manner of someone checking a portrait against the features of the original.

What little satire there is in a film is as likely to be directed at satire as it is at society. The supposedly sentimental ending of *The Conquering Hero,* for example, starts off as a tongue-in-cheek affair as much designed to bamboozle the critics as anything else. It goes out of hand and develops into a series of oddly placed shots of the six Marines, shots which are indeed so free of any kind of attitude as to create an effect of pained ambiguous humanity, frozen in a moment of time, so grimly at one with life that they seem to be utterly beyond any one human emotion, let alone sentiment. The entire picture is, indeed, remarkable for the manner in which sequences are directed away from the surface mood to create a sustained, powerful, and life-like pattern of dissonance. The most moving scene in it—Pang-born's monumentally heartfelt reactions to Bracken's confession —is the product of straight comic pantomime. The Marine with an exaggerated mother-complex sets up a hulking, ominous im-age as the camera prolongs a view of his casual walk down the aisle of the election hall. The Gargantuan mugging and gestur-ing of the conscience-stricken Bracken provokes not only laugh-ter but the sense that he is suffering from some mysterious muscular ailment.

Such sequences, however, though integral to Sturges's best work, do not set its tone. The delightfulness, the exhilarating quality that usually prevails is due to the fact that the relation to life of most of the characters is deliberately kept weak and weightless. The foibles of a millionaire, the ugliness of a frump are all projected by similar devices and exploited in a like man-ner. They exist in themselves only for a moment and function chiefly as bits in the tumultuous design of the whole. Yet this design offers a truer equivalent of American society than can be supplied by any realism or satire that cannot cope with the tongue-in-cheek self-consciousness and irreverence toward its own fluctuating institutions that is the very hallmark of Ameri-can society—that befuddles foreign observers and makes Ameri-can mores well-nigh impervious to any kind of satire.

Satire requires a stationary society, one that seriously be-lieves in the enduring value of the features providing its iden-tity. But what is there to satirize in a country so much at the mercy of time and commerce as to be profoundly aware that all its traits—its beauties, blemishes, wealth, poverty, prejudices, and aspirations—are equally the merchandise of the moment, easily manufactured and trembling on the verge of destruction from the moment of production? The only American quality that can conceivably offer a focus for satire, as the early moviemakers and Sturges, alone among the contemporaries, have realized, is speed. Some of the great early comic films, those of Buster Keaton, for example, were scarcely comic at all but pure and very bitter satires, exhausting in endless combinations of all possible tortures produced as a consequence of the *naif* belief in speed. Mack Sennett was less the satirist of American speed-mania than its Diaghilev. Strip away the comic webbing, and your eye comes upon the preternatural poetic world created by an instinctive impresario of graceful accelerations. Keystone cops and bathing beauties mingle and separate in a buoyant, immensely varied ballet, conceived at the speed of mind but with camera velocity rather than the human body as its limit. Sturges was the only legitimate heir of the early American film, combining its various methods, adding new perspectives and developing the whole in a form suitable to a talking picture.

Since Sturges thought more synoptically than his predecessors, he presented a speed-ridden society through a multiple focus rather than the single, stationary lens of the pioneers. While achieving a more intense identification of the audience with the actors than in the earlier films (but less than the current talking pictures, which strive for complete audience identification with the hero), Sturges fragmented action, so that each scene blends into the next before it comes to rest, and created an illusion of relative motions. Basically, a Sturges film is executed to give one the delighted sensation of a person moving on a smoothly traveling vehicle going at high speed through fields, towns, homes, and even through other vehicles. The vehicle in which the spectator is traveling never stops but seems to be moving in a circle, making its journey again and again in an ascending, narrowing spiral until it diminishes into nothingness. One of his characters calls society a "cockeyed caravan," and Sturges, himself, is less a settled, bona fide resident of America than a hurried, Argus-eyed traveler through its shifting scenes, a nomad in space observing a society nomadic in time and projecting his sensations in uniquely computed terms.

This modern cinematic perspective of mobility seen by a mobile observer comes easily to Sturges because of his strange family background and broken-up youth. He was the son of a normal, sports-loving, successful father and a fantastic culture-bug mother who wanted him to be a genius and kept him in Paris from the age of eight to about fifteen. "She dragged me through every goddam museum on the continent," he has rancorously remarked. Glutted, at an early age, by an overrich diet of esthetic dancing, high-hatted opera audiences, and impressionist painting, Sturges still shows the marks of his youthful trauma.

The most obvious result of his experience has been a violent reaction against all estheticism. He has also expressed fervent admiration for his father's business ability and a desire to emulate him. The fact that he did not, however, indicates that his early training provoked more than a merely negative reaction in him and made him a logical candidate for Hollywood, whose entire importance in the history of culture resides in its unprecedented effort to merge art and big business.

As a moviemaker, the businessman side of Sturges was superficially dominant. He seems to have begun his career with the intention of giving Hollywood a lesson in turning out quick, cheap, popular pictures. He whipped together his scripts in record-breaking time, cast his pictures with unknowns, and shot them faster than anyone dreamed possible. He was enabled to do this through a native aptitude for finding brilliant technical shortcuts. Sturges tore Hollywood comedy loose from the slick gentility of pictures like *It Happened One Night* by shattering the realistic mold and the logical build-up and taking the quickest, least plausible route to the nerves of the audience. There are no preparations for the fantastic situations on which his pictures are based and no transitions between their numberless pratfalls, orgies of noise, and furniture-smashing. A Capra, Wilder, or Wellman takes half a movie to get a plot to the point where the audience accepts it and it comes to cinematic life. Sturges often accomplishes as much in the first two minutes, throwing an audience immediately into what is generally the most climactic and revelatory moment of other films.

The beginning of *Sullivan's Travels* is characteristic for its easy handling of multiple cinematic meanings. The picture opens abruptly on a struggle between a bum and a railroad employee on top of a hurtling train. After a few feet of a fight that is at once a sterling bit of action movie and a subtle commentary on action movies, it develops that you are in a projection studio, watching a film made by Sullivan, a famous director, and that the struggle symbolizes the conflict of capital and labor. As Sullivan and the moguls discuss the film's values and box-office possibilities, Sturges makes them all sound delightfully foolish by pointing up the naïve humanity of everyone involved. ''Who wants to see that stuff? It gives me the creeps!'' is the producer's reaction to the film. When Sullivan mentions a five-week run at the Music Hall, the producer explodes with magnificent improbability: "Who goes to the Music Hall? Communists!" Thus, in five minutes of quick-moving cinema and surprise-packed dialogue, a complex situation has been set forth and Sullivan is catapulted on his journey to learn about the moods of America in the depression.

The witty economy of his movies is maintained by his gifted exploitation of the non sequitur and the perversely unexpected. In nearly every case, he manages to bring out some hidden appropriateness from what seems like willful irrelevance. In *The Miracle of Morgan's Creek,* a plug-ugly sergeant mouths heavy psychiatric phrases in an unbelievable way that ends by sinking him doubly deep into the realm of the psychotic. With nihilistic sophistication, Sturges makes a Hollywood director keep wondering "Who is Lubitsch?" till you are not sure if it is simply fun or a weird way of expressing pretentiousness and ignorance. Similarly, in *The Conquering Hero,* the small-town citizens are given a happy ending and a hero to worship, but they are paraded through the streets and photographed in such a way that they resemble a lynch mob—a device which flattens out success and failure with more gruesome immediacy than Babbittlike satires.

What made Sturges a viciously alive artist capable of discovering new means of expressiveness in a convention-ridden medium was the frenetic, split sensibility that kept him reacting to and away from the opposite sides of his heredity. These two sides are, in fact, the magnetic poles of American society. Accepting, in exaggerated fashion, the businessman approach to films, he nevertheless brought to his work intelligence, taste, and a careful study of the more estimable movies of the past. He also took care to disappoint rigid-minded esthetes and reviewers. Although it has been axiomatic among advanced movie students that the modern film talks too much and moves too little, Sturges perversely thought up a new type of dialogue by which the audience is fairly showered with words. The result was paradoxically to speed up his movies rather than to slow them down, because he concocted a special, jerky, spluttering form of talk that is the analogue of the old, silent-picture firecracker tempo.

Partly this was accomplished by a wholesale use of "hooks"—
spoken lines cast as questions, absurd statements, or explosive
criticisms, which yank immediate responses from the listener.

Sturges's free-wheeling dialogue is his most original contribution to films and accomplishes, among other things, the destruction of the common image of Americans as tight-lipped
Hemingwayan creatures who converse in grating monosyllables
and chopped sentences. Sturges tries to create the equally American image of a wrangle of conflicting, overemotional citizens
who talk as though they were forever arguing or testifying before a small-town jury. They speak as if to a vast, intent audience
rather than to each other, but the main thing is that they un-
burden themselves passionately and without difficulty—even
during siesta moments on the front porch: "I'm perfectly calm.
I'm as—as cool as ice, then I start to figure maybe they won't
take me and some cold sweat runs down the middle of my back
and my head begins to buzz and everything in the middle of the
room begins to swim—and I get black spots in front of my eyes
and they say I've got high blood pressure. . . ."

As the words sluice out of the actors' mouths, the impression
is that they teeter on the edge of a social, economic, or psychological cliff and that they are under some wild compulsion to set
the record straight before plunging out of the picture. Their
speech is common in language and phrasing, but Sturges makes
it effervesce with trick words ("whackos" for "whack"), by
pumping it full of outraged energy or inserting a daft idea like
the Music Hall gag. All of this liberated talk turns a picture into
a kind of open forum where everyone down to the cross-eyed bit
player gets a chance to try out his oratorical ability. A nice word-
festival, very democratic, totally unlike the tight, gagged-up
speech that movies inherited from vaudeville, radio, and the
hard-boiled novel.

Paradoxically, too, his showman's approach enabled Sturges
to be the only Hollywood talking-picture director to apply to
films the key principles of the "modern" revolutions in poetry,
painting, and music: namely, beginning a work of art at the
climax and continuing from there. Just as the modern painter
eschews narrative and representational elements to make his
canvas a continuum of the keenest excitement natural to paint-

ing, or the poet minimizes whatever takes his poem out of the realm of purely verbal values, so Sturges eliminated from his movies the sedulous realism that has kept talking pictures essentially anchored to a rotting nineteenth-century esthetic. In this and other ways, Sturges revealed that his youth spent "caroming around in High-Bohemian Europe" had not been without a positive effect on his work. Its basic textures, forms, and methods ultimately derive from post-Impressionist painting, Russian ballet, and the early scores of Stravinsky, Hindemith, et al. The presence of Dada and Surrealism is continuously alive in its subsurface attitudes or obvious in the handling of specific scenes. Sturges's fat Moon Mullins–type female, playing a hot tail-gate trombone at a village dance, is the exact equivalent in distortion of one of Picasso's lymphatic women posed as Greek statues.

Sturges's cinematic transpositions of American life reveal the outsider's ability to seize salient aspects of our national existence plus the insider's knowledge of their real meaning. But the two are erratically fused by the sensibility of the nostalgic, dislocated semiexile that Sturges essentially remains. The first impression one gets from a Sturges movie is that of the inside of a Ford assembly line smashed together and operating during a total war crisis. The characters, all exuding jaundice, cynicism, and anxiety, work feverishly as every moment brings them the fear that their lives are going to pieces, that they are going to be fired, murdered, emasculated, or trapped in such ridiculous situations that headlines will scream about them to a hooting nation for the rest of their lives. They seem to be haunted by the specters of such nationally famous boneheads as Wrong-Way Corrigan, Roy Riegels, who ran backward in a Rose Bowl game, or Fred Merkle, who forgot to touch second base in a crucial play-off game, living incarnations of the great American nightmare that some monstrous error can drive individuals clean out of society into a forlorn no man's land, to be the lonely objects of an eternity of scorn, derision, and self-humiliation. This nightmare is of course the reverse side of the uncontrolled American success impulse, which would set individuals apart in an apparently different but really similar and equally frightening manner.

Nearly all the Sturges comedies were centered with a sure instinct on this basic drive with all its complex concomitants. Using a stock company of players (all of a queer, unstandard, and almost aboriginal Americanism), Sturges managed to give his harrowing fables of success-failure an intimate, small-town setting that captured both the moony desire of every American to return to the small world of his youth and that innocent world itself as it is ravaged by a rampant, high-speed industrialism. The resultant events are used to obtain the comic release that is, indeed, almost the only kind possible in American life: the savage humor of absolute failure or success. Sturges's funniest scenes result from exploding booby traps that set free bonanzas of unsuspected wealth. In one episode, for example, two automat employees fight and trip open all the levers behind the windows; the spouts pour, the windows open, and a fantastic, illicit treasure trove of food spills out upon a rioting, delightfully greedy mob of bums, dowagers, and clerks. In *The Palm Beach Story,* members of the "Ale and Quail" club—a drunken, good-humored bunch of eccentric millionaires—shoot up a train and lead yapping hounds through Pullmans in a privileged orgy of destruction. This would seem the deeply desired, much fantasied reward of a people that endures the unbelievably tormented existence Sturges depicts elsewhere—a people whose semicomic suffering arises from the disparity between the wild lusts generated by American society and the severity of its repressions.

Sturges's faults are legion and have been pretty well gone over during his most successful period. Masterful with noisy crowds, he is liable to let a quiet spot in the script provoke him to burden the screen with "slapstick the size of a whale bone." A good businessman believes that any article can be sold if presented with eardrum-smashing loudness and brain-numbing certitude. From a similar approach, Sturges will represent hilarity by activating a crew of convicts as though he were trying to get Siberia to witness their gleeful shrieks. To communicate the bawdy wit of a fast blonde, he will show the tough owner of a lunch wagon doubled up like a suburban teenager hearing his first dirty joke. The comic chaos of a small-town reception must be evoked by the use of no less than four discordant bands.

Sturges has been accused of writing down to his audience, but it is more probable that there is too much of the businessman actually in his make-up to expect him to function in any other way. The best of his humor must come in a brash flurry of effects, all more or less oversold because there is nothing in his background that points to a more quiet, reasonable approach to life.

But even these vices are mitigated somewhat by the fact that they provide an escape from the plight of many intelligent, sensibility-ridden artists or entertainers of his period whose very intelligence and taste have turned against them, choking off their vitality and driving them into silence or reduced productivity. The result is that artistic ebullience and spontaneity have all but drained down to the very lowest levels of American entertainment. Even in the movies these days, one is confronted by slow-moving, premeditated affairs—not so much works of art or entertainments aimed by the intelligence at the glands, blood, and viscera of the audience as exercises in mutual criticism and good taste. The nervous tantrums of slapstick in a Sturges movie, the thoughtless, attention-getting antics combined with their genuine cleverness give them an improvised, blatant immediacy that is preferable to excesses of calculation and is, in the long run, healthier for the artists themselves.

As a maker of pictures in the primary sense of the term, Sturges shows little of the daring and variety that characterize him as a writer and, on the whole, as a director. He runs to middle shots, symmetrical groupings, and an evenly lit screen either of the bright modern variety or with a deliberately aged, grey period-finish. His composition rarely takes on definite form because he is constantly shooting a scene for ambivalent effects. The love scenes in *The Lady Eve*, for example, are shot, grouped, and lit in such a way as to throw a moderate infusion of sex and sentiment into a fast-moving, brittle comedy without slowing it down. The average director is compelled to use more dramatic composition because the moods are episodic, a completely comic sequence alternating with a completely sentimental scene. Sturges's treatment is fundamentally more cinematic, but he has not found a technique equal to it. Fluent as a whole, his pictures are often clumsy and static in detail, and he has not learned how to get people to use their bodies so that there is excitement merely in watching them move. In a picture like Howard

Hawks's *His Girl Friday*, Cary Grant uses legs, arms, trick hat, and facial muscles to create a pixyish ballet that would do credit to a Massine. But, when Sturges selects an equally gifted exponent of stylized movement, Henry Fonda, he is unable to extract comparable values from a series of falls, chases, listings to portside, and shuddering comas. Stray items—Demarest's spikey hair, Stanwyck's quasi-Roman nose—clutter up his foreground like blocks of wood. Even dogs, horses, and lions seem to turn into stuffed props when the Sturges camera focuses on them.

The discrepancies in Sturges's films are due largely to the peculiar discontinuities that afflict his sensibility, although such afflicton is also a general phenomenon in a country where whole eras and cultures in different stages of development exist side by side, where history along one route seems to skip over decades only to fly backward over another route and begin over again in still a different period. What Sturges presents with nervous simultaneity is the skyrocketing modern world of high-speed pleasures and actions (money-making, vote-getting, barroom sex, and deluxe transportation) in conflict with a whole Victorian world of sentiment, glamour, baroque appearance, and static individuality in a state of advanced decay. In all probability, his years spent abroad prevented his finding a bridge between the two worlds or even a slim principle of relating them in any other way than through dissonance. A whole era of American life with its accompaniment of visual styles is skimped in his work, the essential problems thus created being neatly bypassed rather than solved.

But his very deficiencies enabled Sturges to present, as no one else has, the final decay of the bloated Victorian world, which, though seemingly attached to nothing modern and destined to vanish with scarcely a trace, has nevertheless its place in the human heart if only for its visual splendors, its luxurious, impractical graces, and all too human excesses. From McGinty to Harold Diddlebock, Sturges gives us a crowded parade of courtly, pompous, speechifying, queerly dressed personages caught as they slowly dissolve with an era. His young millionaires—Hickenlooper III (Rudy Vallee), Pike (Henry Fonda), and rich movie director Sullivan (Joel McCrea)—a similar type of being—are like heavily ornamented bugs, born out of an Oliver

Twist world into a sad-faced, senile youth as moldy with leisure and tradition as an old cheese. Incapable of action, his obsolete multimillionaires gaze out into a world that has passed them by but to which they are firmly anchored by their wealth.

A pathetic creature in the last stages of futility, Vallee's sole occupation consists of recording, in a little black book, minute expenditures which are never totaled—as though he were the gently demented statistician of an era that has fallen to pieces for no special reason and has therefore escaped attention. Fonda as Pike, the heir of a brewery fortune (*The Ale That Won for Yale*), is the last word in marooned uselessness. A wistful, vague, young, scholarly ophiologist nicknamed Hoppsey, Pike's sole business in life consists of feeding four flies, a glass of milk, and one piece of white bread to a rare, pampered snake. In between, he can be seen glumly staring at a horde of predatory females, uncooperatively being seduced, getting in and out of suits too modern for him, sadly doing the oldest card trick in the world, and pathetically apologizing for not liking beer or ale. Oddly enough, his supposed opposite, a fast, upper-class card-sharp (Barbara Stanwyck) is no less Victorian, issuing as she does from a group of obsolete card Houdinis with an old-fashioned code of honor among thieves and courtly old-world manners and titles.

If Sturges has accomplished nothing else, he has brought to consciousness the fact that we are still living among the last convulsions of the Victorian world, that, indeed, our entire emotional life is still heavily involved in its death. These final agonies (though they have gone on so long as to make them almost painless), which only Sturges has recorded, can be glimpsed daily, in the strange, gentle expiration of figures like Shaw, Hearst, Jolson, Ford; the somewhat sad explosion of fervor over MacArthur's return (a Sturges picture by itself, with, if the fading hero had been made baseball czar, a pat Sturges ending); and the Old World pomp, unctuousness, and rural religiosity of the American political scene.

Nowhere did Sturges reveal his Victorian affinities more than by his belief in, use, and love of a horde of broken, warped, walked-over, rejected, seamy, old character actors. Some of these crafty bit players, like Walburn, Bridge, Tannen, made up his stock company, while others like Coburn, Pangborn, Kennedy, and Blore appear only in single pictures. They were never questioned by critics, although they seemed as out of place in a film about modern times as a bevy of Floradora girls. They appear as monstrously funny people who have gone through a period of maniacal adjustment to capitalist society by exaggerating a single feature of their character: meekness, excessive guile, splenetic aggressiveness, bureaucratic windiness, or venal pessimism. They seem inordinately toughened by experience, but they are, one is aware, not really tough at all, because they are complete fakers—life made it inevitable. They are very much part of the world of Micawber and Scrooge but later developments—weaker, more perfect, bloated, and subtle caricatures—giving off a fantastic odor of rotten purity and the embalmed cheerfulness of puppets.

They all appear to be too perfectly adjusted to life to require minds, and, in place of hearts, they seem to contain an old scratch sheet, a glob of tobacco juice, or a brown banana. The reason their faces—each of which is a succulent worm's festival, bulbous with sheer living—seem to have nothing in common with the rest of the human race is precisely because they are so eternally, agelessly human, oversocialized to the point where any normal animal component has vanished. They seem to be made up not of features but a *collage* of spare parts, most of them as useless as the vermiform appendix.

Merely gazing at them gives the audience a tremendous lift, as if it were witnessing all the drudgery of daily life undergoing a reckless transmutation. It is as if human nature, beaten to the ground by necessity, out of sheer defiance had decided to produce utterly useless extravaganzas like Pangborn's bobbling cheeks, Bridge's scrounging, scraping voice, or Walburn's evil beetle eyes and mustache like a Fuller brush that has decided to live an independent life. It is all one can do to repress a maniac shriek at the mere sight of Harold Lloyd's companion in *Mad Wednesday*. His body looks like that of a desiccated 200-year-old locust weighed down by an enormous copper hat. Or Pat Moran's wrecked jeep of a face, and his voice that sounds as if its owner had just been smashed in the Adam's apple by Joe Louis. These aged, senile rejects from the human race are put through a routine that has, in one minute, the effect of a long, sad tone poem and, after an hour, gives a movie a peculiar, hallucinatory quality, as if reality had been slightly tilted and robbed of significant pieces.

No one has delineated sheer indolence as Sturges has with these characters. When one appears on the screen, it looks as if he had wandered into the film by mistake and, once there, had been abandoned by the makers. When a second one of these *lumpen* shows up, the audience begins to sit on the edge of its seat and to feel that the picture is going to pieces, that the director has stopped working or the producer is making a monkey out of it. After a few minutes of lacerated nothingness, it becomes obvious that the two creatures are fated to meet; considerable tension is generated, as the audience wonders what build-up will be used to enable them to make each other's acquaintance. To everybody's horror, there is no build-up at all; the creatures link arms as the result of some gruesome asocial understanding and simply walk off. In *Mad Wednesday*, this technique yields a kind of ultimate in grisly, dilapidated humor, particularly in the long episode which begins with Harold Lloyd meeting the locustlike creature on the greasiest looking sidewalk ever photographed. The two repair to a bar presided over by Edgar Kennedy, who slowly and insanely mixes for Lloyd his first alcoholic potion. This entire, elaborate ritual is a weirder, cinematic version of the kind of "study in decrepit life" for which e. e. cummings is famed; certainly it is at least comparable in merit and effectiveness.

Sturges may not be the greatest director of the last two decades; in fact, it can be argued that a certain thinness in his work—his lack of a fully formed, solid, orthodox moviemaker's technique—prevents him from being included among the first few. He is, however, the most original movie talent produced in recent years: the most complex and puzzling. The emotional and intellectual structure of his work has so little in common with the work of other artists of our time that it seems to be the result of a unique development. Yet it is sufficiently logical and coherent to give it a special relevance to the contemporary American psyche—of precisely the kind that is found in some modern American poetry and painting, and almost nowhere else. Nothing is more indicative of the ineptitude of present-day Hollywood than its failure to keep Sturges producing at his former clip.

FRANK CAPRA 1950

Having won more prizes and recorded more hits in thirty years than any other Hollywoodian, Frank Capra is rated a "cinemagician" whose "masterful comedies" reveal a "tender sense of humor, a quick sense of social satire, and a glowing faith in human nature." Since he is always for the little man (Mr. Smith, Mr. Deeds: helpless, innocent, likable, gawky) against such populist bogies as the Corrupt Politician, Hearstian Newspaperman, Big Tycoon; always in favor of copybook maxims (Be Kind, Love Thy Country, The Best Things Are Free); and spices his sermons with equally stereotyped sentiment and humor (a mild tap by a car salesman and the headlight falls off), Hollywood's best-loved preacher should please anyone who goes for obvious social consciousness, character-building, and entertainment. Actually the only subtle thing about this conventionalist is that, despite his folksy, emotion-packed fables, he is strictly a mechanic, stubbornly unaware of the ambiguities that ride his shallow images.

Riding High (from riches to nags with Bing Crosby) catches some of the jumpy, messy, half-optimistic energy seen around race tracks, but leaves you feeling that you've been taken in like a carnival sucker. For instance, the movie drools democratic pride in Crosby's sugary relationship with his colored stableboy, displaying a sashaying Negro named "Whitey" whose happy slave personality, Sambo dialect (hallelujah), rapid expressions of unctuous love are derived from an old stencil cut out of the deepest kind of prejudice.

Capra's nervous films skip goat-fashion over a rocky *Satevepost* terrain. In *Riding High,* Crosby throws over a dollar-plated job and fiancée to make a stakes-winner out of an underprivileged beast called Broadway Bill (characteristically cast with a gentle, trick-performing horse who doesn't look "diseased with speed"). As in all Capra films, the world is given to the underdog (the 100-to-1 entry, two-buck better, brat daughter—all win over the big, pompous, and rich), but the sleek, pampered technique, the grandiose talk, and eating habits of his down-and-out characters, and even the names (Imperial City, Pettigrew, Brooks) make for a plush, elegant movie that subtly eulogizes the world of powerful wealth. Capra's poverty boys are royalists in ratty boarding houses and leaky stables; when they eat at a hamburger stand, they treat the owner like a witless palace scullion. The gags always revolve about large sums of money, often rib a character for not being a liberal spender, delight in scenes that resemble a busy day at the Stock Exchange. Actually Capra only hates and attacks the humdrum plodder made humble by necessity; his smart-aleck jibes at artless, hard-working waiters or farmers invariably win sympathy where Capra intends you to snicker.

Capra's career-long punching bag has been smug respectability (one of the key lines from *It Happened One Night* was "Twenty millions and you don't know how to dunk"), but he characteristically double-crosses his social criticism. Although Crosby stands for the beautiful freedom of the gypsy (against job slavery, punctuality, table manners, neatness, and bathtubs), he suggests a spoiled little boy more than an anarchic vagabond. Surrounded by male and female sycophants who giggle violently at his jokes and turn up at a crisis with money, food, and good cheer, Crosby looks like a well-kept seal, generally compromises his role with self-confident affectations (he knocks out a cop with a neat, powerless punch) and the secure, aloof expression of one whose mind is on a treasure buried twenty feet from every scene.

The chief sensation in *Riding High* is of a slick, capricious, overtrained life that holds one completely out of the movie as though there were a glass pane between audience and screen. The interesting details have an idiotic element because the director's hand is constantly showing, and the effects are obviously dictated by formulas for keeping an image active, holding the eye, manufacturing excitement in a slight, predictable plot. The idiocy is apparent where Capra energizes static scenes by having Crosby chew gum with jet-propelled jaws, or by photographing the burial of Broadway Bill, who dies crossing the finish line, in a small tornado. Capra is always getting into foolish, capracorny corners and almost edging himself out by suddenly reverting to stark journalistic shots (the horrifying close-up of Broadway

Bill in a ground-piercing nose dive), and carefully anatomized melodrama. One trick scene is the ultimate in surrealism; an extended mid-race examination (the race is so expanded by drama-building close-ups that a camel could have won) of a crooked jockey slyly throwing the race by standing upright in the stirrups and pulling the bit so hard the horse's nose is practically skyward. Despite the exaggerated villainy, the fact that the cameraman should have been trampled to death, and that the jockey is a different, even taller one than the rider who started the race, this is one of the few scenes that pulls you into the movie—as much by spontaneous acting and newsreel photography as by its weirdness.

PARADE FLOATS 1952

By way of the characteristic reticence of John Ford, you probably know that he considers *The Quiet Man*—which, given Ford's influence, should produce some awful offspring notable for female pratfalls, fistfights, and every person a Macy's balloon—to be the best of his 108 pictures. An old-fashioned confection idealizing the scenic beauties and quaint customs of Ireland, it is no better than the supersentimental landscapes and editorial-ridden life in *Grapes of Wrath* (probably the most-bloated-yet version of vocation-oriented films, without any of the looseness of *Slim* or *They Drive by Night*) and a bit worse than the potboiler *When Willie Comes Marching Home*, which was somewhat less hampered by Ford's bellicose barroom sentimentality, the promiscuous dumping of actresses, or falsified by the unstinting use of picturesque, ethnically slanted scenes. Often during *The Quiet Man*, the audience finds something laughable (the town drunkard and gossip muttering when he is offered buttermilk instead of whisky, ''The Borgias would do better''), but mostly the moviegoer has to put up with clumsily contrived fist fights, musical brogues spoken as though the actor were coping with an excess of tobacco juice in his mouth, mugging that plays up all the trusted hokums that are supposed to make the Irish so humorous-sympathetic, and a script that tends to resolve its problems by having the cast embrace, fraternity-brother–fashion, and break out into full-throated ballads.

In the midst of it, is the formless love story of two champion poseurs, one of them a strong, silent ex-boxer from Pittsburgh, Massachusetts (gag), who returns to the thatched cottage of his birth and spends the film wistfully lapping up luxurious scenery around Galway; the other, a hot-tempered, shy country wench who runs through streams clutching her broad-brimmed hat or compulsively glancing over her shoulder as she backs off to the very bottom of the screen. The characters are paper-thin types with traits taken from pulp stories, nineteenth-century novels, and a dozen British films starring members of the Abbey Thea-

ter. The noble close-mouthed hero developed his tungsten muscles in Pittsburgh's mills, learned about Ireland's beauties at his
mother's knee, and lost his urge to fight when he killed a ring
opponent. All this is revealed by way of dialogue, so that there
is nothing for John Wayne to impersonate except John Wayne.
Maureen O'Hara plays the windlike heroine out of *Wuthering
Heights,* and the Ford stock company (Arthur Shields, Ward
Bond, Victor McLaglen, Mildred Natwick, Barry Fitzgerald)
goes through the dated mimicry of such stereotypes as the tip-
pling village cabby, the thick-headed, bellicose squire, and the
jovial village priest, who curses, jokes, and fishes from start to
finish of the film.

Some of the technicolor photography is pretty original—a
dense, gray atmosphere takes most of the hue and intensity out
of the scene and makes for a curious picture that takes place in
daylight yet has some of the sunless, remembered look of a surrealist painting. Ford's ability to lyricize a movie with scenic
effects is manifest wherever the camera moves: Barry Fitzgerald
driving his sidecar beneath a little bridge as the train passes
over it, the old business of the wedding photograph burlesqued
like a quaint valentine, wind delicately whipping a pile of sweep-
ings. But all this padding of what is supposed to be an illusive,
impressionistic study of a land and its people is disturbing because it becomes the underlying motive for the scenes, revealing
the limited significance of every pub brawl, horse race, or pastoral event almost before the scene is under way.

1969

A 1961 cavalry film that is like an endless frontier-day pageant,
Two Rode Together has the discombobulated effect of a Western
dreamt by a kid snoozing in an Esso station in Linden, New
Jersey. Two wrangling friends, a money-grubbing marshal
(Jimmy Stewart) and a cavalry captain (Richard Widmark,
who has the look of a ham that has been smoked, cured, and then
coated with honey-colored shellac), seek out a Comanche named
Parker and trade him a stunningly new arsenal of guns and

knives for a screaming little Bowery Boy with braids who's only bearable in the last shot when the camera just shows his legs hanging limply from a lynching tree.

The movie's mentally retarded quality comes from the discordancy and quality of the parts: it's not only that they don't go together, they're crazy to start with. Each woman and Indian is from a different age in operetta and a different part of the globe. The Indians include an overdeveloped weight-lifter, a sad Pagliacci trying hard not to let his flabby stomach show, plus the above Leo Gorcey tough with his histrionic impression of a monkey on hot coals. The movie wobbles most with Widmark, embarrassed but strangely submitting to courting scenes with Shirley Jones that are filled with temerity and wide-eyed hopefulness. His tomboy sweetheart, a fraulein out of *The Student Prince* with two thick long yellow braids and enough make-up to equal Widmark's, has a fixation on a music box and runs to it at every chance.

The movie is a curious blend of modern blat and a senile impression of frontier culture that derives from the cheapest and oldest movies about prerailroad days in Indian territory. There is a wild, non sequitur quality about the courtship, frontier dialogue, and spitting, thin-skinned, stupidly stubborn Indians taking place in a free-for-all atmosphere in which not one detail or scene goes with another. In general, it is Widmark and Stewart, like two Pinter characters, separated out from a stiff (despite the yelling and flouncing), corny TV-styled production going on behind them. Throughout, these actors barely listen to each other, and, affecting a curious, dragged out, folksy dialect, they take up great amounts of space with words that are from Dimwit's Land. "No! She didn't kill herself, ladies and gentlemen. Not because she was a coward, but because her religion forbade her. Sometimes, it takes more courage to live than to die." Facetiously delivering this speech, Stewart is operating here in a feeble, tensionless mock-up of an officers' cotillion at the local fort. (I kept wondering, Why are they dragging in a dance? Could it be to squeeze that white hypocrisy speech into the remains of a script previously taken up with removing the normal skin tone, stealth, dignity, and clothes sense from Indians?)

It is filled with cliché conceptions: of an Indian camp, a Texas

Guinan seenioreeta who owns the saloon and the town, slow-witted people, an innocent tomboy heroine throwing a barrel of flour over the two Cleggs who come courting her, country bumpkins having a fight in the woods. These one-dimensional impressions could embarrass any actor, but what is staggeringly insensitive about the treatment is the way an actor is made so ridiculous by the camera treatment, either being locked, sliced in two, or frittered away in golden shoe polish by pictorial set-ups. A fine TV soap-opera actress, very good at shading womanly intelligence into irony, showing much more range than Agnes Moorehead in Lady Macbeth–type roles, Jeanette Nolan is murdered long before the Me Comanchah kid gets her by compositions which turn her into unpleasant pleading, cropping her at the hips and hardening her flat, angular face and voice. Mae Marsh, whose frenzied vivacity enriched many Griffith films with improvised, energy-spilling effects, is similarly waylaid, not so much by her corny "I had a white husband once" speech and a make-up job midway between a clown face and Molly Drunk All Night, but by a wigwam composition in which, bent over, she cringes out of a sea of blue ink.

The fascination of the director with lines of action in deep space adds ten lethal minutes here and there of illogicality, to a script that is already overloaded with fat items: capitalist law enforcers, matricide, overbearing mothers. For instance, the Widmark-Stewart team leads a wagon train into the wilderness through bogs of bumpkin comedy and tinsel wooing. Later, after a brief moment at a campsite, all these people are mysteriously back in the fort as though they'd never left it.

It's incredible, the amount of leeway that is allowed. If a prop man locates a bench from an antique store next to a tree in a just-set-up campsite, the scene stays in, though the film for the preceding five minutes has been insisting on formidable wilderness. This is studio moviemaking at its slackest.

All these gauche, careless skills—the uglification of actors (padding a buxom barmaid, Annelle Hayes, so that her bust line starts angling out from the collarbone and doesn't turn in till it reaches her waist), the jerky progress from melodrama to bathos to camp, the TV-Western feeling of no flow, outdoors, or sense of period (Stewart is wearing a jacket from Abercrombie, all Indians and their tents are from a psychotics' Halloween Ball)—are the responsibility of John Ford, a director generally noted for making movies with a poetic and limitless knowledge of Indians, ranging farthest across the landscape of the American past, and being the moviemaker's Mr. Movie.

HARD-SELL CINEMA 1957

One of the major weapons against boredom these days is the joyless rumination one can expend over the success in the "culture underground" of efficient, hard-working mediocrities who threaten to wipe out the whole idea of "felt," committed art. I am referring to the revolution that is occurring simultaneously in jazz (Brubeck, Guiffre, Getz) ; painting (Rivers, Kline, Hartigan, Brooks) ; the novel (Salinger, Bellow, Cheever) ; and films (Chayefsky, Delbert Mann, Kazan). The revolution that has introduced a "new" type into what is known as advanced, radical, experimental, progressive, or, simply, avant-garde art. The figure who is engineering this middle-class blitz has the drive, patience, conceit, and daring to become a successful nonconforming artist without having the talent or idealism for rebellious creation. The brains behind his creativity are those of a high-powered salesman using empty tricks and skills to push an item for which he has no feeling or belief. Avant-gardism has fallen into the hands of the businessman-artist.

The similarities between a Rivers diary-type abstraction, a Brubeck jazz record, and the Lumet-Rose film *Twelve Angry Men* are startling. Each work presents a clever, racy surface, peppered with enough technical smash and speed to make any spectator suspect he is in the presence of a disturbing original talent. However, nothing is explored in depth : Washington does not cross the Delaware in Rivers's famous painting; in fact, this badly composed work barely makes it to a stage of tasteful *joie de vivre* (tentative cobwebby lines, messy water color, and open canvas) that every painting crosses in its early, more facetious moments. By removing the soul from creativity and leaving an easy-to-read exposé of modernity, Rivers paints what amounts to a come-on for every clerk who dreams of greatness in a more romantic occupation. Anyone with necessary brass, drive, restlessness, and lack of taste can not only play the game but become a champion.

An interesting thing about these artists is that they are wonderfully neat and quick technicians. The new jazzmen—Guiffre, Getz, Brubeck—are unbelievably deft and crisp in their run-on gimmicks with instrument and composition. But, by removing everything in accomplishment that gets in the way of technique, they have landed a long way from that which had been planned for progressive jazz by its founding fathers. Without the human involvement and probing of Parker's sax-playing—the pain-wracked attack, as well as the playfulness and sudden spurts of wildly facetious slang—Getz turns the baritone sax into a thing that can be easily mastered, like a typewriter.

It is a mild pleasure simply watching TV director Sidney Lumet's control in *Twelve Angry Men*, bringing a hundred tiny details of schmaltzy anger and soft-center "liberalism" into a clean mosaic. His pointed control and swift exploitation of the beadlike detail is dazzling compared to the slow, camera-milked style of a more perceptive and meticulous Huston, who takes an age of screen time to get across the idea of a stomach growl. In *Giant,* the ponderously traditionalist craftsman George Stevens deliberates through reels of finicky realism to build a slum background for Mexican peons, while Lumet works the same sentimental route to a do-gooder's heart with one line of Reginald Rose dialogue. Within the Stevens triteness (Elizabeth Taylor descending like Miss Nightingale on the poor little adobes of Poker Flat), there are a hundred minor thrills of coloring, tone, texture, time, sunlight, and architecture that are far beyond Lumet's moderate Philco-Hour technique. Nevertheless, it is the shrill tingle of Lumet's counterfeit moviemaking that is helping to drive the Stevens type of architectural craftsmanship into obsolescence.

The most morbid fact about the "revolutionists" is that their leaders are *made* artists, basically blacksmiths who have acquired expedient techniques through long hours of insensitive hard work. Obvious examples of the deadly hand with craft are the current champions of avant-garde fiction whose near best sellers are basically the products of a stale, conservative charm camouflaging an immeasurable vacuity of thought. This *"New Yorker–Partisan Review* axis" writer has built an impressive and odious style that has the solemnity and emptiness of a small-town library room. It features words that are anchored to the page by lead weights, characters who are wobbly, unrecognizable reconstructions of chic art attitudes, and ideas impossible to understand because they come out of a fog of stupidity.

It is hard to say where the business mind first entered the door of modern American creativity. Tracing its antecedents is like working backward across a terrain of quicksand, but one fact keeps thrusting forward: in the rise of cold, short-stack, grounded Macy's artistry, there is an aroma of mean commercial competitiveness.

The new ultrasmooth "radicals" have succeeded on no art front as quickly as they have in films, where fourth-rate talents in compressed flurries of artiness, have made the crucial films of the giant screen. The crews responsible for these films are mostly exiles from Broadway, who developed a rigid, eclectic movie technique to go with mean-spirited "liberalism" that always pretends it is being wonderfully kind, curious, and civic-minded about people from the Upper Bronx, Lower Manhattan, and Pigott, Arkansas. The group discussed here (writers Serling, Chayefsky, Willingham, Schulberg, Rose, Lehman and directors Delbert Mann, Ritt, Mulligan, Lumet, Frankenheimer, Cook, Garfein) started its rise in 1955 with *Marty*, a souped-up, genteel counterfeit of the quaint Preston Sturges–Sam Fuller B-film technique, and continued through a string of successes, each a slightly rougher snap version of something that was controversial in the art of the 1920's and 1930's.

The most immediate effect in each of their hits is that of seeing a fast copy of some art image from the past. In Kazan's *A Face in the Crowd,* there is a preciously knitted shot of two distant silhouette figures walking up a lonely rural road through an atmosphere that suggests barley-textured sunlight, a stock exit that has been a pet of many semigenuine artists (including Chaplin). In the new eclectic style, familiar angles engulf the entire story structure. The social conscience ping-pong in *Twelve Angry Men* is heavily indebted to Steinbeck's tender concern for infinitesimal underdogs. *A Face in the Crowd* makes a lunging sophomoric attempt to show up the boobs and crackpots connected with "jes' plain folks" programs, recalling Sinclair

Lewis's caricaturing and Henry Miller's candid, slapstick sex. The Broadway vultures in *The Sweet Smell of Success* plot each other's destruction with fancy dialogue that bounces Clifford Odets into Damon Runyon and Molly Goldberg. The slick-magazine psychoanalysis of a lonely traitor in *The Rack* and a deranged ballplayer in *Fear Strikes Out* take you back to the late 1930's, when movies like *Blind Alley* were bringing Freud to proletarian art.

The most painfully amusing thing about this devotion to "ancient" modern art is that it also borrows from the big era in TV drama, the early 1950's, which gave the world Chayefsky, Reginald Rose, and many other businessmen "radicals." The scripts that are fed into the noisy films about New York employ concision and coercion maneuvers that were invented so that a full-scale drama could be squeezed in between the commercials of such hour shows as the Kraft Cheese program. By using these same maneuvers in full-length films, the picture-makers have invented a new type of play-movie and also managed to produce the most vertical movies in film history.

The story is unfolded by savage emotionalizing and trouble-injecting dialogue while two people are in between the events of life (i.e., walking from the cloakroom of the 21 Club to the table of the big-shot columnist). As in the Dr. Rex Morgan comic strip, life is a horrible mess that transpires in the speeches of upright citizens who seem to be glued against a gray backdrop that is always underlit and hard on the eyes. Their run-on speeches ("I don't know what's the matter with me, I keep getting so depressed. I'm going to quit night school. My nerves are shot") invariably touch some trouble that is supposedly bothering each spectator in the theater. For this reason, many people, including the critics of *The New Yorker* and *Time*, think the movies are full of "ideas"—"disturbing," "offbeat," and even "three-dimensional."

Nevertheless, the basic fault of the New York film is that it has no living at all. Though the screen is loaded with small realities—flickering hands, shadows, grunts, squirms, spinal sag, lip-clenching, an old brassiere in a bum's suitcase, homely first names like Sidney and Charley repeated endlessly—the New York films seem to shriek for one ordinary casual action, realistically performed, such as Bogart's succinct repairs on the overpopulated tank in *Sahara*.

No matter how hard the actors try to hide under a mantle of ordinariness, an extraordinary conceit pours from them in timing, emphasis, posture, and mood. It shows up in the smirking, overcooked accent of a pregnant wife in a housing project. It even creeps into the unusually humble acting of Henry Fonda, who, as a tender-hearted intellectual on the jury of *Twelve Angry Men*, knocks off his Nero Wolfeian crime analyses as though he were swatting flies. The actors and directors of these New York films tunnel through problems as though they were made of paper. In *The Sweet Smell of Success*, the dialogue spills out of realistically mannered mouths before you expect it. The ''dumb-blonde'' cigarette girl minces and whines in a quick unfolding as though she had been cranked like a toy. Newspapers are read and flung away in a violently stylish way and the frozen-lipped delivery of repartee makes the columnist look like a pompous orangutan. It is inconceivable that this high-glossed, ultrasophisticated drama hinges on a dope-planting act in a nightclub that is carried on with as little difficulty as water has finding its way through a sieve. The self-confidence of these new picture-makers is of a kind that feels the audience's eye will accept anything, no matter how dull or unconvincing, if it is dressed up in some sort of trappings borrowed from ''Art.''

The characters in New York films are usually nonentities, the kind that have been filmed only occasionally, as in Preston Sturges's earliest low budgets—a meek old man whose only individuality is a horrible glint of self-satisfaction in his eye, an untalented baton-twirler who has nothing except a determined leg kick and a hawklike opportunism in her limply pretty high-school face. Starting with something in their favor, these faceless characters remind you of the dried-up, joyless atavisms inhabiting the great comic strips of middle-class defeat: ''Out Our Way,'' ''Boarding House, ''The Bungles,'' ''Colonel Hoople.'' After being mauled by what *Life* and the *New York Post* call ''New Talent,'' these average characters are the most schmaltzed-up, pushy group of unlikables to cross the screen, far worse than the money-soaked glamour that traipsed up and down the Georgian staircases of MGM and Irving Thalberg.

The New York films, which make an almost useless item of the camera, are carried to popularity by their pop-pop-pop type of masochistic acting, which is usually in the hands of Strasberg-influenced performers. The idea behind their florid act is to exploit the worst in people until the effect is like spit, pus, or garbage. The idea of intense character criticism is all right, but the way the New York films do it is close to sickening. No matter how modest or quiet the acting seems—Paul Newman's traitor in *The Rack* or Pat Hingle's hard-rock plebe in *The Strange One*—there is a priggish, superior-smart feeling underlining the performance and making it unbearable. When these actors put a character under the light, the result is apt to be a comic-strip characterization rather than a movie figure. The bulges, bumps, and bubbling in Newman's doubting, worrying, unaggressive soldier are like the short-stroked venom that is scratched into the form of a Colonel Hoople. Though the figure is in constant play, there is no movement or characterization. Newman's job is made up solely of torment, much of it interesting and all of it irrelevant to the idea of a continuously developing, forming personality.

Except for a few interesting situations like the delicately drawn web of secretarial malice, jealousy, and insecurity around a water cooler in *Patterns*, the most obvious ruts are followed to expose types that have been victimized in American art as far back as Horatio Alger. It is actually a comic-strip world for stereotyped victims—the domestically hounded bookkeeper, slug-headed football star, pimple-brained ball fan, oily fixer—with acting clichés piled on top of a stock character. In sparking two films with his baseball-rowdy bit, Jack Warden does fascinating things with scorn and world-weariness, but his basic attack is so rancidly corny as to kill the mobility of the role. There is only one word to describe such inverted acting that whipsaws nothing but triteness, the word being "corrupt."

Also, the acting has so much pitch and roll that there is overflow with each performance. From Pat Hingle (mild smirking), Ben Gazzara (facial showboating), Tony Perkins (coy simpering fragility), Don Murray (boyish earnestness), Anthony Franciosa (well-oiled glibness), E. G. Marshall (superiority), John

Cassavetes (aggressive conceit), and Paul Newman (surreptitious modesty), the spectator gets a load of self-consciousness along with the piles of role-bitching sawdust. Thus, one of the neatest jobs in New York films, Lee Remick's ungifted, eye-wandering baton-twirler in *A Face in the Crowd,* is marred by a slight knowingness that surrounds an otherwise unpolished sex-bomb miniature living in a small-town nowheres. Another good effort, the nonactorish playing of academy troublemakers in *The Strange One,* is nearly ruined by Gazzara's self-satisfied pantomime and three bit players who use banality to plug up the slapdash generalizing of Willingham's script. The result: there hasn't been a dumber "dumb tackle," a more weasely crawler, a snottier mamma's-boy snot. For people who like the taut, life-worn fluidity of Dailey-Nolan-O'Brien-Marvin-Cagney-Bogart-Armstrong-Darro-MacLane acting, the New York film portraiture, which made its debut in some early Judy Holliday films, sweats too much around the edges.

The Kazans and Schulbergs of the "Talent Revolution," who glory in their grasp of American ordinariness, are incapable of touching any figure or locale with warmth, charm, or respect. Where modestly skillful Pat Neal is ground into tightness by the Kazan-Schulberg brass knuckles in *A Face in the Crowd,* the fate of newcomer Andy Griffith, who plays a cute hillbilly crashing his way to the top of TV and then falling off, is more like massacre. Off his comically "hick" records of a few years back, Griffith should be a close fit for the soft-shoe backwoods joker, a-wailin' and a-wanderin' Rhodes, who is supposed to be the hero-villain of this barrel-house epic. Instead, Griffith is put in a hyperbolic strait jacket by Kazan's predilection for "mean-animal" acting; only one scene—Rhodes's first encounter with the camera—is played close to the truth of the Ernie Ford type of left-field TV entertainer.

In that scene, as Griffith cuddles with the technicians, makes obvious jokes about the complicated TV machinery, and likens the camera eye to his uncle's drink-soused orb, he scores the only troubling notes in a boringly seething film. In mid-stride, the scene then crumbles into a Capraesque carnival of hokey "documentary shots"—little Americans throwing coins at the needy;

Negroes in silent gawking at Rhodes's democratic "dare" and sure-shot confidence. The professionally sly fumbling and stop-go improvising of the hayseed smoothie is never again seen in a film that is supposedly dedicated to revealing the hypnotism of such performers.

These new ambassadors to Hollywood concentrate on the fleetingly seen situation and itinerant figures that must supply most of the immense backlog of material that feeds into dreams. The situations are like stray bits of nothing picked up out of the corner of the eye: the party of drunken office workers at the largest table in a crowded Italian restaurant, a mysterious conversation amongst jazz buffs in the dark alley behind a nightclub, an attempted pickup in the center of a jammed subway car, the jazz-infected body of a slim delinquent stretched across the stairway in a precinct station-house, a tourist couple seen at the end of a hotel hallway, evidently teetering on the edge of some problem. Each film has one or two expanded episodes that break the rhythm of these veiled impressions, a big scene that usually involves a complicated attempt at prostitution, promiscuity, or, as in *A Face in the Crowd*, some long-distance wooing that transpires between a judge and contestant in a baton-twirling contest at the local football stadium. It is in these big-deal moments, where the movie suddenly switches from quickly gimmicked sketches to a fully developed event, that the New York film technique shows up in all of its rickety melodramatic thinness.

Though the New York films like the side-of-the-eye perception, each director makes sure that his film is cluttered with classy examples of "self"-expression. Thus, it is not hard to locate those effects that show the director breathing hard on the story. In each film, one notices that the handling—Delbert Mann's use of spongy acting in an otherwise stiff nighttime scene, Mackendrick's svelte, speeded-up stylizations of the "money-mad American" cliché, Garfein's heavily ironic direction of actors, which seems to stretch characters to a stock Greek-tragedy size —is as sleek as glass, and that it differs from old-fashioned Hollywood direction in that the style parades in front of the film instead of tunneling under a seminaturalistic surface. In other words, from Mulligan's ethereally delicate ballplayer to

Mackendrick's mannered columnist, the salient effect is precious-ness.

In each story, a marred character stumbles heavily over most of the hurdles, eaten up by a fashionable sickness, like megalo-mania, a hunger for great financial security, a cowardice brought on by the absence of parental love. An Iago-type hipster, in *The Strange One,* runs a military academy as though it were an easy game of sadistic checkers. A ballplayer breaks down under an unbearable perfectionist load placed on him by a demanding father. A shrewd personnel manager rises like helium in a Wall Street firm while despising the tactics of his patron saint and boss. One doesn't mind the crawling acceptance of cures, motives, troubles that have been rubber-stamped by endless usage in fic-tion and plays as much as the mechanical feints made at the idea of human complexity.

The most consistently used maneuver in these scripts is the one that throws a switch on characterization. It is predictable that the hard, sure, convoluted sadist in a Southern academy will at some point show a small-scale worry, cowardice, and need for friendship; that the malevolently biased cop will be switched to simply an overworked humanist; that the outspoken "geetar" player, who befriends a homeless Negress at 2 A.M. on the corner of Beale and Handy, will end up shouting incredibly written filth—"dressed-up black monkeys"—at his help.

But the most tiresome of all Chayefsky-Willingham-Rose ma-neuvers is the voyeurlike use of supposedly daring material. Manhattan types are always tiptoeing towards a seamier LIFE but never opening its green door. Prositutes, lesbians, bathroom culture, sordid bedroom setups, strippers, pornography, and immoral cops move into the orbit of the central characters so that the production team can mince, tickle their toes in the kind of subject that is supposed to give an enormous boost to those who want to reach the avant-garde circle. The peak of movie-script boredom is reached when, in the long *Bachelor Party* funeral through Greenwich Village, a groom's sex trouble is taken up every stair of a prostitute's walk-up, through tons of fear, nausea, and doubt and finally taken downstairs, without encountering one detail that could "realistically" occur any-where in the world. In terms of all-around inflexibility and genteel observation, the whole scene is reminiscent of the insipid, stiff jerkiness of Charley Chase boxing in two-reel comedy with Jim Jeffries.

Although the new TV exiles to Hollywood are cagey and deft in their social-conscience sell, the New York films, at their best, do a cold deviling of the middle class. Chayefsky creates an unbearably cute prison camp in which pale-gray New Yorkers are humiliated intellectually, shrunk in courage, robbed of wit and grace, given a variety of Freudian pimples and scars, and generally misused in a tender way. There is a half-minute bit in *Twelve Angry Men* in which the halo-wearing minority vote on the jury, a pinch-faced architect (Henry Fonda), is seen carefully drying each fingernail with a bathroom towel. It is a sharply effective, stalling-for-time type of adverse detailing, showing the jury's one sensitive, thoughtful figure to be unusually prissy. Unfortunately, this mild debunking of the hero is a coldly achieved detail that sits on the surface of the film, unexplored and unimportant. After being exposed to such overplanned thrusts at a host of enemies—prejudice, stupidity, Madison Avenue affectation, sadism, meek conformity, perfectionism—the spectator leaves the theater feeling mildly entertained by clever craftsmanship, and slightly ill from swallowing rancid education in good citizenship.

The same type of repetition that drives TV fans crazy during the commercial is used in "New Talent" films. One trip to the market of trouble isn't enough for Chayefsky's Little Fear character; he keeps cutting back, circling, returning to the same trouble, until you feel he's caught in a series of revolving doors. In *The Young Stranger*, the handsome bowlegs (James MacArthur), who punches a movie-owner and ends in a police court, keeps renewing the experience. A worried indigestion (Begley) in *Patterns* keeps swallowing pills for heart sickness and feeling guilty about not taking the kid to see the Giants. The peculiar note in this repetition, which gives a treadmill effect to the scenario, is that it is played with the overstated vehemence of a TV spieler. The actors—Begley, MacArthur, Tony Curtis, who, as Sydney in *The Sweet Smell of Success*, breaks the Olympic record for fast acting—don't chew their roles so much as storm past them, like a train going through a nightmare tunnel that never ends, and with a grating monotony about the forward-motion performance, in which actions and words seem hardly to affect the acting. One leaves these films with a buzzing head, plus a feeling that the jingle-jangle of hard-sell cinema is a long way from the complicated art of simple picture-making, as it has been employed by the unrecognized Hawks, Walsh, Anthony Mann, and John Farrow.

The worst TV play has more on-the-spot invention than the best hard-sell film, and occasionally on TV one notices a Hollywood oldie that is haunting for the fact that it is completely the product of quiet improvisation in the face of a miserable, pulpish story. In such TV "repeats" can be seen the amount of natural, uncompromised picture-making that has been displaced by the new hack saws of artiness. One of the fixtures on TV movie shows, a lovely Raoul Walsh film called *The Roaring Twenties*, journeys with niggling intricacy and deceptive footwork in a lot of grayed rice pudding, capturing the most poignant aspects of the twenties' background and movement. One pounds along with a broken gun on walks and fights that are tensely coiled with forlorn excitement. They are not walks so much as anatomical probings of densely detailed backgrounds that give a second level of formed life to a movie about the last throes of Capone-type gangstering.

Watching the detailing and steering in Walsh's most minor shot of a worn-out *chanteuse* singing "Melancholy Baby," the viewer can estimate the damage of the Kazan-Chayefsky tribe. These newcomers, in being so popular and influential, have all but destroyed background interest, the gloved fluidity of authentic movie acting, and the effect of a modest shrewdie working expediently and with a great camera eye in the underground of a film that is intentionally made to look junky, like the penny candies sold in the old-time grocery. In place of the skillful anonymity of *Pickup on South Street*, *The Lusty Men*, or *The Thing*, there is now a splintering and caterwauling that covers gaping holes with meaningless padding and plush.

The mess we are facing in movies and other media promises to be the worst era in the history of art. Not even the ponderously boring periods, similar to the one in which Titian and Tintoretto painted elephantine conceit and hemstitched com-

plication into the huge dress-works affair called Venetian painting, can equal the present inferno of American culture, which
is so jammed with successful con men. One can only glance
back in wonderment at those sinkings in each art form where
the ''shrewdster'' gained a decisive entrance. In painting, it
occurred in the late 1940's, when certain eruptions combined to
bring about a glib turning in avant-garde painting (art-dealer
Putzel's death, stylistic hardening of the introsubjective leaders, arrival of businessmen appreciators like Soby, Sweeney,
Kootz, Janis, and backing of the entire radical school by all
kinds of high-powered critics and publications).

In movies, the Ice Age started to set in with another weird
combination of forces (giving up the experimental ''B,'' the
ultraconservative turn of big shots like Huston, the decline of
the action directors, and explosion of the gimmick: big screen,
the ''liberal'' insight, Freudian symbols, arts-and-crafts Wellesian photography). In the case of each medium, the crucial
moment occurred when immense popularity became an important factor in the field of difficult, naturally talented expression.
At that moment, the businessman-artist appeared with his quick
formulas for achieving ''daring,'' the ''original look,'' and his
skills for maneuvering into, and holding, favorable corners in
the world of high culture.

Now that the middle class has found serious art, it is almost
impossible for a natural talent—good, bad, or in between—to
make any headway. In other words, if you are wondering what
has happened to the tough, impersonal, against-the-grain in-
novator in our times—the type of artist who has the anonymous
strength of a Walker Evans, the natural grace of a James Agee,
the geographic sense of an Anthony Mann, the bitingly exact
earthiness of a J. R. Williams, the suavely fluid humanism of a
Howard Hawks—he has been hidden by a fantastic army of commercial fine-artists, little locustlike creatures who have the
dedication of Sammy Glick, the brains of Happy Hooligan, and
the joyful, unconquerable competitive talents of the Katzen-
jammer Kids.

DON SIEGEL 1969

Considering the automatic high coloring of his vermin, the anxious hopping around for the picturesque, the hokey scripts with worn-out capers and police-routine plots, why write about Don Siegel? Having made a few good modest-budget films—*Baby Face Nelson, Flaming Star* with Elvis Presley, *The Invasion of the Body Snatchers*—that aren't shown in art theaters, he has been wrongly deified by auteurists, though he's basically a determinedly lower-case, crafty entertainer who utilizes his own violence to build unsettling movies with cheap musical scores that leave in their wake a feeling of being smeared with bilge. Not as good as Hawks before *Red Line 7000*, probably better than Blake Edwards (*Gunn*), another manipulative sockbam director, not as gutty or lyrical as the Sam Fuller of *Pickup on South Street,* he is interesting only if he's left life-size and unhaloed.

What is a Don Siegel movie? Mainly it's a raunchy, dirty-minded film with a definite feeling of middle-aged, middle-class sordidness. Every cop, prostitute, and housewife is compromised by something: the pimp in *Madigan* is compromised by his connection to the police; the police commissioner keeps company with the society matron when her husband is on a camping trip with her son, and so on. There are elements of the *Brighton Rock* Graham Greene (the suspension between melodrama and farce in *Baby Face Nelson*), Robert Louis Stevenson (the odd feeling for desert grayness and squalor in *Flaming Star*), and Al Capp (cartoon exaggeration in the Daisy Mae, who services Coogan of *Coogan's Bluff* in a Mojave shack's wooden bathtub). With these elements and the fact that Siegel's a commercial director who's good at his job, the movie works out so that it has something more than push and slime.

Siegel's movies are spiritually as opportunist and crafty as the grafting cops, cheating wives, and winged hoods who make up the personnel. They are also zesty, hard-working entertainments with good nervy second bananas (Don Stroud, Steve In-hat) working alongside the wooden, sat-upon Widmark (Siegel normally discourages his expensive actors from becoming anything but wooden replicas of themselves), unsettling camera work with a lot of zooms, high-angle shots, zigzagging action scenes that make devastating cut-away material. (The last thing heard in a police station is the line "I know it was him, Officer, because this is his shoe.")

While using as his movie basics the same ingredients that rattle around in a TV crime drama—a twenty-minute wait for a decent Stirling Silliphant line, two stiff-brainless-righteous cops who are like Hoboken lawyers, with everything being played for its sensational value—Siegel gets at least one scene, in *The Lineup*, as sensitive as Robert Frank's still shots. What is so lyrical about the ending, in San Francisco's Sutro Museum, is the Japanese-print compositions, the late afternoon lighting, the advantage taken of the long hallways, multilevel stairways in a baroque, elegant, glass-palace building with an exposed skating rink, nautical museum, and windows facing the sea with eye-catching boulders. It's a minor masterpiece of preplanning by an assistant director and an extensively structured pictorial tour by Siegel, expediently using Hitchcock's *Foreign Correspondent* (the interesting, relaxed use of girls from a convent school, a dummybody carefully described in its three-story drop) and Welles's *The Lady from Shanghai* (nice glass cases with miniature boats). The Siegel touch is always apparent in the excessive number of viewpoint shots, the nice feeling for an eroded structure with awkward angles, a sad reliance on edgy Broadway acting (Eli Wallach overworking his nervous-leering eyes) and especially the fascination with a somewhat mannered athleticism seen from above, in which the body is poised or moving against background action that is a violent contrast in space, tone, movement.

Siegel is a director who stays strictly outside of people, away from their ideas, emotions: the scripts from the bottom of a TV-office barrel concern impulsive, nervous-energy types who live strenuously and usually die fast in scenes that are cluttered with their cronies and enemies. Individually rather shallow creations, they pick up color from contact with one another. It's symbolic that Dancer, main criminal of *The Lineup*, becomes hysterical when faced with a noncommunicative stone-faced hawk in a wheelchair who is supposed to receive the cache of heroin. The man's absolute refusal to be familiar drives Dancer to shove man and wheelchair off the balcony into a somersault that ends three floors below on an ice rink. (If someone won't talk to a Siegel character, the effect is literally a mortal insult.)

Though Siegel doesn't let his star actors seek their own level of expression, Betty Field and Don Stroud, mother and son in *Coogan's Bluff,* can literally tear the screen apart with ribaldry while being squashed. "That wasn't nice, that wasn't nice at all. I show you the coat my son bought for me and you say things like that. You talk like that to a mother." Always surprised, strident, Field here is a great comic caricature trying to rid her territory of a hostile intruder. Stroud has this evasive, rabbity quality, as though people were harassing him and he's had just about enough. "Leech off," the old high school expletive for shrugging off a pest, has never been varied more ways than in Stroud's writhing-lifting maneuvers. Siegel's lopsided discourse on the cantankerous New Yorker has sweetness, kookiness, and, behind its stiffly parodied face, enough lyrical humor to almost cover the roughed-through feeling of a TV production.

Siegel has a way of suggesting chains of rapport and intimate knowledge, from a police commissioner down to the pimp and teenaged thrill addict in the hinterlands of Brooklyn. Much of the interest comes from the swift connection between weirdly separated types. A tough Manhattan prostitute walks into the hotel room of a just arrived Phoenix cop: "Hi, sugar, will you zip me up?" The opening of *Coogan's Bluff* is a slambang parody of Kubrick's *2001* start: space-devouring images, a sheriff's jeep whipping across the desert floor, and a ravaged-faced Indian hopping around in the hills, setting up his arsenal to destroy the world as the jeep approaches. The first line of dialogue has a funny intimacy that establishes the sheriff's snide antihero character in seven small words: "OK chief, put your pants back on," and the pants fly into the shot, landing at the feet of a most eccentric Apache—very stocky, battered face, hair cut with a tomahawk.

Siegel's concept of what a secondary player can do is more idiosyncratic and inventive than Peckinpah's boisterous use of

Strother Martin and Warren Oates in *The Wild Bunch,* who always stand for earthy, beer-guzzling, whoring health of life. The real humor in Siegel perhaps stems from his putting second leads into roles that reverse their real natures in compositions that have a rowdy off-kilter vigor: sensitive-gentle-practical Betty Field as a popeyed bat out of Hell's Kitchen. How does one explain the wild fun in the scenes between Lee J. Cobb, a New Yorker with not one minute of patience left in his harassed body, and Clint Eastwood (Coogan), a cunning non-verbal actor who makes most of his acting scores by going cool-faced while others talk at him. ("Look Tex, you're not a cop here. How many times have I got to tell you? There's a plane leaving for Phoenix in three hours. If you're not on it I'm putting you in jail.") The real punch comes from the strange intimacy: this precinct cop uptown on the West Side acts as though he's been putting up with the annoyance of Eastwood's stubbornness and clear blue eyes for a lifetime. He acts tired of Coogan from the moment Eastwood, totally polite and civilized, enters his office.

SAMUEL FULLER 1969

Though he lacks the stamina and range of Chester Gould or the endlessly creative Fats Waller, Sam Fuller directs and writes an inadvertently charming film that has some of their qualities: lyricism, real iconoclasm, and a comic lack of self-consciousness. He has made nineteen no-flab, low- or middle-budget films since 1949, any one of which could be described as "simple-minded corny stuff . . . but colorful," a bit of John Foster Dulles, a good bit of Steve Canyon, sometimes so good as to be breathtaking. *Pickup on South Street* is a marvel of lower-class nuttiness, Richard Widmark as a pickpocket working with a folded newspaper in the subway, almost all of it at night and each all-libido character acting uncorked, totally without propriety checks. Besides being a slow, awful movie, *Steel Helmet,* with its insane hero, a big-faced character, fighting a war against everybody but a little Korean boy, exemplifies the way Fuller touches everything with iconoclasm, turning it into black comedy. *Run of the Arrow,* one of the two movies that still embarrasses Rod Steiger (a mulish Confederate with a mysterious Irish accent and a hatred of Yankees that drives him into joining the Sioux nation), is totally unpredictable and always fresh.

The simplest way to describe his best film, *Pickup on South Street,* is to talk about his movie eye. A blunt melodrama about microfilm, stoolies and Soviet agents (Fuller's scripts are grotesque jobs that might have been written by the bus driver in *The Honeymooners*: "OK, I'll give you five minutes to clear out. If you're not out, we're going to burn the place down"), its quite long segments in a subway have a devilish moodiness, spareness, quietness. While Widmark's Skip character goes to work in a crowded subway car, there is this light touch and satisfying balance between build-up and attention to the moment. Bresson in his own *Pickpocket* film doesn't get close to the directness or the freshness: the ability to keep a scene going without cuts or camera tricks, fastening on enormously pungent faces, Widmark's fine-boned and tight-skinned youthfulness, the way he moves through the car, approaching his victim, Jean Peters, and, in one of the most unexpected detail shots, his hand becomes like a seal's sensitive flipper, dropping down below a newspaper and into a pocketbook. Part of the fun is the not-sure consternation on the faces of the two FBI agents who are following the girl and have no expectation of seeing an expert pickpocket at work.

The movie is filled with good images (the girl walking across the avenue, Widmark standing in his river shack drinking beer) that are always dependent on a trademark coziness to draw the spectator's attention. Little nests or lairs instead of apartments, a hammock instead of a bed, a box lowered into the river in place of a refrigerator, violence that is never interrupted and includes Widmark's friendly grin after nearly decapitating Jean Peters. Fuller's concentration has the curiosity of a kitten: the fine thing about Peters is that her nervous defiance, her guileless and garrulous jabbering seem the pensive, unfortunate traits of a private person rather than an actress's tricks.

Fuller is typically enthralled by material that George Stevens or Capra would consider hopelessly drab. He makes great scenes out of an aged woman's talk about her fatigue. A conventional scene of spies questioning an unwitting accomplice becomes the meanest hotel scene, reminiscent of Diane Arbus's camera eye, her obsession with picking up the down side of American life. The hub of the scene is its directness, the lack of fastidiousness with setting, people, dialogue. The stolid furniture is Moscow, 1940, the three men are square *sauerbraten* types, and Peters is a keyed-up, frenzied dame working through a debris of untalented dialogue: "Boy, you'll never believe it. You know what he thinks we are: Commies. Can you beat that? There sure are nuts walking around."

Once you've seen any of the uncut scenes or heard the blunt cartoon names (Short Round, Lucky Legs), it is impossible to forget the grotesque artist, the wackiness of his films. The movie is sincere about inexplicable mush: Nat King Cole at a crossroads in Asia, expending lavish concern shining a rifle, overpowered by his GI costume, singing about lost love at the China Gate. For a movie that is inordinately white supremacist, it is wild seeing Cole's ecstatic grin at being an American solder in a torn-up Asian battlefield.

All of his war films, loaded with fatuous brotherhood, show this unstomachable condescension of whites toward blacks, Orientals, and Sioux, plus Cole's type of demented happiness at being part of the white man's inane projects, such as capturing a pointless pagoda in endless, scrubby woods. Apart from the madness for Oriental art work that has an undressed look and has been dropped onto an unlikely spot from a helicopter (after being constructed overnight by a single blind carpenter), the craziness of these propagandist films is that the white hero is such trash: unprincipled, stupid, loud-mouthed, mean, thinking nothing about mauling women or any man a foot shorter. Zack, who starts *The Steel Helmet* as a helmet with a hole in it, a bit like a turtle until the helmet rises an inch off the stubbled field to show these meager, nasty eyes slowly shifting back and forth, casing the area, is like someone born on Torment Street between Malicious and Crude. Brueghel has a study of a peasant on crutches, drawn from behind, that suggests the sunk-in-earth, tired squatness. One of F. M. Ford's descriptions of Tietjens, "his body seemed to be constructed of meal sacks," gets close to the soft leadenness, the rancidness with which he's portrayed by Gene Evans, one of the most raucous guys in films. Evans plays the hot-headed showing off, the endless chewing on a cigar stump, with the blast effect of water issuing from a whale's spout, bestial and grotesque as a charm spot in a film dedicated to the U.S. infantry.

With its mangy, anonymous sets, lower-class heroes who treat themselves as sages, and the primitivism (the lack of cutting, rawness with actors, whole violent episodes shot in one take), *Steel Helmet* antedates Godard's equally propagandist work. From the bald and bereft sets to the ponderous, quirky messages that are written on small bits of paper and mailed out of the film like little newspapers (Please help Baldy to grow some Hair), his mangy characters are stubborn cousins to the similarly blocky ones that fight a war near Godard's Santa Cruz. The countries involved are just as unknown, and below both careers is this obsession with renegades, people straddling two worlds, the sane and insane (*Shock Corridor*), the bourgeois and the revolutionary (*La Chinoise*). What's good about his films is lovable; the daring, uninhibited use of semidocumentary techniques that save the movie from Fuller's mind, an unthinking morass at best. Against so many insane scenes (Cameron Mitchell standing in a fake teahouse and screaming, "I'm your Itchi-ban, not him! I always sat next to you!") there is a straight technique that seems all movie, with no tie-ins to other media. No one has been so sly at inserting an animated cartoon into a fiction screen: showing the trajectory of an arrow through drawing when, if photographed, the arc would have been invisible. Blunt and abstract, he often measures a scene into stylized positions and chunks of time.

There are two instances of this nonillustrative composing in *Run of the Arrow*. A whole town stands on a bridge looking into the river, while a counterpoint conversation goes on between Rod Steiger and his mother, building a slow, pastoral effect and a haunting time sense. Another third into the movie and this classical scene almost repeats itself: Steiger and Brian Keith sit at right angles to one another, staring into the prairie, neither party looking at the other. Keith says, "You can't turn your back on your own people," while Steiger is locked in his nursery-rhyme verbal incantation, "I don't like Yankees," etc., etc. It's a lovely scene: Steiger repeats this jingle in fifteen quiet, solidly stubborn ways, just as Godard has it done at a service station in France in *Weekend* ("You killed my boyfriend, he was beautiful and you're ugly," etc., etc.).

Fuller is one of the first to try for poetic purity through a merging of unlimited sadism, done candidly and close up, with stretches of pastoral nostalgia in which there are flickers of myth. The opening scenes in *Run of the Arrow* establish one man's bitterness toward the North, his vision of the South and a maximum heart-throbbing romanticism about General Lee (seen from a blacksmith's shop on a prancing white horse), and it's all done with lines and masses, a correct positioning of woods and fields and the decorum of Corot. There is so much of this offbeat visual posturing, but the question remains: how much of it occurred accidentally?

Fuller has no aptitude for foreign milieu, but, with his lingering passion for the exotic, he can't stay away from it. It's touching and ludicrous to see him lingering over bric-a-brac until he mauls the pagoda or the Buddha out of shape. (His Buddha, the highest one ever built out of wood, should have been sold to Macy's for its Thanksgiving Day float.) There are a few other traits: a fixation about children, blunt violence, the lurking feeling that he'd like to do a movie all in close-ups. *China Gate* is so absurd that it becomes an enchantment to the camp taste. The whole opening is impossibly nutty: an adorable tot and his puppy run through a ruined city, being chased by a figure in black silk pajamas and ballet slippers who is ready to butcher the boy's flop-eared pup for breakfast. A voice over all this says, "In this ravaged city where people are starving, all the dogs have been eaten except one."

WHITE ELEPHANT ART VS. TERMITE ART 1962

Most of the feckless, listless quality of today's art can be blamed on its drive to break out of a tradition while, irrationally, hewing to the square, boxed-in shape and gemlike inertia of an old, densely wrought European masterpiece.

Advanced painting has long been suffering from this burnt-out notion of a masterpiece—breaking away from its imprisoning conditions toward a suicidal improvisation, threatening to move nowhere and everywhere, niggling, omnivorous, ambitionless; yet, within the same picture, paying strict obeisance to the canvas edge and, without favoritism, the precious nature of every inch of allowable space. A classic example of this inertia is the Cézanne painting: in his indoorish works of the woods around Aix-en-Provence, a few spots of tingling, jarring excitement occur where he nibbles away at what he calls his ''small sensation,'' the shifting of a tree trunk, the infinitesimal contests of complimentary colors in a light accent on farmhouse wall. The rest of each canvas is a clogging weight-density-structure-polish amalgam associated with self-aggrandizing masterwork. As he moves away from the unique, personal vision that interests him, his painting turns ungiving and puzzling: a matter of balancing curves for his bunched-in composition, laminating the color, working the painting to the edge. Cézanne ironically left an exposé of his dreary finishing work in terrifyingly honest watercolors, an occasional unfinished oil (the pinkish portrait of his wife in sunny, leafed-in patio), where he foregoes everything but his spotting fascination with minute interactions.

The idea of art as an expensive hunk of well-regulated area, both logical and magical, sits heavily over the talent of every modern painter, from Motherwell to Andy Warhol. The private voice of Motherwell (the exciting drama in the meeting places between ambivalent shapes, the aromatic sensuality that comes from laying down thin sheets of cold, artfully clichéish, hedonistic color) is inevitably ruined by having to spread these small pleasures into great contained works. Thrown back constantly on unrewarding endeavors (filling vast egglike shapes, organizing a ten-foot rectangle with its empty corners suggesting Siberian steppes in the coldest time of the year), Motherwell ends up with appalling amounts of plasterish grandeur, a composition so huge and questionably painted that the delicate, electric contours seem to be crushing the shalelike matter inside. The special delight of each painting tycoon (De Kooning's sabrelike lancing of forms; Warhol's minute embrace with the path of illustrator's pen line and block-print tone; James Dine's slog-footed brio, filling a stylized shape from stem to stern with one ungiving color) is usually squandered in pursuit of the continuity, harmony, involved in constructing a masterpiece. The painting, sculpture, assemblage becomes a yawning production of overripe technique shrieking with preciosity, fame, ambition; far inside are tiny pillows holding up the artist's signature, now turned into mannerism by the padding, lechery, faking required to combine today's esthetics with the components of traditional Great Art.

Movies have always been suspiciously addicted to termite-art tendencies. Good work usually arises where the creators (Laurel and Hardy, the team of Howard Hawks and William Faulkner operating on the first half of Raymond Chandler's *The Big Sleep*) seem to have no ambitions towards gilt culture but are involved in a kind of squandering-beaverish endeavor that isn't anywhere or for anything. A peculiar fact about termite-tapeworm-fungus-moss art is that it goes always forward eating its own boundaries, and, likely as not, leaves nothing in its path other than the signs of eager, industrious, unkempt activity.

The most inclusive description of the art is that, termite-like, it feels its way through walls of particularization, with no sign that the artist has any object in mind other than eating away the immediate boundaries of his art, and turning these boundaries into conditions of the next achievement. Laurel and Hardy, in fact, in some of their most dyspeptic and funniest movies, like *Hog Wild,* contributed some fine parody of men who had read every "How to Succeed" book available; but, when it came to applying their knowledge, reverted instinctively to termite behavior.

One of the good termite performances (John Wayne's bemused cowboy in an unreal stage town inhabited by pallid repetitious actors whose chief trait is a powdered make-up) occurs in John Ford's *The Man Who Shot Liberty Valance.* Better Ford films than this have been marred by a phlegmatically solemn Irish personality that goes for rounded declamatory acting, silhouetted riders along the rim of a mountain with a golden sunset behind them, and repetitions in which big bodies are scrambled together in a rhythmically curving Rosa Bonheurish composition. Wayne's acting is infected by a kind of hoboish spirit, sitting back on its haunches doing a bitter-amused counterpoint to the pale, neutral film life around him. In an Arizona town that is too placid, where the cactus was planted last night and nostalgically cast actors do a generalized drunkenness, cowardice, voraciousness, Wayne is the termite actor focusing only on a tiny present area, nibbling at it with engaging professionalism and a hipster sense of how to sit in a chair leaned against the wall, eye a flogging overactor (Lee Marvin). As he moves along at the pace of a tapeworm, Wayne leaves a path that is only bits of shrewd intramural acting—a craggy face filled with bitterness, jealousy, a big body that idles luxuriantly, having long grown tired with roughhouse games played by old wrangler types like John Ford.

The best examples of termite art appear in places other than films, where the spotlight of culture is nowhere in evidence, so that the craftsman can be ornery, wasteful, stubbornly self-involved, doing go-for-broke art and not caring what comes of it. The occasional newspaper column by a hard-work specialist caught up by an exciting event (Joe Alsop or Ted Lewis, during a presidential election), or a fireball technician reawakened during a pennant playoff that brings on stage his favorite villains (Dick Young); the TV production of *The Iceman Cometh,* with its great examples of slothful-buzzing acting by Myron McCormack, Jason Robards, et al.; the last few detective novels of Ross Macdonald and most of Raymond Chandler's ant-crawling verbosity and sober fact-pointing in the letters compiled years back in a slightly noticed book that is a fine running example of popular criticism; the TV debating of William Buckley, before he relinquished his tangential, counterattacking skill and took to flying into propeller blades of issues, like James Meredith's Ole Miss-adventures.

In movies, nontermite art is too much in command of writers and directors to permit the omnivorous termite artist to scuttle along for more than a few scenes. Even Wayne's cowboy job peters out in a gun duel that is overwrought with conflicting camera angles, plays of light and dark, ritualized movement and posture. In *The Loneliness of the Long Distance Runner*, the writer (Alan Sillitoe) feels the fragments of a delinquent's career have to be united in a conventional story. The design on which Sillitoe settles—a spokelike affair with each fragment shown as a memory experienced on practice runs—leads to repetitious scenes of a boy running. Even a gaudily individual track star—a Peter Snell—would have trouble making these practice runs worth the moviegoer's time, though a cheap ton of pseudo-Bunny Berigan jazz trumpet is thrown on the film's sound track to hop up the neutral dullness of these up-down-around spins through vibrant English countryside.

Masterpiece art, reminiscent of the enameled tobacco humidors and wooden lawn ponies bought at white elephant auctions decades ago, has come to dominate the overpopulated arts of TV and movies. The three sins of white elephant art (1) frame the action with an all-over pattern, (2) install every event, character, situation in a frieze of continuities, and (3) treat every inch of the screen and film as a potential area for prizeworthy creativity. *Requiem for a Heavyweight* is so heavily inlaid with ravishing technique that only one scene—an employment office with a nearly illiterate fighter (Anthony Quinn) falling into the hands of an impossibly kind job clerk—can be acted by Quinn's slag blanket type of expendable art, which crawls along using fair insight and a total immersion in the materials of acting. Antonioni's *La Notte* is a good example of the evils of continuity, from its opening scene of a deathly sick noble critic being visited by two dear friends. The scene gets off well, but the director carries the thread of it to agonizing length, embarrassing the viewer with dialogue about art that is sophomorically one dimensional, interweaving an arty shot of a helicopter to fill the time interval, continuing with impossible-to-act effects of sadness by Moreau and Mastroianni outside the hospital, and, finally, reels later, a laughable postscript conversation by Moreau-Mastroianni detailing the critic's "meaning" as a friend, as well as a few other very mystifying details about the poor bloke. Tony Richardson's films, beloved by art theater patrons, are surpassing examples of the sin of framing, boxing in an action with a noble idea or camera effect picked from High Art.

In Richardson's films (*A Taste of Honey*, *The Long Distance Runner*), a natural directing touch on domesticity involving losers is the main dish (even the air in Richardson's whitish rooms seems to be fighting the ragamuffin type who infests Richardson's young or old characters). With his "warm" liking for the materials of direction, a patient staying with confusion, holding to a cop's lead-footed pacelessness that doesn't crawl over details so much as back sluggishly into them. Richardson can stage his remarkable seconds-ticking sedentary act in almost any setup—at night, in front of a glarey department store window, or in a train coach with two pairs of kid lovers settling in with surprising, hopped-up animalism. Richardson's ability to give a spectator the feeling of being There, with time to spend, arrives at its peak in homes, apartments, art garrets, a stable-like apartment, where he turns into an academic neighbor of Walker Evans, steering the spectator's eyes on hidden rails, into arm patterns, worn wood, inclement feeling hovering in tiny marble eyes, occasionally even making a room appear to take shape as he introduces it to a puffy-faced detective or an expectant girl on her first search for a room of her own. In a kitchen scene with kid thief and job-worn detective irritably gnawing at each other, Richardson's talent for angular disclosures takes the scene apart without pointing or a nearly habitual underlining; nagging through various types of bone-worn, dishrag-gray material with a fine windup of two unlikable opponents still scraping at each other in a situation that is one of the first to credibly turn the overattempted movie act—showing hard, agonizing existence in the wettest rain and slush.

Richardson's ability with deeply lived-in incident is, nevertheless, invariably dovetailed with his trick of settling a horse collar of gentility around the neck of a scene, giving the image a pattern that suggests practice, skill, guaranteed safe humor. His highly rated stars (from Richard Burton through Tom Courtenay) fall into mock emotion and studied turns, which suggest they are caught up in the enameled sequence of a vaudeville act: Rita Tushingham's sighting over a gun barrel at an amusement park (standard movie place for displaying types who are closer to the plow than the library card) does a broadly familiar comic arrangement of jaw muscle and eyebrow that has the gaiety and almost the size of a dinosaur bone. Another gentility Richardson picked up from fine *objêts d'art* (Dubuffet, Larry Rivers, Dick Tracy's creator) consists of setting a network of marring effects to prove his people are ill placed in life. Tom Courtenay (the last angry boy in *Runner*) gets carried away by this cult, belittling, elongating, turning himself into a dervish with a case of Saint Vitus dance, which localizes in his jaw muscles, eyelids. As Richardson gilds his near vagrants with sawtooth mop coiffures and a way of walking on high heels so that each heel seems a different size and both appear to be plunged through the worn flooring, the traits look increasingly elegant and put on (the worst trait: angry eyes that suggest the empty orbs in "Orphan Annie" comic strips). Most of his actors become crashing, unbelievable bores, though there is one nearly likable actor, a chubby Dreiserian girl friend in *Long Distance Runner* who, termite-fashion, almost acts into a state of grace. Package artist Richardson has other boxing-in ploys, running scenes together as Beautiful Travelogue, placing a cosmic symbol around the cross-country running event, which incidentally crushes Michael Redgrave, a headmaster in the fantastic gambol of throwing an entire Borstal community into a swivet over one track event.

The common denominator of these laborious ploys is, actually, the need of the director and writer to overfamiliarize the audience with the picture it's watching: to blow up every situation and character like an affable inner tube with recognizable details and smarmy compassion. Actually, this overfamiliarization serves to reconcile these supposed long-time enemies— academic and Madison Avenue art.

An exemplar of white elephant art, particularly the critic-devouring virtue of filling every pore of a work with glinting, darting Style and creative Vivacity, is François Truffaut. Truffaut's *Shoot the Piano Player* and *Jules et Jim*, two ratchety perpetual-motion machines devised by a French Rube Goldberg, leave behind the more obvious gadgetries of *Requiem for a Heavyweight* and even the cleaner, bladelike journalism of *The 400 Blows*.

Truffaut's concealed message, given away in his Henry Miller–ish, adolescent two-reeler of kids spying on a pair of lovers (one unforgettably daring image: kids sniffing the bicycle seat just vacated by the girl in the typical fashion of voyeuristic pornographic art) is a kind of reversal of growth, in which people grow backward into childhood. Suicide becomes a game, the houses look like toy boxes—laughter, death, putting out a fire—all seem reduced to some unreal innocence of childhood myths. The real innocence of *Jules et Jim* is in the writing, which depends on the spectator sharing the same wide-eyed or adolescent view of the wickedness of sex that is implicit in the vicious gamesmanship going on between two men and a girl.

Truffaut's stories (all women are villains; the schoolteacher seen through the eyes of a sniveling schoolboy; all heroes are unbelievably innocent, unbelievably persecuted) and characters convey the sense of being attached to a rubber band, although he makes a feint at reproducing the films of the 1930's with their linear freedom and independent veering. From *The 400 Blows* onward, his films are bound in and embarrassed by his having made up his mind what the film is to be about. This decisiveness converts the people and incidents into flat, jiggling mannikins (*400 Blows, Mischief Makers*) in a Mickey Mouse comic book, which is animated by thumbing the pages rapidly. This approach eliminates any stress or challenge, most of all any sense of the film locating an independent shape.

Jules et Jim, the one Truffaut film that seems held down to a gliding motion, is also cartoonlike but in a decorous, suspended way. Again most of the visual effect is an illustration for the current of the sentimental narrative. Truffaut's concentration on making his movie fluent and comprehensible flattens out all complexity and reduces his scenes to scraps of pornography —like someone quoting just the punchline of a well-known dirty joke. So unmotivated is the leapfrogging around beds of the three-way lovers that it leads to endless bits of burlesque. Why does she suddenly pull a gun? (See "villainy of women," above). Why does she drive her car off a bridge? (Villains need to be punished.) Etc.

Jules et Jim seems to have been shot through a scrim which has filtered out everything except Truffaut's dry vivacity with dialogue and his diminutive stippling sensibility. Probably the high point in this love-is-time's-fool film: a languorous afternoon in a chalet (what's become of chalets?) with Jeanne Moreau teasing her two lovers with an endless folksong. Truffaut's lyrics—a patter of vivacious small talk that is supposed to exhibit the writer's sophistication, never mind about what—provides most of the scene's friction, along with an idiot concentration on meaningless details of faces or even furniture (the degree that a rocking chair isn't rocking becomes an impressive substitute for psychology). The point is that, divested of this meaningless vivacity, the scenes themselves are without tension, dramatic or psychological.

The boredom aroused by Truffaut—to say nothing of the irritation—comes from his peculiar methods of dehydrating all the life out of his scenes (instant movies?). Thanks to his fondness for doused lighting and for the kind of long shots which hold his actors at thirty paces, especially in bad weather, it's not only the people who are blanked out; the scene itself threatens to evaporate off the edge of the screen. Adding to the effect of evaporation, disappearing: Truffaut's imagery is limited to traveling (running through meadows, walking in Paris streets, etc.), setups and dialogue scenes where the voices, disembodied and like the freakish chirps in Mel Blanc's *Porky Pig* cartoons, take care of the flying out effect. Truffaut's system holds art at a distance without any actual muscularity or propulsion to peg the film down. As the spectator leans forward to grab the film, it disappears like a released kite.

Antonioni's specialty, the effect of moving as in a chess game, becomes an autocratic kind of direction that robs an actor of his motive powers and most of his spine. A documentarist at heart and one who often suggests both Paul Klee and the cool, deftly neat, "intellectual" Fred Zinnemann in his early *Act of Violence* phase, Antonioni gets his odd, clarity-is-all effects from his taste for chic mannerist art that results in a screen that is glassy, has a side-sliding motion, the feeling of people plastered against stripes or divided by verticals and horizontals; his incapacity with interpersonal relationships turns crowds into stiff waves, lovers into lonely appendages, hanging stiffly from each other, occasionally coming together like clanking sheets of metal but seldom giving the effect of being in communion.

At his best, he turns this mental creeping into an effect of modern misery, loneliness, cavernous guilt-ridden yearning. It often seems that details, a gesture, an ironic wife making a circle in the air with her finger as a thought circles toward her brain, become corroded by solitariness. A pop jazz band appearing at a millionaire's fête becomes the unintentional heart of *La Notte,* pulling together the inchoate center of the film—a vast endless party. Antonioni handles this combo as though it were a vile mess dumped on the lawn of a huge estate. He has his film inhale and exhale, returning for a glimpse of the four-piece outfit playing the same unmodified kitsch music—stupidly immobile, totally detached from the party swimming around the music. The film's most affecting shot is one of Jeanne Moreau making tentative stabs with her somber, alienated eyes and mouth, a bit of a dance step, at rapport and friendship with the musicians. Moreau's facial mask, a signature worn by all Antonioni players, seems about to crack from so much sudden uninhibited effort.

The common quality or defect which unites apparently divergent artists like Antonioni, Truffaut, Richardson is fear, a fear of the potential life, rudeness, and outrageousness of a film. Coupled with their storage vault of self-awareness and knowledge of film history, this fear produces an incessant wakefulness.

In Truffaut's films, this wakefulness shows up as dry, fluttering inanity. In Antonioni's films, the mica-schist appearance of the movies, their linear patterns, are hulked into obscurity by Antonioni's own fund of sentimentalism, the need to get a mural-like thinness and interminableness out of his mean patterns.

The absurdity of *La Notte* and *L'Avventura* is that its director is an authentically interesting oddball who doesn't recognize the fact. His talent is for small eccentric microscope studies, like Paul Klee's, of people and things pinned in their grotesquerie to an oppressive social backdrop. Unlike Klee, who stayed small and thus almost evaded affectation, Antonioni's aspiration is to pin the viewer to the wall and slug him with wet towels of artiness and significance. At one point in *La Notte,* the unhappy wife, taking the director's patented walk through a continent of scenery, stops in a rubbled section to peel a large piece of rusted tin. This ikon close-up of minuscule desolation is probably the most overworked cliché in still photography, but Antonioni, to keep his stories and events moving like great novels through significant material, never stops throwing his Sunday punch. There is an interestingly acted nymphomaniac girl at wit's end trying to rape the dish-rag hero; this is a big event, particularly for the first five minutes of a film. Antonioni overweights this terrorized girl and her interesting mop of straggly hair by pinning her into a typical Band-aid composition—the girl, like a tiny tormented animal, backed against a large horizontal stripe of white wall. It is a pretentiously handsome image that compromises the harrowing effect of the scene.

Whatever the professed theme in these films, the one that dominates in unspoken thought is that the film business is finished with museum art or pastiche art. The best evidence of this disenchantment is the anachronistic slackness of *Jules et Jim, Billy Budd, Two Weeks in Another Town.* They seem to have been dropped into the present from a past which has become useless. This chasm between white-elephant reflexes and termite performances shows itself in an inertia and tight defensiveness which informs the acting of Mickey Rooney in *Requiem for a Heavyweight,* Julie Harris in the same film, and the spiritless survey of a deserted church in *L'Avventura.* Such scenes and actors seem as numb and uninspired by the emotions they are supposed to animate, as hobos trying to draw warmth from an antiquated coal stove. This chasm of inertia seems to testify that the Past of heavily insured, enclosed film art has become unintelligible to contemporary performers, even including those who lived through its period of relevance.

Citizen Kane, in 1941, antedated by several years a crucial change in films from the old flowing naturalistic story, bringing in an iceberg film of hidden meanings. Now the revolution wrought by the exciting but hammy Orson Welles film, reaching its zenith in the 1950's, has run its course and been superceded by a new film technique that turns up like an ugly shrub even in the midst of films that are preponderantly old gems. Oddly enough the film that starts the breaking away is a middle-1950's film, that seems on the surface to be as traditional as *Greed*. Kurosawa's *Ikiru* is a giveaway landmark, suggesting a new self-centering approach. It sums up much of what a termite art aims at: buglike immersion in a small area without point or aim, and, over all, concentration on nailing down one moment without glamorizing it, but forgetting this accomplishment as soon as it has been passed; the feeling that all is expendable, that it can be chopped up and flung down in a different arrangement without ruin.

THE DECLINE OF THE ACTOR 1966

The strange evolution of movies in the last ten years—with the remaining studios ever more desperate, ever more coordinated —has brought about the disappearance of something that reviewers and film theorists have never seemed to miss: those tiny, mysterious interactions between the actor and the scene that make up the memorable moments in any good film. These have nothing to do with the plot, "superb performance," or even the character being portrayed. They are moments of peripheral distraction, bemusement, fretfulness, mere flickerings of skeptical interest: Margaret Sheridan's congested whinny as a career woman sparring with Kenneth Tobey (Christian Nyby's *The Thing*); Bogart's prissy sign language to a bespectacled glamour girl through the bookstore window (Howard Hawks's *The Big Sleep*); or Richard Barthelmess's tiredly defiant dissolute slouch when he enters the *cabaña* in *Only Angels Have Wings* (also by Hawks). Such tingling moments liberate the imagination of both actors and audience: they are simply curiosity flexing itself, spoofing, making connections to a new situation.

Even so-called photographed plays—for instance, George Cukor's *Dinner at Eight*—could once be made to produce that endless unreeling of divergence, asides, visual lilts which produce a vitality unique to the movies. With the setting and story of a Waldorf operetta, Cukor was able to get inflections and tones from the departments that professional cinematicians always class as uncinematic: make-up, setting, costumes, voices. Marie Dressler's matronly bulldog face and Lee Tracy's scarecrow, gigolo features and body are almost like separate characters interchangeable with the hotel corridors and bathtubs and gardens of Cukor's ritzy and resilient imagination. Cukor, a lighter, less sentiment-logged Ernst Lubitsch, could convert an obsession or peculiarity like Jean Harlow's nasal sexuality, or Wallace Beery's line-chewing, into a quick and animating caricature—much as Disney used mice and pigs in his 1930's cartoons.

Lately, however, in one inert film after another, by the time the actor moves into position, the screen has been congealed in the manner of a painting by Pollock, every point filled with maximum pungency, leaving no room for a full-regalia performance. No matter what the individuality of the actor may be —an apprehensive grandstander (Jeanne Moreau) with two expressions: starved and less starved; an ironing board (Gregory Peck) who becomes effective in scenes that have been grayed, flattened, made listless with some domesticity; a defensively humble actress (Anne Bancroft) who overvalues her humanism and eloquence—and no matter how fine the director's instincts may be, the result is invariably almost the same. In a situation where what counts is opulence and prestige—a gross in the millions, winner of the Critics' Award, Best Actor at a film festival—the actor has to be fitted into a production whose elements have all been assembled, controlled, related, like so many notes in a symphony. As a full-blooded, big-wheel performer rolling at top speed, the actor would subvert this beautiful construction, and so the full-blooded, big-wheel performance has become an anachronism.

Item: David Lean's *Lawrence of Arabia* is almost a comedy of overdesign, misshapen with spectaclelike obtrusions: the camera frozen about ten feet in front of a speeding cyclist, which, though it catches nice immediate details of his face, primarily shows him fronted on screen for minutes as a huge gargoylish figure; the camels, by far the most exciting shapes in the movie, photograph too large in the "cineramic" desert views; an actor walking off into fading twilight becomes the small papery figure of an illustrational painting; Jack Hawkins's General Allenby, so overweighted with British army beef, suggests a toy version of a Buckingham Palace guard. While the other technicians are walloping away, the actors, stuck like thumbtacks into a maplike event, are allowed—and then only for a fraction of the time—to contribute a declamatory, school-pageant bit of acting.

Item: Another prime example of this sort of thing is Serge Bourguignon's *Sundays and Cybele,* whose two leading players are made to resemble walking receptacles for the production crew. The story (Patricia Gozzi, a twelve-year-old, goes on little outings to the park with Hardy Kruger, an amnesiac) is made into a rite of style consisting mainly of layer-on-layer compositions in which the actors become reflected, blurred, compartmented, speckled, through some special relation with apparatus, scenery, a horse's body, windshield wipers. Such things as the tilt of a head or a face reflected in a drinking glass become so heightened, so stretched, that they appear to go on echoing, as if making their effect inside a vacuum. Yet all this is in the service of the kind of role that consists of little more than being delightful with a sniffle or looking transported while walking through trees carrying a child who is cutely imitating a corpse.

The new actor is, in fact, an estranged figure merely jiggling around inside the role. Sometimes he seems to be standing at the bottom of a dark pit, a shiny spot on his pomaded hair being the chief effect of his acting. Or he may be a literate fellow riffling the clutter on his desk. But, in either case, performance is invariably a charade: the actor seldom makes his own sense. He is no longer supposed to act as close to credible as possible; he is a grace note or a trill; he is a dab of two-dimensional form floating on the film surface for photogenic purposes.

Item: Keir Dullea's acting of the psychotic student in Frank Perry's *David and Lisa* is broad, swingy, without a moment that suggests either curiosity or the macabre homeliness, jaggedness, that might be expected in a disturbed kid. The set-piece handling of each scene usually finds Dullea's Frank Merriwellish, chalk-white face in the empty stillness, holding to an emotion for an unconscionable time. His tantrum when a doctor pats him on the back takes so long in evolving that the performance of it (crying, a face rigid with intensity, a stiff-handed wiping at his clothes to get rid of germs) seems to be going backward in slow motion.

The only good acting in recent films has been lavished on the role of the eternal sideliner, as played by John Wayne (the homesteader in John Ford's *The Man Who Shot Liberty Valance*) or by George Hamilton (as the liquescent juvenile in

Vincente Minnelli's *Two Weeks in Another Town*). These actors salvage the idea of independent intelligence and character by pitting themselves against the rest of the film. Standing at a tangent to the story and appraising the tide in which their fellow actors are floating or drowning, they serve as stabilizers —and as a critique of the movie. Mickey Rooney's murderously gloomy, suspicious acting in Ralph Nelson's *Requiem for a Heavyweight* is another case of superior sidelining, this time among the lunatic effects of apartment scenes that are pitch black except for a 40-watt bulb, a huge hotel sign blinking on and off, actors photographed as eucalyptus trees being ogled from the ground by tourists.

While today's actor is the only thing in the film that is identifiably real, his responses are exploited in a peculiar way. His gaucheries and half-hitches and miscalculations are never allowed their own momentum but are used self-consciously to make a point—so that they become as inanimate and depressing as the ceaseless inventories in Robbe-Grillet novels. Jean-Paul Belmondo, the cool cat car thief in Jean-Luc Godard's *Breathless,* is seen standing before the stills at a theater entrance, doing a smeary Bogart imitation that leans on false innocence instead of developing spontaneously. Monica Vitti, a frightened erotic drifter in Antonioni's *Eclipse,* does a scene-hog's cheerful reaction to a dog's trick walk, full of "meaning" that upstages the characterization.

Falling out of the film along with the actor as performer are other related devices that once had their value. Compare, for example, the heavy, weighted masks of the actors in *Lawrence* with the caricatured features of William Powell, Cary Grant, or Edgar Kennedy, features that served to offset and counterpoint what might otherwise have been precious, sour, or effete about them. Powell, an artist in dreadful films, would first use his satchel underchin to pull the dialogue into the image, then punctuate with his nose the stops for each chin movement. He and Edgar Kennedy, who operated primarily with the upper torso, were basically conductors, composing the film into linear movement as it went along.

Another loss is the idea of character that is styled and constructed from vocation. In Kurosawa's *Yojimbo* (a bowdlerized version of Dashiell Hammett's *Red Harvest*, with a bossless vagabond who depopulates a town of rival leaders, outlaws, and fake heroes), the whole superstructure of Hammett's feudal small town is dissolved into an inchoate mass of Goyalike extras whose swarmings and mouthings are composed with naïve pictorialism. Swarming, moreover, seems to be the full-time occupation; you never see interiors, work, or any evidence of everyday life. The exposition of character through vocation has completely evaporated and been replaced by a shorthand of the character's daily habit, jotted into a corner of the role by set-designer, costumer, author. Jean Seberg's journalistic career is merely wedged into appropriate notches of *Breathless*: a *Herald Tribune* sweat shirt, a quick question to a celebrity novelist at the airport. The source of Monica Vitti's well-tended existence in *Eclipse* is snagged in a one-line footnote about her translator's work. The idea of vocations is slipped into the spectator's acceptance without further development.

The idea of movement per se has also lost its attraction to moviemakers. The actor now enters a scene not as a person, but like a Macy's Thanksgiving balloon, a gaudy exhibitionistic fact. Most of those appurtenances that could provide him with some means of animation have been glazed over. The direct use of his face as an extension of the performance has become a technique for hardening and flattening; and the more elliptical use of his face, for showing intermediate states or refining or attenuating a scene, has vanished, become extinct. In fact, the actor's face has been completely incapacitated; teeth—once taken for granted—or an eyeball, or a hairdo, have all become key operators. They front the screen like balustrades, the now disinherited face behind.

The moving body, too, in its present state of neglect has become a burden—particularly on foreign directors, who seem to realize that their actors might be mistaken for oxen, pillars, or extensions of a chaise longue and, so, give each of their films a kind of late, sudden, jolt. Toshiro Mifune suddenly comes alive toward the end of *Yojimbo,* throwing daggers into the floor of his hideout. Before this, he could usually be seen in one of those compositions Kurosawa prizes of three heads sticking out of their respective potato bags watching one another's faces while waiting for the lunch whistle to blow and break up the photography. *Eclipse* has a parody, very exciting, of people using their arms and hands in a stock exchange scene; most of the time these actors working on telephones, sandwiches, penciling, seem to be trying to fling their hands away. The *Lawrence* ensemble travels over literally half a continent with almost no evidence that any legs have been used. No actor is ever trusted with more than a few moves: a thin path having been cleared for him to make his walk down a dune, or to pontificate around porch furniture, he is then choreographed so that each motion, each bit of costume creaks into place.

Item: The lack of athleticism in *Requiem for a Heavyweight* is, under the circumstances, peculiarly comical. The cast seems made up of huge monolithic characters being held in place, incapable of a natural movement—particularly the overrated Anthony Quinn. Walking down a lonely street sparring at the sky or mumbling while he puts on shirt and tie, Quinn plays the role as though the ground were soft tapioca, his body purchased from an Army-Navy store that specializes in odd sizes.

The late work of certain important directors—Cukor's *The Chapman Report,* Huston's films since *The Roots of Heaven,* Truffaut's *The 400 Blows*—shows a drastic change into the new propulsive style. Every element of the film has been forced into serving a single central preoccupation, whether of character (gelatinous frigidity), metaphysic (elephants are the largeness and mystery of life), or situation (the kid as misunderstood delinquent). A key, symbolic feature of the new style is the transformation of dialogue into a thick curtain dropped between the actor and the audience. The words spoken by Alec Guinness in *Lawrence* (prissily elocutionary), by Montgomery Clift in Huston's *Freud* (mashed, faintly quivery), by Laurence Harvey's Washington journalist in John Frankenheimer's *The Manchurian Candidate* (girlish, whispering) sound like valedictory speeches coached by Archibald MacLeish or the way Indians talk on TV Westerns. The peculiar thing is that each word has been created, worked over by a sound engineer who intercepts the dialogue before it hits the audience. There is no longer the feeling of being close to the actor.

Joan Crawford—despite the fact that each of her roles was

played as if it were that of the same dim-witted file clerk with a bulldozer voice—always seemed hooked up to a self-driving sense of form which supplemented exactly what the movie couldn't give her. The current population of actors must probably be said to have more real skills than Crawford, but they don't come off as authentically. Geraldine Page, for instance, an actress of far greater sensibility and aplomb, must go through an entire glossary of mouth-shifting, sinus-clearing, and eye-blinking to make her character in *Sweet Bird of Youth* identifiable as anything. The difference between Crawford's tart in *Grand Hotel* and Page's obsessed ex-star is as great as that between George Kelly and William Inge. The effect of Miss Page's increased power and leisure, which expects no resistance from the movie, is to eviscerate the entire film. The same is true of Gregory Peck's pious Lincoln impersonation in *To Kill a Mockingbird* and of Angela Lansbury's helicopterlike performance in *The Manchurian Candidate,* in which every sentence begins and ends with a vertical drop.

The first sign of the actor's displacement could be seen in a 1952 Japanese film whose implications were not made clear until the New Wave, Antonioni, and others incorporated them into that special blend of modern-art cliché and Madison Avenue chic that now makes such good business. Just about every film aimed at American art theaters has come to be a pretentious, misshapen memory of *Ikiru* that plays on the double effect of the image in which there is simultaneously a powerful infatuation with style and with its opposite—vivid, unstoppable actuality. The fantastic clutter and depression of a petty government office; mouthed-in tepid talk that dribbles endlessly (as in John O'Hara's fiction, where dialogue now devours structure, motive, people, explanation, everything); the poor ghosts who crawl in trying to push a request for a playground in their spot of a slum —each of these items in *Ikiru* seem overrun by a virus of creativity without concern for its direction, everything steaming together into an indictment of drudgery that finally muffles the actors.

The same funguslike creativity and narcissistic style appear in an almost dead-handed way in *Freud, Lawrence of Arabia,* and *Eclipse.* Here the actors show up as rugs, or an entire battle scene is converted by artful lighting into an elongated shadowy smear. Just as *Ikiru* moves from a white emptied abstract death ceremony to a jammed city scene, *Lawrence* employs the split between desert and crowded Cairo to accent the peculiar density of each, and Antonioni juxtaposes the frenzied stock exchange with inarticulate lovers in emptied streets. Even in the crudely constructed *Divorce, Italian Style*, a din of diverse technical energy moves over streets, trains, the very bodies of the acting team. Mastroianni's face, sleep-drenched and melancholic, stares out of a dining car at the flat, parched Sicilian fields; and few actors have looked so contaminated by sleaziness, a draggy kind of living: it is the whole movie that is sitting on him. *Divorce, Italian Style* is like a parody of the realism in *Ikiru;* there is nothing to touch this unfunny farce for the sheer jarring effect of eager-beaver technicians charging into one another, trying to put in *more*—more funny stuff, more realistic stuff, more any kind of stuff.

Most directors have been pushing Kurosawa's invention to the extreme of treating actors with everything from the fancy tinker-toy construction of *Lawrence of Arabia* to the pure sadism of *The Manchurian Candidate*. One of the wildest films in its treatment of actors, *The Manchurian Candidate* is straight jazz all the way through—from the men who are supposed to be brainwashed to the normal ones in army intelligence. When Sinatra, for instance, moves in a fight, his body starts from concrete encasement, and his face looks as though it were being slowly thrown at his Korean houseboy opponent, another freak whose metallic skin and kewpie-doll eyes were borrowed from a Max Factor cosmetic kit. Janet Leigh seems first to have been skinned and stretched on a steel armature, and then compelled to do over and over again with hands and voice things supposed to be exquisitely sexual. The audience is made to feel unclean, like a Peeping Tom, at this queer directional gamboling over bodies. And Sinatra's romantic scenes with Miss Leigh are a Chinese torture: he, pinned against the Pullman door as though having been buried standing up, and she, nothing moving on her body, drilling holes with her eyes into his screw-on head.

In one advanced film after another, we find an actor being used for various purposes external to him—as a mistake, a pitiful object, a circus sight. The most troublesome aspect of Peter O'Toole's Lawrence is that the story moves faster and further than the actor, who is not unlike the Tin Woodsman of Oz (O'Toole starts with a springing outward movement, to walk over the world, and then turns into a pair of stilts walking in quick, short strides). Consider also the squashy ineffectual performance by Peter Ustinov in *Billy Budd* (which he himself directed) or the pitiful ones by Jeanne Moreau in Orson Welles's *The Trial* and Truffaut's *Jules et Jim.* A frightened actress, Miss Moreau is never there with enough speed, sureness, or grace, but her directors realize that her inadequacies can be exploited photogenically. Watching her stretch out in a sexy bed pose, or teeter on a diving board, or climb up a bridge abutment, stand poised, and then leap off, you get the feeling that her feeble creaking is intentionally being underlined as something to sorrow over.

What we have, then, is a schizoid situation that can destroy the best actor: he must stay alive as a character while preserving the film's contrived style. Thanks to this bind, there are roughly only two kinds of acting today. With the first, and the least interesting, type, the actor is hardly more than a spot: as in Antonioni's films, where he becomes only a slight bulge in the glossy photography; or, as in the endless gray stretches of Truffaut's, where his face becomes a mask painted over with sexual fatigue, inert agony, erosion, while his body skitters around weightlessly like a paper doll. Huston's work, too, has moved in a progression from the great acting of, say, Bogart and Mary Astor in *Across the Pacific* to no acting at all: in *Freud,* the actors do not escape for one moment from the spaces Huston has hacked out of the screen for them in order to make an elegant composition.

The second style of acting turns up in fairly interesting films. Here the actor does a movie-full of intricate acting by turning his back to the camera. He piles a ferocious energy and style into sorrowful characters who have lived through dismal orphanages, or alcoholism, or life membership in Alcatraz—precisely the characters who should have nothing in common with his kind of joy in performing, happy animal spirit, all-out vigor.

The result is that there is no communication at all between the setting—which is flat and impressively accurate—and the actor, who splatters every second with a mixture of style and improvisation. Blake Edwards's *Days of Wine and Roses* drags unbelievably while Jack Lemmon kicks in a liquor store door or stares drunkenly at the dirty sea water. Lemmon in this movie is a blur of pantomimic skill, though with enough cynicism in his performance to cut the mechanical writing of the role. However, inside all the style, the actor seems to be static, waiting around sourly while the outer masquerade drags on.

There has, finally, never been worse acting nor more mistakes made by actors being given impossible things to do. A fan's memory gets clouded by these weird performances: a jilted intellectual (Francisco Rabal in *Eclipse*), who goes through an entrance gate as though he had learned to walk by studying an airplane taking off; a U.S. Senator imitating Lincoln at a costume ball (James Gregory in *The Manchurian Candidate*), picking up his didactic acting from several garbage heaps left over from the worst propaganda films of World War II. The poor actor today stands freezing, undone, a slab of beef exposed to public glare as never before. Clift's Freud may be hidden behind a beard, buried in a tomb (his walk to the cemetery must be pulled by earth-movers), but he is still unmercifully revealed as an unused performer. Some actors, like Jackie Gleason in *Requiem for a Heavyweight,* haven't yet moved into their act. And Kirk Douglas, as a gesticulating, angry ex-actor in *Two Weeks in Another Town,* is a body on display, one now shrinking in middle age while the mind of his employer is fixed on other things. Criticism of acting has always been quick to cover a performance with a blanket word, but trying to consider today's actors as auxiliaries of the story in the pre-1950's sense is like analyzing post–Jackson Pollock painting with an esthetic yardstick that esteems modeling.

CARTOONED HIP ACTING 1967

The kooky thing about film acting is its uncontrolled, spilling-over quality. The meat of any movie performance is in the suggestive material that circles the edge of a role: quirks of physiognomy, private thoughts of the actor about himself, misalliances where the body isn't delineating the role, but is running on a tangent to it.

Burt Lancaster's stationmaster in *The Train*—a semireluctant fighter in the Resistance stationed in Nazi-occupied France —is an interesting performance because it has almost no center. Seven-eighths of his time is spent occupied at work tasks, scrambling around the countryside. The basic information of his role is impatiently dispatched to the audience: a man pissed off at the absurdity of total sacrifice to save a carload of Van Goghs and Picassos, the "glorious French heritage." The overtone in a Lancaster performance is that of a man who seems to disappear into concentration when he has to work with his hands. The amount of work, involvement, that goes into a Lancaster action is fairly ravishing: he seems perversely committed to sidetracking quietly (no one's going to notice this) the fantastic leonine head, the overrated nimbleness of his body. Lancaster half ruins his performance with innocent sincerity, but at that point where the script stops and Lancaster has his task before him, he sinks into it with a dense absorption. His energy of concentration is like a magnet that draws the atmosphere into the action of his hands.

The opposite of Lancaster's energy-expending performance is everywhere in *Bonnie and Clyde*. Where Lancaster's *Train* performance is filled with small bits of invention to entertain himself while the movie progresses, Faye Dunaway glides, drifts like a vertical sashay. She goes into the movie at one end, comes out the other, leaving a graceful, faint, unengaged wake behind her. (Lancaster, at movie's end, has left behind him a map of zigzagging tracings and small clusters of intense activity.) The idea that this pastel dream of the Depression days is "perfectly cast and edited" is nonsense, and the proof of it is Miss Dunaway. She could have been folded neatly and quietly by the real Bonnie Parker (a very tough ex-waitress), slipped gently into an envelope, and posted to the Lincoln Center Repertory Company from whence she came. If movies were dependent on an "intelligent," exact rendering of a believable character, Miss Dunaway's vanilla charm would be a single-handed blight. At her best, she is too clean, blossoming. Catherine Deneuve–ish, nurtured in luxury, she'd shrivel up in the dirt crumbiness of the 1930's. (For perfect casting you'd need the butch short-order cook at Howard Johnson's: "Hey, Clyde, come pick up your A.C. on toast!")

The movie starts with the aroma of a French Agnes Varda bedroom scene: Miss Dunaway lying belly down on a bed, in heat, restless, with no action in town, West Dallas. "Hey there, that's my momma's car you're stealing!" She flies down the stairs, the camera staring up her billowing skirts. The movie picks up now that it's out in the open air, an authentic small town street with covered sidewalks: pseudo–folk conversation, spiffed-up Warren Beatty doing that coy shuffle in which his face loses itself inside a boyishly fake half-grin.

The fluke of Dunaway is that her body moves uncannily in harmony with the film's movement. While Beatty-Pollard-Hackman are muscular, earthbound, scurrying and plodding in skit-like business that is both entertaining and synthetic, she is almost air.

The point is that, in both Lancaster's and Dunaway's acting, there is little center, i.e., deep projection of character. Though a great deal of interpretation can be plied into the written role of a kid uneasy and bored in West Dallas, trying to become a celebrity through bank robbery, the center of the role, just a step from the sexy, flamboyant gun-moll role in *White Heat*, is a static, negligible thread.

The only kick in *Reflections in a Golden Eye* comes also from extras: Taylorisms and Brandoisms that shoot the film away from Carson McCullers's story and into the careers of two stars: his mulishness, her shrewishness. According to the daily newspapers, this is a "dirty movie" but "magnificently acted." When you meet the "gross, termagant wife" and her "pompous, purse-lipped major," the major is building his chest measurements by lifting weights, his wife is on her way to another ride into the hay with her next-door neighbor. Mostly what is seen is girth, the inert mass of Brando's elmlike body, the eyebrows moving in a slat face. Then cut to the stable area: much material about Taylor's riding gig and how she gets on a large white stallion.

Reflections is a clawingly bland movie about two army officers and their wives: amongst their quiet routine are such diversions as horse-beating, clothes-sniffing, nude bareback-riding, nipple-snipping with garden shears, masturbation fantasies with the beloved's discarded Baby Ruth wrapper, daily adultery in the woods. Given these In-gredients, this story of a seldom seen Army camp is Stalesville, due to the neuterization of the locale, the dated use of symbols (a close-up straight into the pupil of an eye to sink home the voyeurism of a young soldier standing outside a living room looking at a nude female). The people here are treated with a symbolic scorn that has cobwebs on it: a bobbing behind on an army saddle to suggest that Weldon (Brando) is Major Impotence.

Then there is the corny literalism of the color to go with the Golden Eye of the title (every word of McCullers's title is insultingly reiterated). The movie's color is that of caterpillar guts, and its 14-karat image is a duplicate of the retouched studio portraits that could be obtained in Journal Square, Jersey City, in 1945. Here and there, the color is vulnerable to rose pink. For instance, during the scene in the stables, there are any number of people, horses, buildings, but the local color that registers in the all-over yellowed monochrome is the rose pink of Liz Taylor's shetland wool pullover and a faint flush of the same pink in her cheeks.

The tough ad for *Point Blank* is misleading. An Andy Warhol silk-screen effect, Lee Marvin's Planter's Peanut head is seen alongside a gun barrel pointed at Times Square. This smashing blue-red-black-white ad suggests Action, in the Hammett-Chandler tough-cop tradition. You sort of expect to see Sleet Marvin and Angles Dickinson. They're there in recognizable form only.

Whatever this fantasy is about, it is hardly about syndicate heist artists, nightclub owners, or a vengeful quest by a crook named Walker (Marvin) for the $93,000 he earned on the "Alcatraz drop." The movie is really about a strangely unhealthy tactility. All physical matter seems to be coated: buildings are encased in grids and glass, rooms are lined with marble and drapes, girls are sculpted by body stockings, metallic or velourlike materials. A subtle pornography seems to be the point, but it is obtained by the camera slithering like an eel over statuesque women from ankle across thigh around hips to shoulder and down again. Repeatedly the camera moves back to beds, but not for the purposes of exposing flesh or physical contact. What are shown are vast expanses of wrinkled satin, deep dark shadows, glistening silvery highlights. The bodies are dead, under sedation, drugged, or being moved in slow-motion stylistic embraces. Thus, there's a kind of decadent tremor within the image as though an unseen lecherous hand were palming, sliding over not quite human humans. It's a great movie for being transfixed on small mountains which slowly become recognizable as an orange shoulder or a hip with a silvery mini-skirt.

In a sickening way, the human body is used as a material to wrinkle the surface of the screen. Usually the body is in zigzags, being flung, scraped over concrete, half buried under tire wheels, but it is always sort of cramped, unlikely, out of its owner's control. At one point in the film, Marvin walks over to a public telescope at Pacific Palisades and starts squinting at a whitish skyscraper. It is one of the mildest scenes since the births of Sam Spade and Philip Marlowe, but after the endless out-of-control cramping of bodies, the serenity of the composition and the reasonable decorum make for a fine blissful moment.

The fact that Academy Award Lee Marvin is in the film hardly matters. His blocklike snoutlike nose makes itself felt, also the silvery snakelike hair that doesn't look like hair, and the implacable, large-lipped mouth. Particular parts of his body and face are used like notes in a recurring musical score. His body stays stiff, vertical, very healthy and sunburned, but he is not actually in the movie. The syndicate is ripped apart by a psycheless professional who never moves except in a peculiar way

—like a mechanical soldier quick-stepping through a Bauhaus corridor; a memorable mystical moment has him flying slow-motion through a bathroom door, his arm waving a blasting Colt 45.

Point Blank is an entertaining degenerate movie for its bit players: Michael Strong as a used used-car dealer, Lloyd Bochner and his sharkskin style of elegant menace. There are fine tour-de-force action compositions: a woman berserk with rage, beating a man from head to toe, a car salesman being tortured in his own used Cadillac as it is bounced between concrete pillars (a take-off on the Huston-Hawks gangster beating in which the victim is jabbed back and forth between two people in black).

However, with all its visual inventions and dreadfully fancy jazz, the movie really belongs to a composite image of look-alike actresses. As the dawn goes further down over the old notion of acting as a realistic portrayal, Angie Dickinson's flamingolike angles can be seen one-half foot away from the despised Mal, all debauched beef-cake. They are seated on an orange chaise, like two book ends; his left hand reaches over two acres of sumptuous material and starts descending down the buttons of Angie's mini-dress. It is a surprisingly delicate scene (considering the camera-made massiveness of the two figures), and it has almost nothing to do with the actors.

If one's mind focuses momentarily on any of the acting personnel in the abovementioned films, one's reaction is not in terms of over-all evaluation, the role played. The movie experience is a magical, intimate recognition of some small intimate trait or traits that are unique to the actor. In the current papers, some blazing performances have been credited to actors whose persona is an imperceptible excrescence that bubbles up alongside the role: Elizabeth Taylor (spunky shrillness), Warren Beatty (natty dreamer), Rod Steiger (sweaty know-it-all), Alan Bates (bucolic shrewdster).

The actors, in other words, are erroneously built up as migratory statues, but in reality their medium has the blur, the shifting nonform of a series of ant hills in a sandstorm.

DAY
OF THE
LESTEROID 1966

There has no doubt been an upheaval in films during the 1960's, but almost nothing has been said about the Department Store styling or Modiste's Sensibility which seems to be causing the upheaval. Near the beginning of *Help*, the Beatles are seen walking up paths to identical red-brick houses, which, inside, turn out to be one long arcade of opulence, most of it vulgar and on display at any department store. It is typical of Beatledom that, while the spectator gets a distinct impression of modern goodies —an electric organ complete with comic books, a lot of food dispensers, a sunken bedroom for John Lennon—the scene itself is hardly touched.

During the night, Ringo does a funny crawl and talk when he is thrown from his bed by a ring-removing device, and later John Lennon does some dead-pan phoning, but on the whole their wild talent for goonish comedy is scarcely tapped by their director, Richard Lester.

Although there is a critical notion about Lester, a poor-man's Prospero showing us our wilder dreams, the fact is that he has been getting farther away from fantasy in any stereotyped sense and closer to a rather depressing comic-strip world of his own.

It is a world of Display Cases in which—like the old-fashioned Harold Teen or Katzenjammers—the humor is melancholy and the zaniness forced. Despite the frenetic postures, there is no real movement, and the chief effect is a sad, gray, frustrated technology. There is hardly a smidgeon of fun in any of these "cool" scenes (as in *The Knack*) where the actors have an embarrassing lachrymosity and limpness like drooping flowers or candles.

Lester's trademark is a kind of thickness of texture which he gets purely with technique, like the blurred, flattened, anonymous, engineering sounds which replace actors' voices, plus the piling up of finicky details, as in the scene of the Beatle shaving his friend's image in the mirror. A Harold Lloyd would have milked this gag by lengthening it; Lester goes to the opposite extreme of such radical foreshortening that the spectator is in danger of losing the scene.

In his exploitation of camera-editing devices, Lester has used his advertising-film background with such intensity that he leaves the idea and feeling of movies. What he creates is a new, assertive, hard-pushed Nowness that makes one feel out-of-it with a syntax of restlessness, cacophony, Gothic toys, gadgets as gadgets rather than plot mechanisms, and, most of all, a Fu Manchu feeling that comes from heavy costuming-cosmetic jobs that hardly allow an actor to exist.

Master of the Erector Set effect, Lester is a compendium of tricks and traits used by other Macy's directors who give a movie experience that veers between a catalogue of posh-vulgar items for licentious living (*Thunderball*) and a wildly imaginative Cecil Beaton notion of the twenty-first century in which Mastroianni, with his French's mustard skin and hair, manages to be the only decent actor despite a puckish notion that he is as doll-like as the mechanical porcupine that he uses for skin massager, gun bearer, and pet (*The 10th Victim*).

Louis Malle, in *Viva Maria,* shares with Lester the notion that any item, from the brass bedstead which Lester's unclowns push across the spectator's dormant spirit to a bronze horse in Malle's Mexican courtyard, can be turned into a causeless sight gag. Laboring under the delusion that he is Mr. Malleable, the director takes dozens of implacable items, including a miscast Jeanne Moreau, and piles up toothless slapstick effects. A typical priceless moment: a priest beheaded by a grenade, the pay-off being a shot of the torso descending the stairs, the head lodged in the man's hands while smoke issues from his cowl.

Thunderball never lives up to its prologue special, a water ballet involving silhouetted nudes in strawberry punch, a fishbowl effect that has some authentic eroticism and sets the Commodity tone of the ensuing mess. Lesterizing the Bond movie, the director has achieved something even Malle doesn't quite do in his *House-and-Garden* version of a 1912 banana republic: A marriage of the tinker-toy and the human in which the very air seems to turn into high-priced leather.

When Bond flies off via a missile corset, the interesting item isn't the stiff take-off, as though he had been ascending into the air by way of an escalator, but the dead-air effect behind him. It is exactly the same non-air that is used in the Alpine high jinks with the Beatles, the interesting difference being that the far-from-gilt-edged Bond director intentionally stops far short of credibility so that the spectator, like a buyer, can study each construct: the clipped square eyebrows that Sean Connery shifts in a placard effect, the frothy bubbles that spin up from an underwater love act.

The 10th Victim is by far the best neo-Lester film in that it totally accepts the idea of a department-store film and in certain nonplot scenes comes close to the perfumed eroticism that is always promised in painting by Rothko or Jasper Johns but never delivered. The good scenes are those that move away from the one-plot idea of legalized murder into a burnt-color madness in which the male is not only emasculated but turned into a sort of Vogue-designed vapor that the Amazon female lugs, hauls, shoves.

Lester's idea basically is a film that doesn't grow organically, but is postbuilt and prebuilt by a team of design specialists who are only bothered by the fact that they have to use actors inside their blue-white gauzemanship and painter's-dream sets. The Italian combine behind *Victim* actually blasts this Group-Ther-wrappy notion into disturbing poetry that is only grounded by the plodding and oddly arranged musculature that Ursula Andress exhibits as a female Mr. America.

Lester's syntax involves a relentless enterprise with photography (zoom, helicopter view, hand-held camera, changing the speed by removing frames) worked against a careful compartmenting. In this schizoid presentation, the actor is only a ploy in a program where the audience's ordinary view of a scene is constantly destroyed while he is held stationary against a maniacal engine which may be a bus-station storage locker (Lester's worst sight gag) or a black-white image of the Beatles at work which serves as a target for colored darts.

The bounciness and terrible rigidity is found in all the sub-

Lester works, the most schizoid being *The Chase,* an America-stinks number written by an old-time specialist in that area, Lillian Hellman, who here turns one small Panhandle town into a manic-depressive hell of lechery, Frugging, car-madness, Sin-town shakes and quivers à la Beatledom: At peak moments the streets get piled up with hell-raisers in new Chevrolets, all heading in different directions.

In the queen bee of vignette scenes, in which two or three moralistic scolds bitch each other in interesting dialogue, Miss Hellman has caught the Lester sickness: she has borrowed the kaleidoscopic effects in *Help* and chopped her script into a mass of Small Town filigrees, miniature versions of *The Little Foxes.* Some of her 100 per cent masochists and sadists drive in from the most distant reaches: the stray gum-chewers and Coke-drinkers who idled around gawking at the lynch scene in *Fury.* The weirdest borrowing: one beaten up wagon from the Our Gang comedies and the fake piety Negress, who discolored so many 1920's films, telling her child to pay no attention to those white folks and their criminal acts.

This diced conglomeration Middle Class Theater that forces its director to mimic scenes from *On the Waterfront* and *Ice Palace* is pure department store. Where Malle uses two actresses to play one starved role, Miss Hellman has written three and four of everything: Two near ghosts who walk uninvited into any-one's office or living room just to kibitz the action; three Robin Hoods in reverse who beat up anyone who looks lawful; two sex-pots who have little flesh but manage to divide the good and bad males between them; three huge revels that go on simultane-ously. The only nonduplicate is an escaped convict who sneaks home one night and is played with sneaky movie-stealing cheeri-ness by Robert Redford.

The chase, near the end, suddenly gives up the Lester ghost and becomes a wonderfully sinuous inside depiction of a fire in a car dump that leads into a perfectly timed version of the Lee Oswald murder. Swatchlike characters who automatically move into place (as a Miserable Drunken Bag, Martha Hyers at her lowest as an actress) give way to a complicated unfolding in which there is an unpredictable exit and entrance of shockingly beautiful images. One fiery moment with Brando working his way toward Redford penned in by thugs in a lakelike inferno is a stunner. No one has died more perfectly or surreptitiously than Redford, but hardly anyone in this Day of the Lesteroid has been allowed to act, i.e. to sift his way within a panoramic unfolding. In the Commodity program which Lester Help-ed engineer, every situation has a beginning-middle-end development that murders an offbeat actor (Marlon Brando) who thrives on working away from Systems and has based his throwaway talents on being able to grab attention from any Chevrolet or sequin gown that the lower technicians throw in his way.

THE WIZARD OF GAUZE 1966

When did movie directors decide that boredom was part of the game? The first mushrooming took place long before *The Red Desert* in a steady parade of overrated classics made in France: the metaphysical masquerades of Julian Duvivier, the under-visualized blues ballads of Marcel Carné.

Punctuating his films with tremolo effects, using voices like flute music, and turning shootings, escapes, flights into echoes, Carné (in the 1930's) created movies that eluded a direct gaze like the light from a subway train. What he did was grayer, less battering, with more romantic longeurs than the new Bondishness of *Ipcress File*. However, many of his techniques, such as using Arletty as a public image rather than an actress, are not too different from Sidney Furie's scaled-down work in *Ipcress File*.

This is a Chandleresque thriller that has no thrills, with an antihero who is more like a sugary flavor than an actor doing a Philip Marlowe. For his ticket, Furie's customer tries to pretend that set designs in chic colors are adding up to a movie. Actually, the only suspense is how slowly an effeminate knight (nonplayed "superbly" by Michael Caine) can put dimes in a parking meter, crack eggs in a skillet, or flatfoot his way through a library. This is something like watching Rod Steiger in *The Mark* trying to substitute a prop coffeepot for a decently written part.

Alfred Hitchcock, one of the most dogged of entertainers, hit a fallow period in the 1940's when he anticipated the kind of humorless playfulness we now find in such French prizes as *Zazie* (comic strip techniques) or *Breathless* (satires of acting styles, self-conscious parodies of Cagney-Bogart films). Trying to make the studio film pliable again, Hitchcock hit on esthetic accidents that aroused queer sensations: for example, an elusive sense of size (how large is the lifeboat in *Lifeboat*?); the claustrophobic sensation of being caught for two hours in the deadly orange-peel harmony of *Rope*; a speeding car in which the only thing moving is Ingrid Bergman's overteased coiffure; a scene fastened to the back of Michael Wilding as he walks through a ballroom; a succession of shots in which actors pop into and out of the frame, like shooting-gallery figures; the spooky-looking guests being introduced to Miss Bergman at Claude Rains's party; Cary Grant appearing upside down to the morning-after perspective of a sobered heroine.

Somewhere on the road between Hitchcock's cumbersome *Lifeboat* period and the latest glutted diversions, there has been a general desire among directors to (1) feed their vulgarity on the material of old Hollywood films, (2) replace tempo and form with unfunny satire, and (3) surround the spectator by film, as by a volley of buckshot, attacking him from all sides.

Using a Ziegfeldian chorus with nudes in classic Mr. Clean poses and reviving the chiclet colors that didn't work for George Sidney when he directed MGM musicals, Federico Fellini tyrannizes the audience in *Juliet of the Spirits*. The apparent idea, if it isn't to prove himself a cinematic Bellini, painter-director of overstuffed masquerades, is to provide the spectator with an additional stomach, a gastric passage that imbibes the billows of fake chatter and color without the mind having to contend with them. Like Godard-dammerung's chatter, Fellini-Bellini doesn't focus one's attention on unnoticed reality, but dissolves the spectator's capacity for noticing. Before his Pillow Case Special has moved past the scene in which an oversaccharine Joan Blondell type has been chopped (hidden with Curtiz's mirror and Orson Welles's trick of unspooling ticker-tape dialogue from unopened mouths), the spectator feels he is being pushed through an endless, unexciting crowd.

Any film that starts out with Giulietta (one-expression) Masina as a devoted wife beginning to doubt her husband's fidelity is in trouble. Her sexless acting is a parlay of Bambi's stiff motion, Harry Langdon's large ball-bearing eyes, and Spring Byington's ability to exude goodness, patience, and domestic cleanliness with a raspberry valentine smile. The movie leaks entertainment as this tender smile under an inverted souptureen hat falls half asleep at the beach (in harmony with the spectator) or flies to the wall in terror when a Liberace in mint-green toga gazes at her in miniscule eroticism.

A Jack-the-wrapper director, who grabs the spectator's throat in the first shot and doesn't let go until he has used every sexual-fantasy item from a leatherette boa constrictor to stiffened tongues, Fellini has boldly, willfully transformed a single idea (wife in a torment of phantasmagorical thoughts) into a hundred cliché-packed scenes. Every night scene employs an excruciating cricket noise to imply Country. The key scene in Spencer Tracy cycles—a gliding fox trot through admiring ballroomites while someone plays Their Song—is stylized into glassiness, made creepy by lengthening the moves, deadening the husband (Mario Pisu), who wears more eye-mouth make-up than his wife and holds her in the angelic no-touch embrace that is standard for Fellini antiquarianism.

Fellini is the only enthusiast for old Hollywood Muzak who doesn't believe in syncopation or its absence. A sort of mentholated accordion sound (like rain with dead raindrops) is bent forward and moved fast, but it doesn't have any beat.

He is also afflicted with a sort of equalism that makes every object as loudly important as the people. At least a tenth of the film takes place above, below, or in the neighborhood of an oversized baroque hat which has no life but outacts the glazed face beneath. While people are walking under these chic Barney Google creations, everything is stationary, and the spectator wanders under the tentlike brim, pursuing time.

Such lidded echoes of the floats in Pasadena New Year's Day parades are only one of the many cotton bandanna devices for diminishing people. Dead skin, feet that don't touch the ground, kids expanded and overdressed. A simple walk from a front gate to a doorway suddenly becomes a Big Scene (any older director would have skipped it). An iron bellpull carries as much import as the whole clutter around a decayed mansion.

Fellini reverses the old Warner Brothers theory in which a talented bit player provided a great deal of the scenery, built the pace, and served as a foundation for the movie's structure. The bit players here are used as wasteful clutter. Instead of individuals, they become wiggles, clown effects: e.g., an expanse of fiendishly concentrated enthusiasm on a face posed artfully against a bright orange umbrella.

Fellini's own distaste and ennui creep into the film in the form of a Gauze Wonderland of meaningless decor. Objects, transparent stuff, a basketwork lift for getting customers to a tree platform for minor orgies are brought forward actually to degrade, lessen the actors who have to cart them around. This personification of objects and depersonalization of people was fairly serviceable in *M. Hulot's Holiday*—or, for that matter, in Keaton's *Navigator*—but all it does for Fellini is to suggest some failure of moral intelligence. He can't seem to distinguish between the importance of a dark blue wickerwork lift and the actress who's riding in it.

The antithesis of these globular confections can be found in *What's New, Pussycat?*: especially in its handling of supporting cast (Capucine's tense nympho, Paula Prentiss's suicidal stripper). Clive Donner's direction gets a hardness of line, a whiplike individuality by compressing his actresses into a murderously confined space. Keeping the tempo fast, Donner has them almost on tiptoe, with no time to overpromote their Hollywood traits.

Woody Allen's writing, too, often appears as the obverse (funny) side of the bed-sheeted surrealism of Juliet in Remorseville. Despite too many Sennett chases in an overlong finale, Allen and Donner between them manage a punched-up college-humor style which really is funny. When they are not merely kidding the old two-reelers but trying hard for real Sennett or Keaton, they give us such moments as the Siegfried funeral with Sellers (wrapped in a flag) planning to launch himself out to sea.

Fellini's characters, on the contrary, generally look as though they were operating under the same ideological burdens as their director: Valentina Cortese, piled high with romantic garbage, a wig that ends in daisies, huge frilly chokers, Billie Burke's chattering gaiety. It is impossible to have all this and a Bergman Festival, too. Actresses staggering under this amount of trickery are not at their best while diving ecstatically through the morning dew.

Fellini's best image in recent years is still the opening of *8½*, a berserk Madison Avenue type hopelessly trying to climb through a cab window while life and/or the movie business streams past. This at least had dramatic meaning, which is not found in *Juliet of the Spirits*. Even the images have a kapok-padded puffiness that Claes Oldenburg gets in his pop-art sculptures of fried potatoes. For pure uninspired nothingness, openness within pacelessness, this *shtick* may be the closest meeting between the commercial art film and the Andy Warhol idea of shooting buildings or real-life situations with a stationary camera, not trying to make a movie.

The result: A film that surrounds the spectator with canned beauty and surprisingly indicates that the New Cinema is in one sense a kitchy-coo throwback to that old convention in painting, now abandoned—a windowlike opening on a scene of pillowy shapes representing Nature. Fellini's circusy image, remarkable as it is for luminosity and seamless continuity, offers the eye and mind far less than *International Showtime,* a Saturday TV fixture with foreign clowns and gymnasts.

THE COLD
THAT CAME
INTO THE
SPY 1966

What is interesting about the Cultural Exposition is that, while the public has become cognizant of the geniuses in each art form, the works themselves have been losing their separate identity as painting, TV comedy, or film.

As Abstract Expressionism moved into history, it became glaringly evident that its brand names, De Kooning & Co., were involved in a dilemma which dated their works without resolving the problem: a hang-up between no-environment painting and a much thinner wall-covering that shuns all the mannerisms of the Masterpiece.

Similarly with TV. The only original brand of humor in this medium was developed on the late-night talk shows from Jerry Lester to Johnny Carson. By turning its back on the more obvious TV possibilities (probably a good thing) and concentrating, like *Pussycat,* on the format of a nightclub routine, Don Adams's *Get Smart* is one of the few half-hour shows which manage to be both funny and successful. As a klutz version of James Bond and the U.N.C.L.E. agents, Adams's comedy is at once lower (the voice of a canary spieler), faster (the razzing one-liner of the night-clubs), and higher (originally geared to fewer people) than anything except the more inspired ad-libs of the Allen-Paar-Carson-Griffin variety shows.

In the last five years, movies have reached the point achieved in painting some ten or fifteen years ago. No moviemaker wishes, in other words, to be caught dead making a movie. If you compare *Life at the Top* with its parent, *Room at the Top,* you can see how much ground has been covered in a hurry. Instead of the corny, old, candid scene of adultery in the earlier film, we now have that floor-walker's inventory of "camp" objects (Good Godard!) plus a cockeyed notion of how a husband reacts to being cuckolded. Adultery is neither represented nor symbolized in traditional terms; it is rather triggered like Pavlov's dog by a series of associations which remind us of earlier movies.

Instead of plot or characters—in place of old-fashioned acting or directing—all the film-maker needs to do now is exhibit a string of objects reminiscent of old cinematic love affairs: the discarded shoes, the half-eaten remains of what passes for a champagne supper, the "telly" rolling an old Astaire film and (most nostalgic of all) one punchy shot of the cuckolded Laurence Harvey wearing a child's mask of Disney's dog Pluto and holding the lover's discarded tie.

Jean Simmons's total feminism, faultlessly played, is the one redeeming reality in the drifting, witless dramatization in an Englishy version of O'Hara's Country: hapless married people ensnared, sort of scratching around in superfluous plumbing, croquet sets; Antonioni's morbid strip-tease, done twice without cuts; and, mostly, car scenes that are nearly pointless whether the inevitable Rootes product (the movie's hero) is moving or parked. Oddly enough, what all this emphasis on decor at the expense of people suggests most is the social realism novel that appeared before Edison invented the camera.

This is particularly apparent in *The Spy Who Came in from the Cold*, which is also a striking example of a bookish movie issuing from a cinematic book. Less a routine spy story than a novel, the fascination of Le Carré's book was precisely in a film-like quality which managed to combine the complexities of *Herzog* with the mobility and eyewitness technique of Hitchcock at his *Vertigo* best. Ten years ago, any reader would have thought, "What a great movie this would (will) make." But today all this cinematic quality is wiped out in favor of something else.

Although Martin Ritt has done an interesting job of bringing out the dull, pudgy side of Le Carré's hero, this is at the expense of Leamas's equally important other side, which is one of great physical and spiritual strength. Burton's big face is not too well cast as the "faceless hero," and the pulverizing attempt to get rid of all his box-office glamour seems to have shriveled the actor considerably beyond the author's intention.

Despite this handicap, Burton has some memorable scenes with whisky bottles, drunken talk, and particularly in one final court-room close-up when he realizes he's been sold out by his own superiors. Burton and Ritt deserve a good deal of credit in going against the actor's grain here—he is not even allowed to use his biggest asset, his voice. And even though they don't quite manage to make Le Carré's character come through, it still remains a powerful projection of something so rocklike and stubborn in Leamas's character as to be good in its own right.

What is more interesting, however, is the manner in which current techniques succeed in turning a slow filmlike book that grips the reader into a "terse, swift" screenplay that is solemn and often dull. For one thing, the script is condensed like an accordion, with scenes either dropped out or briefly suggested in a manner which destroys any subjective identification.

Hitchcock, for example, got his subjective effects from using normal time: The spectator is there, living through a scene and seeing only what he would see as an eyewitness. The new vogue does just the opposite. Although the plot flashes by with almost meaningless rapidity, there is no impression of speed or move-ment—of many different scenes being compressed, as in *Tom Jones* or *The Knack*.

It's more like reading a five-page precis of *War and Peace* while sitting in a handsomely decorated library. The camera lingers interminably, like a Winslow Homerish version of the nineteenth century, on some studiously squared detail of emotion or decor, but there is such an absence of identification with the actor as to suggest the word "objective" in its worst scientific sense.

The cold that's now in *The Spy* was put there by a writing team (Guy Trosper and Paul Dehn) who have the notion that Leamas is an up-to-date Cold War version of the burnt-out figure who infests books by Arthur Koestler and Graham Greene: always demoralized and dehumanized by a rotten system.

The film's most telling frame shows Burton, humiliated by the East German head of counterespionage and manacled hands-to-feet in a bare cell. Ritt has prepared this shot as though it were the Last Supper, yet Burton manages a surprisingly truthful effect of middle-aged discomfort and defeat, like a sort of grounded, misshapen sea monster. What is dropped from the script here is a brilliantly worked out scene in which Leamas— far from being the sodden depressed cipher so often portrayed by Charles Boyer or James Mason in Graham Greene movies— maneuvers one of his captors into a dark room and, outthinking him with a wonderful chair gimmick, destroys him with his own brand of superjudo.

It is typical of the new-style film that any scene so actable as this is automatically too melodramatic or corny and must be dropped. Instead, we get innumerable beginnings and endings of scenes (like the above), all done in a slow friezelike genre style, which makes it impossible for the actors to get any complication inside their roles.

Leaving out so much self-explanatory action makes it necessary to explain the plot with a good deal of improbable dialogue. Even when the dialogue comes verbatim from Le Carré, it must be encircled with traffic lights to make sure the audience gets every plot idea from the loaded speech. The chief device for tying these fractional views and mobilizing the continuity is a door that flaps people in and out with a constancy recalling an old-fashioned play.

The book opens with a chase-and-kill scene in which Leamas's prize agent is gunned down cycling towards Checkpoint Charlie. Anyone reading this was hooked by Leamas's view, which becomes Dostoyevskian in its realization of all the pigeons, all the cheating, and hopelessness involved in a mucked-up operation.

The movie has scrubbed this viewpoint, which would have filtered Leamas's personality into the event. In its place is a perusal of the storefront scenery and an enthralling music-hall enactment of the bicycling, but the movie loses its one chance to identify Leamas as not merely depressed but as also a subtly talented technician in a squalid Looking Glass job. After Burton has been squeezed into his role, the same undercutting goes on with Claire Bloom and Oskar Werner, who never get to act themselves into the Cold War scene.

When the bearded East German intelligence official (Werner)

asks Leamas for his forged signature, a typically Hitchcock moment is set up with two professionals absorbed in the intricacies of handwriting. This scene, the kind that can be acted into a killing bit and realized best with a subjectively used camera, is not milked at all.

As Leamas disintegrates according to a fantastic plot arranged by his Control, he moves through a London underworld, employment office, crackpot library, prison. Le Carré made these moments into great bouts of acting. A fussy librarian gets tangled in his stubbornness as a bum, his garbage and smell, even the problem of spelling his name on pay checks. Burton could have acted this highbrow Bowery comedy into the area of Falstaff's humor, but it has all been displaced or tersed up by obsessive need for a dour, relentless movie.

An actor who can defeat this chilling style has to be a master at working in needlepoint. There is a tantalizing stretch when Burton reports back to his prissy, devious boss, and the actor (Cyril Cusack) gets more inflection with his glued-together lip motion on ''Quite so'' or ''mental fatigue'' than Errol Flynn does in the whole underrated movie about Gentleman Jim Corbett.

Werner, as the tough Jewish questioner, does a weirdly clever job of being just what he should be (like a terrier, slight and agile). Most of his virtuoso-ish hocus-pocus is done by obliterating one word to emphasize a raised syllable or accented laugh, and it is managed within a whiskery mask that should deaden his talent for eloquence.

The Spy may not be as stylish as *Eva, Help!,* or *Giulietta of the Syrups,* but it has an aftereffect that is surprisingly pungent and more provoking than the other movies. Despite the cold literary treatment of *The Spy,* a few of the fragments are so precisely verisimilitudes, both in relation to Le Carré and to life, that they succeed in themselves in making this a hard movie to forget.

RAIN IN THE FACE, DRY GULCH, AND SQUALLING MOUTH 1966

The obvious fact about any movie image is that it can be read for any type of decisive, encapsulating judgment. A library has been poeticized about Keaton's diluted Sitting Bull face, the horizontal hat, and the rigid sags of his clothes, an automatic "personality" which fades from view as the real Keaton works inside the frozen "armor." Regardless of the occasion, Keaton uses the tar drop eyes, the discouraged fish-mouth (held closed by an act of will) like a slot machine to make a viable situation out of whatever lemon turns up in the scene. Critics sentimentalize Keaton into a wish-fantasy of poetic comedy—superimposed upon what they cannot help observing. They thereby attempt, also, to separate this intensely pragmatic, though original, craftsman from the movies in which he appears, and from the kind of crass opportunism which these comedies, the best of them at that, represent.

Keaton, a re-enactment of the silent film era by a crude writer, is a joy to read when Rudi Blesh is setting the scene at Keaton's studio, presenting a clown who is a clutter of versatility (bridge shark, third baseman, lover) and directly opposite to the deadpan artist eulogized in film books. This is a fabulous book, but, when Blesh starts analyzing the comedies as great laugh machines, the pages become stiff, hard to assimilate. Much of Keaton isn't meant for laughs, and what has been said about his sad, motionless pantomime, the famous frozen kisser, now is irrelevant. The shingle face, at the rare times when Keaton uses it in place of his angled body, is used as an efficient florid syrup, an acting weapon much beloved by its owner.

Blesh's images of these comedies as a roller coaster of energy, a machine gun of perfectly manipulated gags, doesn't have anything to do with Keaton's normal zigzag. *Sherlock Jr.* is a slow scroll, a coiling together of short movements in which Keaton's native fixation on mechanics and slow-witted concern for his own talent works as a drooping agent on the action. The prefabricated Sennett slapstick, which may have been energetic before it became worked into automatic maneuvers by constant repetition, appears to be moving in slow halt-go rhythm; in fact, the pavane-like motion sometimes is standing still. The disappointment now produced by Keaton comes from the fact that there is no real victimization from the disasters. Also, this world that has breath-taking reality and nowness—Santa Monica in the 1920's—is hardly touched by the action, which is faded, automatic, over-decided.

There is a dreadful notion in criticism that movies, to be digested by esthetes, must be turned from small difficulty into large assets and liabilities. James Agee, who always paid out tribute like a public-address system, is never precise, but his fastidious pricing of a Lauren Bacall gave the reader the secure feeling that Bacall could be banked at the nearest Chaste National.

Henry Fonda, during a recent run-through of his films in New York, doesn't add up as "one hell of an actor" (as Bill Wellman declared in a *Cinema Magazine* interview), but he is interesting for unimportant tics: the fact that he never acts one-on-one with a coactor.

When Glenn Ford is a boneless, liquidy blur as a cowboy dancer in *The Rounders,* Fonda fields Ford's act by doing a Stan Laurel, suggesting an oafish bag of bones in a hick foxtrot. Again, in *The Lady Eve,* Sturges kids this Fonda-ism of opposing his playmates in a scene: Fonda's Hoppsy is a frozen hopsicle, a menace of clumsiness, while Eric Blore and Eugene Pallette are clever acting dervishes playing scintillating types.

Fonda's defensiveness (he seems to be vouchsafing his emotion and talent to the audience in tiny blips) comes from having a supremely convex body and being too modest to exploit it. Fonda's entry into a scene is that of a man walking backward, slanting himself away from the public eye. Once in a scene, the heavy jaw freezes, becomes like a concrete abutment, and he affects a clothes-hanger stance, no motion in either arm.

A good director must chop Fonda out from his competition:

John Ford isolates Fonda for a great night scene in *Young Mr. Lincoln,* communing with himself on a Jew's harp; there is another one, in *The Ox-Bow Incident,* where Fonda explodes into a geometrical violence that ends in a beautiful vertical stomping. Left on his own, Fonda gets taller and taller, as he freezes into a stoical Pilgrim, sullenly and prudishly withdrawing while he watches another actor (Lee Tracy in *Best Man*) have a ball.

Fonda's man-against-himself act was noticeable in his first films during the 1930's, when his twenty-year-old Tom Joad–Slim-Lincoln were aged into wizened, almost gnomelike old folks by an actor who keeps his own grace and talent light as possible in the role. During the 1940's, in *Daybreak* and *Ox-Bow,* Fonda starts bearing down on the saintly stereotype with which writers strangled him. In a typical perversity, he edges into the bass-playing hero of *Wrong Man* with unlikable traits: nervousness that is like a fever, self-pity, a crushing guilt that makes him more untrustworthy than the movie's criminal population. Almost any trait can be read into his later work. From *Mr. Roberts* onward, the heroic body is made to seem repellently beefy, thickened, and the saintliness of his role as an intelligent naval officer–candidate–President shakes apart at the edges with hauteur, lechery, selfishness.

The peculiar feature of these later Fonda performances, however, is that he defeats himself again by diminishing the hostility and meanness—so that they fail to make us forget the country-boy style in which they are framed.

In his best scenes, Fonda brings together positive and negative, a flickering precision and calculated athleticism mixed in with the mulish withdrawing. Telephoning the Russian premier, desperate over the possibility of an atomic war (*Fail-Safe*), Fonda does a kind of needle-threading with nothing. He makes himself felt against an indirectly conveyed wall of pressure, seeping into the scene in stiff, delayed archness and jointed phrasing—a great concrete construction slowly cracking, becoming dislodged. It is one of the weirdest tension-builders in film, and most of it is done with a constricted, inside-throat articulation and a robot movement so precise and dignified it is like watching a seventeen-foot pole vaulter get over the bar without wasting a motion or even using a pole.

Before it reaches its two strippers at midway point, *The*

Rounders shows Fonda in urbane-buoyant stride, but, even a second-team bit player, Edgar Buchanan, outfences him during a funny exchange in which Fonda explains the name Howdy. Eugene Pallette (*Lady Eve*), a buoyant jelly bowl moving skyward as he goes downstairs, is a magical actor, and nothing in Fonda's divested vocabulary is equipped to produce that kind of spring-water bubbling and freshness.

The decisive encapsulating opinion in movie reviews comes usually from reading a plot that is all but hidden by molecular acting and direction. *Who's Afraid of Virginia Woolf?* is an example of Kaleidoscopic Limited, an ordered mélange with not too many pieces but each of them colliding against its neighbor, and all of them hitting like flak into the famous Albee play. The most famous scene is an erotic nondance, which is neither erotic nor dancelike, in which Elizabeth Taylor suggests a gyrating milk-bottling mechanism. Part of the problem here is that the view is top-heavy, and, while her pinchy face and Orphan Annie hairdo are very noticeable, there is no feeling of fatness in action. All the little effects—the acorns in her cheeks, cushion bust, tiered neck—mitigate against the story idea that this is a Bitch Wife drawn to an impotent Science Boy.

That the all-important George name is screamed, belched, panted at a non-George shows once again that movies must not be read as stories. The mangled name (even Miss Taylor yowls or jowls it, seeming not to know who it belongs to) is never acted by its supposed owner, a cyclonic acting-machine named Richard Burton. Burton is pleasing, but the emerging character is not Albee's, or Martha's, George.

This is not to say that Burton, who is far ahead of his co-workers in this movie, doesn't add up to intensely absorbing, complex terrain. Alongside the mushy Taylor performance, Burton is without self-consciousness as a drinker, and, unlike his wife, who moves like a three-dimensional playing card, he fills a scene with body, talk, face. Everything flows around Burton, though at no point is he a masochistic, mediocre ultimate in soft, ineffectual husbands.

Miss Taylor's Martha is also a perfect example of the error in trying to surround a performance with an imprisoning judgment. The role has been castigated as crude, monotonous, prankish, but

there are at least two scenes in *Woolf* where she's close to humor
and uses the fat lips and lines enclosing them to fill the screen
with credible humanity. Her opening mimicry of Bette Davis
reacting to a messed-up bedroom should become an unforgettable
movie bit, probably because it suggests Burton's mentoring. The
bit involves the expression ''Wha-ta dum–puh!'' said with a com-
plain-y, whine-y little girl effect in which Miss Taylor ends up
handing you the puh sound in dump; Miss Davis, a blatant blend
of Sophie Tucker and Eleanor Roosevelt, should be jealous. Miss
Taylor is even more haunting later in the film, when, after sleep-
ing with the visiting professor (George Segal), she suddenly
starts using the kitchen as a workable locale. Moving from counter
to fridge to sink, her hips become a hub around which the kitchen
appears to be moving.

Shifting Albee's play into a Warner Brothers movie brings on
a curious ambivalence. There is a need to make every surface intensely touchable or realistic in the manner of every rackets-film
photographed by James Wong Howe. At the same time, opposing
this old Warners trick is an abstract theatricalizing, a negation
of scene and scenery when the play moves outdoors and into non-
scenes: yards without neighbors, streets without cars or people,
and a juke joint without customers. Yet the surfaces are intensely
specific as air, bark, skin—even moon surfaces. A movie about
intellectuals, sophistication, high verbosity, rattles with images
of blindness, papier-mâché settings out of children's operetta,
streets ridden with street lamps and blinking signs that don't
light, and people staring into these fake lights without seeing
anything, à la Orphan Annie and her blank circle eyes.

Thus, the movie loses reality by disallowing terrain, but picks
up interest when people are treated as terrain. The movie's
pivotal scene is a long monologue, Miss Taylor weaving back and
forth, using the word ''snap'' to suggest the final disruption of
her marriage. Her weavelike motion, the lights moving kaleidosco-
pically on her face, a hairdo like a great tangled bird's nest—
the whole effect is a forest of tangled nasoid speech and crafty
motion that doesn't record as talk, but makes insidious impact as
shifting scenery.

PISH-
TUSH 1966

Something died in the movies when TV, wide screen, and the New Wave film made the bit player expendable. Watching Rita Tushingham or Jeanne Moreau makes one think wistfully of Frank McHugh's eyebrows, Eugene Pallette's humpty-dumpty walk, Edgar Kennedy's mad wounded-bull heavings, and all the others. Whatever happened to Eric Blore?

The great strength of the movies in the 1940's was the subversive power of the bit player. Movies that have become classics, rightly (*The Lady Eve*) or wrongly (*Casablank*), are never more savage and uninhibited than in those moments when a whirring energy is created in back of the static mannered acting of some Great Star.

Casablanca shifts into high gear as soon as Bogart's glum face hits the surrealistic Yiddish energy of Leonid Kinsky. *The Lady Eve* is charmingly acted by Stanwyck and Fonda, but that looney Dickensian spirit that was Sturges's trademark came from brief moments with people like Blore, Pallette, and Demarest. Most of these subactors were short on range, but the explosiveness of their Brief Moments more than made up for it: Frank McHugh, using his hands, eyebrows as though they were wings; Edgar Kennedy, mixing drinks like a barker playing a shell game; the electric-fan velocity with which William Demarest counteracted the monotony of his voice.

As opposed to these midget giants, we find something more nearly the opposite today. Tushingham, Moreau, and especially Giulietta Masina—three tiny women—swell their proportions to giantism with gestures and decor. Moreau, for example, in *Bay of Angels,* piles herself with outsized boas, eyelashes, cigarette lighters, corsets, wigs. This is supposed to prove that she's psychologically doomed.

There is good acting today, but it is very different from the Tushingham-Moreau approach, in that it stays within the modesty and infiltrating of good bit-playing: Oskar Werner's precise melancholia in *Ship of Fools*; James Fox's toughness immersed in a soft-sweet intellectualism in *King Rat*; Robert Shaw's scene-stealing in *From Russia with Love,* which is done alongside Sean Connery, who is a master in his own right in the art of sifting into a scene, covertly inflicting a soft dramatic quality inside the external toughness.

Thus, the current movie, like the current cocktail party in which one or two cultural Big Shots take over, tries to get along with a few big actors doing star turns. *Repulsion,* a Mittel-Europa case history modeled on Hitchcock's *Psycho,* is often convincing and horrific, but the star, Catherine Deneuve, is a too glamorous actress, incapable of blending herself into the street scenes, which lack bit players to make them credible. Just as the best thing in *The Hill* is the hill itself, so the best things here, substituting for the old bit performances, are background minutiae such as wall cracks, dripping faucets, distant views of a playground.

A good actor is usually one who has picked up the tricks that made Lee Tracy better than Spencer: a talent for (1) retreating into a scene, (2) creating an effect of space, and (3) becoming a combination of fantasy figure and the outside world, but always a fragmental blur. For the same reason, a good straight man is nearly always a better actor than the star comic: Dean Martin, George Burns.

A bad example of an actor who has nothing of Tracy's sifting is Simone Signoret, Werner's partner in the *Fools* film, a female Lionel Barrymore sullenly encased in a blocklike girth. She shows nothing but perspiration to pull herself into the scene. An even worse example of the megalomaniac star who can make the simplest action have as many syllables as her name is Rita Tushingham.

The myth that a director breaks or makes a film is regularly disproved by this actress who does a sort of Body Unpleasant act of turning herself into a Duck Bill Blabberpuss (*The Leather Boys*) and carrying on a war of nerves against the other actors. In a somewhat gentler vein (*The Knack*), she adds a gratuitous spookiness, which makes every gag seem to last forever. While this film has been accused of having too many jokes, the fact is that the actress smothers every joke with a goonish nasality and by peering overlong at the grown-ups.

Similarly, it is not the director's fault if she Tushingham's everything up with her particular brand of pathology: being sullen when she should have been airy, simulating the fevers of lust with a wooden body. She injects a grotesquerie into her love scenes, which has more to do with dirty Puritanism than with real sex. In *A Taste of Honey*, Tony Richardson's direction was unfairly blamed for this: he was accused of being too "moralistic" to bring out the "lyrical, childlike, *gamine*" qualities of his heroine. But Tushingham's lyricism is always more gamey than *gamine*. For example, the scene with her unlovely aging mother in the bathtub is made unnecessarily cruel and embarrassing merely through the daughter's appraising stare of distaste.

Actors, too, have been unjustly accused of a certain crudity when playing against Rita (and "against" is the word). Peter Finch has never looked more like a marooned dirigible than in *The Girl with the Green Eyes* when he either beds down or drinks tea with this hard-eyed adolescent. (Olivier, in a similar situation, was allowed by his fellow actress to gain sympathy for his Entertainer.) It's not that Tushingham hogs the screen exactly, but she does chew her way through another actor's scene with bulldog incisors.

The difference between good acting and the Tush treatment is evident in that Richardson film, *The Entertainer,* where Olivier and Alan Bates are working typical Tushingham material: ugly faces, a cesspool existence, meandering narrative, and a grainy *Breathless*-style photography. Here the tawdry beach resort picks up something of the wonder of Chaplin's *Gold Rush* cabin or the dentist's quarters in *Greed*.

There is no moralizing in Olivier's low-comic treatment of a lower-depth character, as there always is in Tushingham's overplaying. In other words, the actor is not always pinning placards on himself explaining: "This is a Bourgeois, this is a Proletarian, this is a Lovable Child." Olivier avoids every stereotype of the tawdry show-biz has-been in order to give his Entertainer some of the magical complexity of a real-life Chaplin. In fact, Osborne's "liberal" clichés that were thrown away by Olivier were overplayed by Tushingham in *A Taste of Honey*.

Like Richardson in *Taste of Honey,* Sydney Furie has never been a more luckless director than in *The Leather Boys.* The best thing about this film is the performance of Dudley Sutton, who plays the homosexual with real old-fashioned elegance, like a bit player. Compared to this, Tushingham plays her lower-class sex kitten with a wild inappropriateness which might look better in a comic strip than in a movie.

Tossing her head about like a basketball and nasally, toothily spewing scorn at her high school teacher, she seems a cross between an adolescent Maggie Jiggs and a delinquent Orphan Annie. A few shots later, abed with her teenage lover, there is the same wild improbability about her sexuality. No one, except possibly Anne Bancroft, can outdo her in a bed scene.

It may be unfair to expect a young and relatively inexperienced actress to exercise her own discretion on a bad script. But actors such as Olivier are flexible enough to improve on the author's intention; others make a bad intention worse.

Furie, a Martin Ritt–type director, who works with submiddle-class people in overstrained wrangling situations, sets up one Tushless situation in an early winter boardwalk that serves as a chaser for Miss Tushingham's presence. The scene involves a potential (Colin Campbell) and committed homosexual (Sutton) picking up a pair of unsentimentally sexy blondes, who have a rowdyism the movie needs and a convincing manner at Ski Ball.

The matter-of-fact presentation of these birds—who recall Howard Hawks's birds of passage in *The Big Sleep*—gives the feeling of a 1940's film made twenty years too late.

The scene moves about with a roughed-in, wind-blown looseness, fanning out into several corners of Coney Island. The comic-strip sexology of Miss Tushingham reappears, and the film veers back into didactic acting and working-class scenes shod or shoddy with leather.

There were moments in high 1940's films—Elisha Cook in *The Big Sleep*—when a supporting player hit his peak and managed to dry out whatever juicy glamour and heroics were in the film so that it took on a slatelike hardness. The art in this Cook-type acting—played from left field—is miles beyond the studiously ill-mannered Reo Rita, who is not only old-fashioned, but who, with her special brand of pushing and ham, manages to rob the film of its space, background, and the effect of being made with a camera.

THE SUBVERTERS 1966

One day somebody is going to make a film that is the equivalent of a Pollock painting, a movie that can be truly pigeonholed for effect, certified a one-person operation. Until this miracle occurs, the massive attempt in 1960's criticism to bring some order and shape into film history—creating a Louvre of great films and detailing the one genius responsible for each film—is doomed to failure because of the subversive nature of the medium: the flash-bomb vitality that one scene, actor, or technician injects across the grain of a film.

The Ultimate in a Director's Film, *Strangers on a Train*, now seems partly due to Raymond Chandler's talent for creating erotic eccentrics like the quarrelsome sex bomb who works in a record shop. Nothing in Hitchcock's file of female portraiture has the realistic bite of this Laura Elliott role, nor does any other Hitchcock film show the shady Los Angeles eye for transportation and suburbia.

Inside Daisy Clover, a thoroughly soft Hollywood self-satire, has one scene that is dynamite as anti-Hollywood criticism and the only scene in which Natalie Wood, snapping her fingers to get in time with a giant screen image of herself, is inside the Daisy role with the nervous, corruptible, teenage talent discovered years ago by Nick Ray.

The crassest film, *The Oscar*, has a bit performance by Broderick Crawford, in which he creates his boillike effects of degeneration, vileness. Crawford's corny lolling performance of a small-town sheriff suggests a career of hard-won professionalism, the kind of inside movie technique this Sammy Glick film is supposed to exude but never touches.

King and Country is generally credited as a Joe Losey film, one that is stained with his loathing and casts the spectator in the center of a rat-infested muddy horror known as trench war. It may be a "very good movie," but, within its didactic, humorless images that seem to brood themselves out of a Rembrandt darkness, there is almost nothing that is fresh for Losey, the actors, or Larry Adler, who did the lachrymose music. From the opening harmonica solo, which is pure bathos and standard for little characters crushed by their superiors, to the final Freudianism in which a gun is placed inside the deserting soldier's mouth to finish off what the firing squad started, this is a photographed play with overtrained bits, particularly from Losey's catalogue of male-female symbols.

Just as *Paths of Glory* is indebted to Tim Carey's smart-alecky performance and Calder Willingham's talent for edgy words, obscenity-skirting dialogue, Losey's new films are given a great lift by Dirk Bogarde and the tepid intellectuality he inflicts by dragging back on his lines, going silent before quietly spacing his words, in a manner that suggests some fear or sensitivity pulling the words down his throat. Bogarde is woodenly interesting, and, to a lesser extent, so is Tom Courtenay repeating his specialty, a face that has the stiff, convicted homeliness of a wanted criminal on the Post Office bulletin board, plus a chewing, swallowing dialect in which every fourth word gets home to the spectator.

However, aside from the acting, there is a small reward in Losey's ability to bring out a suffocating intimacy, apparent long ago in Hollywood films Losey made about a prowler, wet-back, and green-haired boy. Nobody gets such a feeling of worshipful hovering, but it is the disconcerting coldness of a Losey that he doesn't touch his doomed material but just polishes the surfaces.

The Flight of the Phoenix has as its dominant image a group of unstinting character actors strapped like horses to a small airplane or pieces of a larger one. This repeated shot and another fine one of the same hard-working line of actors resting against a plane's fuselage, each one choked with realistic gimmicks and fervor, suggest that almost any Robert Aldrich film is based largely on the wild, sloppy life that a Dan Duryea ensemble player can ply around the edges, trying to budge a huge, flabby movie script.

Aldrich's movie is not only built on the idea of subversive acting, it is pure entertainment that balances the director's shortcomings as a highly personal technician against an unerring instinct for the type of filigree electricity that makes a film but never gets discussed in the *Cahiers* interviews with great directors. The major project—flatly recounting the building of a small plane from bits of a larger one—is flubbed in faulty coloring, *Lawrence of Arabia* shots of the desert, some miscasting with two French actors who lack the hard, antimovie approach of a typical Aldrichite, and the curious fact that Aldrich, who can sift the landscape into the faces and emotions of his actors, goes dead on anything strictly involved with setting.

The film's excitement comes from baroque latticework, unimportant bits of action that seem to squeeze through the cracks of large scenes: The freakish way in which Hardy Kruger's Germanic gabble works over a sun-cracked lower lip; the job-type sensation of watching work procedures from the perspective of an envious, competitive colleague; Ian Bannen doing a monkeyish prancing and kidding around the German; a great deal of letter-perfect hatred of authority by Ronald Fraser as a butterball sergeant; the weird effect of Jimmy Stewart veering back and forth between the slow Charley Ray affectations that made him an unbearably predictable star and a newer Stewart who has a middle-aged doggish look and threads his way along a complicated moment in a peering tricky fashion unrelated to script or acting.

Watching Duryea quietly pin down his Milquetoast role without the usual Duryea aggression of a corny trumpet effect in his upper palate, enjoying the queer pogo-stick jumps of Fraser when a dead engine slowly comes alive, a critic might hope for a new award at the year's end: Most Subversive Actor. This is possibly the only way that justice can be afforded the real vitality in film.

Instead of the overreported people in faulty projects—the Lumets, Steigers, Claire Blooms—the moviegoer is pointed toward the fantastic detailing of Ian Bannen as a toadying liberal officer in *The Hill;* Michael Kane doing a forceful amalgam of silent cunning and subofficer deviousness as the "Exec" in *The Bedford Incident;* Eleanor Bron's mugging, put-on acting that just skirts sickening cuteness as the fake Indian girl in *Help.*

One of the joys in moviegoing is worrying over the fact that what is referred to as Hawks might be Jules Furthman, that behind the Godard film is the looming shape of Raoul Coutard, and that, when people talk about Bogart's "peculiarly American" brand of scarred, sophisticated cynicism they are really talking about what Ida Lupino, Ward Bond, or even Stepin Fetchit provided in unmistakable scene-stealing moments.

CARBONATED
DYSPEPSIA 1968

A big sour yawn pervades the air of movie theaters, put there by a series of tired, cheerless, low-emotion heroes who seem inoculated against surprise, incapable of finding any goal worthy of their multiple talents. The yawn is built into people who seem like twins though they are as various as the teetering scriptwriter in *Contempt,* the posh master crimester of *The Thomas Crown Affair,* and that ultimate in envy and petulance who is the philosophy professor approaching middle age in *Accident.* Each of these three heroes (Michael Piccoli, Steve McQueen, Dirk Bogarde) shifts constantly in a voluptuous way between mobility—driving trickily in flashy little cars, making fast-cut repartee while rushing into an airport—and its opposite, the most deadening kind of innocuous living.

The disenchantment that sweeps over the theater is also caused by a series of technicians who are quite literally emptying the screen of conventional tension and rules. These technicians, who range through a realistic cameraman (Raoul Coutard) whose ability for candidness seems mercurial, a master of concision in scriptwriting (Harold Pinter), and a bite and bitterness director (Luis Buñuel), seem totally cynical about the pre-1960's notion of good and/or profitable movie creation. The Coutard-Pinter technician has contrived a lighter-the-better film, in which the attack is on the industry and the middle class, and the method includes turning the action toward the spectator, using people as walking-talking editorials, making positional geometry of the most mundane, piddling actions.

Accident is filled with positional constructs, one centered around an omelette whipped up at midnight, a nice kitchen crisscrossed with anger, embarrassment, brutal rudeness, as well as paths of action. Similar geometry, exercises in movement using the screen as a floor, are set up around the packing of a suitcase and hedge-clipping. *Band of Outsiders,* a parody of a sex triangle, its people not real, but more like fleas, is also crammed with ricochet movements; a Madison danced in a two-

bit bar with its nonsense trio led by Sami Frey, building a
spacious rectangle over and over, punctuating the construction
with a witless hop and clap at one corner, and a foot stamp at
another.

. One of the funnier scenes last year involved a zinged-out Albert Finney, comatose on the living room sofa, blearily looking
at the Telly. ''Charlie, you look awful. Don't you get any
sleep?'' Charlie, hangdog, gets up, heads for the bedroom. The
seedy-sexy Billie Whitelaw says: ''Charlie, come back here and
sit down.'' He returns just as docilely as he left. This is a very
low-key, high-humor scene; the bemusing things come mostly
from positioning, the automatic moves that Charlie perpetrates
every time his tough, all-woman ex-wife goes into her top-ser-
geant act. There is also something perversely sardonic about
the lush-sour woman, an incongruous health addict wearing
satin on a zoo-farm in the country, appearing more spent and
ravaged than the city-corrupted Charlie.

Charlie is one of the many reputedly gifted and successful he-
men who, poleaxed by the ironies and vagaries of life, appear for
most of their screen life with a creased and deflated expression.
This face, which might seem to be thinking of Black Power, Mc-
Carthy's chances, or what they mean by ''the art of the Real,''
is more likely chewing on the question: ''What can I do with
myself for the two hours between now and dinner?''

The Stare has devoured a great deal of screen time in movies. Benjy the Graduate, ex-college-magazine editor and track
captain, leads a split life on screen; half the time he's hung up
between Mrs. and Miss Robinson, the other half he's at half
mast: a flattened silhouette, descending an escalator, staring
at a fish tank or lying on a raft silhouetted against the pool.

The Stranger, a man who takes quick naps on his feet while
eating, sitting vigil over his mother's coffin, is a handsome office
worker in Algiers. Bereft of ambition, there's always the definite feeling that this escapist intellectual, as torpid as they
come, is working and living below his mental structure. This is
one of the most interesting performances, so filled with the
materials of sensuality and lassitude. Mastroianni not only does
the curious, innocuous routines that now make up the life of the
Inactive Hero, but he gets the most intense sybaritic pleasure

from simply a smoke after lunch, a swim, the dozing-off ride on a bus, or the slow movement of the street below his beaten-up hotel room. He is a snake, slowly, luxuriously unwinding. But in the midst of this tantalizingly sensual, pleasure-driven acting, and below the staring, is the frightful aspect of bottomless emptiness, aimlessness.

Actually, it could be said that the whole riverbed of films shifted somewhere in the early 1960's, at the time of Antonioni's rise, when the rudiments of nausea, apathy, jaundice, heart soreness were examined by actors. Movies suddenly changed from fast-flowing linear films, photographed stories, and, surprisingly, became slower face-to-face constructions in which the spectator becomes a protagonist in the drama. In 1961, while actors like Jeanne Moreau in *La Notte* were sinking into self-absorption, miserable doubts about their past careers, the movie became determinedly psychological and, more important, the face of the screen as well as the actors emptied, flattened out. Now, whole characterizations, like those of the active-passive duo in *Persona*, tied together in an identity struggle, are based on a kind of prolonged staring, not only at life but into oneself. What is more exciting is that the movie has almost accidently arrived at the beauties, handsomeness, of banalized emptiness. A whole book could be written about the exquisite beauties of the one scene in *Persona*, comprised of Bibi Andersson in a 1950's bathing suit, a sunny courtyard scene, and not much action. The whole drift of the scene is based on flat, yawning stretches of skin, silence, sunlight, and, behind it all, particularly, is The Stare.

Although used to put a virtue-wins-out pulp story, like *Graduate* or *Band of Outsiders*, in the area of sensitivity and conscience, the stare is much more interesting for what it means in movie technique. When this pensive, larger-than-life profile, back of the head, or full face, fills the screen with a kind of distilled purity, the image becomes purified abstract composition, a diagram, and any soul-searching is secondary. The movie, in a mysterious fashion, diverts at this moment from the clutter and multiplicity of story-telling, naturalism, to a minimal condition. The screen is reduced to a refined one-against-one balance, and the movie's excitement has shifted strictly into a matter of shape against shape, tone against tone.

Prior to the 1960–62 outburst of debut films, the material of the screen—shadow, people, the sound, too—gave the comforting sense of a continuous interweave of action in deep space. Today, an elementalism has taken over. When the pointed starkness of a Greek statue is moving slowly against a flat, bludgeoning stretch of blue sky (*Contempt*), it is similar in syntax to the flat eroticism of Faye Dunaway's silky stride and body as it is seen as one all-over matlike shape against the loneliness of a 1920's Dallas street. In both cases, a kind of primitive block-against-block composition is being worked for a singing, coloristic impact.

The movie today has been turned around, flattened out, the most obvious sign of this re-arrangement being the prevalence of pictures within pictures: instead of one continuous image, the scene appears to fragmentize: an evil husband watches witchlike activities on a TV screen; his wife worries about the shadow-rimmed square on the wall where a portrait once hung; a revenge-driven bride, camouflaged by make-up and wrong wigs, appears to come together in drawings and paintings; the teenaged careers of an intellectual circle are recounted in still photographs; an unconfident husband mimics and discusses the brashness of the Dean Martin gambler in *Some Came Running*; a homely peasant wife plasters a fashionable brassiere ad against her body. In effect, this image-within-image marks the advent of a movie that is no longer an evolving scene but singular confrontations between actor and spectator (a psychological effect that is not a great deal different from the question-answers confrontation that goes on in therapy between psychiatrist and patient).

There is now a distrust of unity, continuity, and it shows itself in what appear to be calculated thrusts at the spectator. These synthesized fragments, placards of propaganda, are often precious editorials that seem isolated, self-contained, aimed at the audience's soul. Groups of decaying Kiwanis types displayed in fancy hotels like a Natural History exhibit, motel rooms loaded with vulgar energy-savers, computers and IBM machines, highways that are diseased and sign pocked with modernity, material (nuns, wigs, orgiastic discothèques, splendiferous luggage) that has a built-in scene-satirizing point, bloody sports events, all-night supermarkets, the carrying of unlikely mirror-bed-tuba objects through crowded streets, an alienated person wandering in an industrial wasteland, standing against an empty wall.

Sometimes, these dislocated items represent the Muck of the Establishment, sometimes they are Escapes from it, but they are always treated as a kind of magic.

In one film, the image slides from sports cars and their owners in Esquire clothes into an idol effect: a Negro in white coveralls who tends cars in an underground garage. This somber, statuesque attendant is examined as though he held some crucial message: seated in a chair against a wall, looking somewhat like an electrocution victim.

Julie Kohler's scarf and Bubbles's balloon are escapes from the labyrinth; in structural terms, they are film-within-film segments in which the movie abandons story progression and talks directly to the spectator. A white scarf billows over a French seacoast town, a pastel journey, overextended and precious, that ends when the straight line of a jet crosses the soft-focus image. Pre-figured in some wall prints earlier in the film, an aerostatic Goya balloon comes to rest at the end of a film. The mesmerically improbable object, plus the perfect pastoral landscape, draws the gutted hero out of his lethargy into a more promising life.

Nausea is everywhere in movies today. Yet, there is a great distance between this negative feeling on screen and the anti-Establishment nihilism that has made such thought-provokers as a clean, grace-filled sort of gorgeous, cartoony, facetious film (*Contempt*), a beautifully grainy, intimate, limpid survival fight (*Persona*), and another movie of real suffering (*Accident*) that is clever, delicate, and urbane with the most elegant infighting in acting between Dirk Bogarde and Stanley Baker.

For both the nullity rampant in movies today as well as the simplistic image, the most advanced and volcanic are the latest from the Warhol factory. Behind *Nude Restaurant, Bike Boy,* and, particularly, *4 Stars,* is a morbid, flesh-bound, self-reviling vision: the films crawl with an obsessional pursuit of rancid pleasures. By just presenting rambling Ondine or National Velvet as isolated, spoiled fruits, stripping away their connections to personal drama or outside world, and by languidly exposing jig-acting situations (tangled bodies on a mattress, gargantuan make-up scenes, a crazy telephone scene with a witchlike gypsy, her maddening horsey smile flashing on and off like a neon sign), the picture becomes a drum-beat of the film concept that the Moment's the thing, and, also, that what's Now is pretty sickening.

There is no story-telling form imposing its pressure on the screen. When Brigid Polk, hippopotamus of sin, sprawls in a bathtub in white bra and blue jeans, and talks to someone just outside camera range about the drug-curing scene in different hospitals, the image is free, for itself, and wide open: the spectator, as well as the actor, can almost vegetalize inside the frame. Everything is stopped as the movie engulfs itself in a fuck-off atmosphere. With giggling hysteria, fag expressions, the most pathetic bravado voice, she explodes the screen outward by giant abandon and cravenness. The camera milks the paleness of her slack flesh, a cheap cotton brassiere cuts into the doughy torso, the image is the most underrated phenomenon in films: a blast of raw stuff.

It's not only Brigid Polk or her counterpart Jason in the underground film firmament, but their flesh-obsessed self-exposure (both diarylike and diarrhetic in that bits of decaying self are flung out) has become a standard role in films everywhere. This confessional acting is abetted by a voyeur camera which does not enhance, but feeds on, every flaw: the actor stands crucified in front of the camera. A detective's wife turns a seduction scene into a flat head-on encounter with the audience: a pinched and dried Lee Remick under a humiliating light, seems disrobed for a flagellation rather than a love scene. Truffaut's Bride, supposedly a male-gobbling Mata Hari, is tortured by an insensitive wig-maker and her own recalcitrant, slipping flesh. She becomes a series of static parodies filling the screen, stark presentations, almost processed before your eyes, of someone's middle-aged aunt. Good or bad doesn't matter in a screen presence that comes across like an Easter Island sculpture: the Dread C. Scott performance of a kook-hooked brain surgeon isn't actually a performance: a tortured larger-than-life face seems to be dazed as it moves occasionally right or left.

As soon as these versions of the Underground Man and Oblomov start reviling and revealing themselves, the spectator is hooked. While bathing him in remorse, the picture cathartically immolates him in a new kind of connection to the screen. What happens is that everything becomes open ended: time is untempered and boundless; characters are left engimatic, full of the complexities of a single moment; photography is deliberately raw, uncentered, violently push-pulling against the confines of the screen.

ONE-TO-ONE 1968

Besides being a brazen movie with a built-in sneer, particularly for the older denizens of Coin Flats, Beverly Hills, *The Graduate* is another in a series of Sandwich Specials. Clyde wins Bonnie over hamburgers; Perry and Dick, the *In Cold Blood* murderers, relax with hamburgers before and after the Clutter massacre; in *Bedazzled,* Dudley Moore and Eleanor Bron are a cook-waitress team in a Wimpy Bar. All this chopped steak is a give-away on the new tone in films; unless the material is thoroughly banal, it isn't considered chic.

A life of innocuousness marches over the spectator and greenhorn hero. A little stump of a man, dragging himself around with weighty reluctance (he walks toward something as though going away from it), Dustin Hoffman is laid out like an improbable menu. People are always darting into his periphery to point him out as a boy wonder, from captain of the track team to debating captain and literary editor. Benjamin, as it turns out, is Bill Bradley crossed with Denny Dimwit.

The most literate sound Benjy makes is a short pup's whimper, which is overplayed in the same way as his panicky rabbit's expression, whenever a demanding or threatening adult hovers in sight. The simplest sentences have trouble surfacing through this lipless mini-man, who, despite Hoffman's intelligence-within-contrivance acting, adds up to a facile, hardly original put-down of the whole affluent class. If vulgarity is being shown up in *The Graduate,* it's on both sides of the camera.

Resembling George Segal's sculptures of a banal Everyman, generalized and locked in a few trademarks of his job, Benjy the Ordinary is the direct opposite of the eclectically hopped-up movie he inhabits. Goalless, not possessed of much wit or intelligence, lacking stature or bearing, he is a champion of the Lacklustre, along with the simple-minded, gullible nurse, Sister Alma, in *Persona.* This chunky tomboy (Bibi Andersson) is morbidly grounded in the commonplace. In a two-character movie, it is Alma's not too bright, undeveloped gush that holds the screen, does all the talking.

Andersson's Jean Seberg face has always been a slightly awful fixture in Swedish cinemah for button-featured beauty. In this film, it becomes a curtain to compose the Acropolislike screen, while the zealous miss gets button-hooked to the pedestrian task; she props up pillows, turns on radio, gets into bed, carries a tray. And undercutting the role further is an X-ray image (perfected through a string of late Bergman films) that denatures her face of its health, lustre, and, at the same time, gives it a formal elegance.

The irony of these movies, which cherish ordinariness, not allowing a speck of glory to their earth-bound characters, is that the activities dull while the syntactic invention shoots skyward. In a vast expanse of ultramarine, the parents—Mr. and Mrs. Gruesome—present their prize graduate ("who is soon to continue his studies as a John H. Alpington scholar") to the adult world. The father is a goggle-eyed irritant, the mother is a shrill veteran of beauty parlors, and both are acted with shattering glibness. Yet the factor that dominates these son-parent collisions is the Image: a whole scene of clean, glistening, expensive materials.

It would be hard to overestimate the ultrafluorescent image and its involving power. The hero is usually grounded, Antonioni fashion, silhouetted against a canvas float, some shutters in a darkened hotel room, the wall of a swimming pool. The movie takes on a near science-fiction excitement and presence, half today, half a year from tomorrow, an uncluttered cube of overpowering color and glowing cosmeticized skin.

There has been little or no attempt to keep up with the syntactic development in such imagery. While critics analyze the Sturgeslike satire of *Graduate,* the cheap fictional moves of *In Cold Blood,* the puzzling psychology of *Persona* (are the two characters halves of one schizoid personality?), the screen is being designed into one that has more grip per inch than ever before. One to one haunts the screen today, a condensing of persons, places, those one-prop compositions in *Graduate,* everything boiling down into a single symbol of itself. Given these symbolic units (all four Clutters flattened into one stretch of pseudo-Kansas cloth), the screen gets manipulated into a dynamite-laden rectangle of superreality.

With its strong performance by Bibi Andersson, *Persona* is an obvious example of a one-to-one syntactic conception. The opening, like a quick run-through of the old Ingmar Bergman, is a penny arcade of one shots: a man's hand being spiked to the table, shots of people's heads in the manner of Mantegna's dead Christ, a spiked fence, the countdown of numbers that precedes an amateurish movie, the ripping sound of film flying around the sprockets. Everything that follows this surreal Ensorish gallop is its clean, cool white, unpopulated reversal. And within this section, which is the movie proper (two seemingly opposite women in a forced, highly-charged confrontation with each other), the screen is a march of bare, stringent compositions.

Perhaps this composition should be detailed, because it appears in film after film: *Red Desert, Le Départ, Knife in the Water*. Antonioni must have invented it: the human figure as an island silhouetted against a sharp drop of unsympathetic scenery. There are two or three delineated elements, none of which act as support for the other. Antonioni uses a wall or building as a menace; in *Persona,* the background is a disinterested one; in *The Graduate,* the subordinate detail is manipulated into placards of American vulgarity.

In these oned-up scenes, the design play becomes as important as the story theme. As seldom happened in pre-1960's naturalism, the movie is constantly drumming a pattern in which dominant and subordinate are contested. The most fascinating pornography springs out of a low-keyed, lackluster setting: a nurse and her ward lounging in a darkened summer place. The camera, desultory in its moves, shuttles between the two women, each in a sort of Whistler's Mother pose. The nurse's verbal description of a four-way sex act between two young women and two boys on a sunny, vacant beach springs into flagrant physicality. On screen, there is nothing but a dry interior.

In Mike Nichols's film, there is a studied effort to make everyone exotic and nutty, like walking fish tanks. A coarse deadening and simplification goes on, so that a whole string of aged, overdressed people march through a hotel as one gingerbreaded

gaggle. A cookie-cutter is used on Benjy, cutting away all ambiguous edges, fixing him in place. Grown-ups, wherever they
appear—at Benjy's welcome-home party, around a hotel lobby,
in a campus boardinghouse—seem eight feet tall, misshapen,
bolted to prefab versions of themselves. Hoffman and his plagu-
ing environment of adults are indented into the screen with a
diamond drill, glistening and hollow at the same time.

A total agnosticism permeates all the above films: a disbelief
in the romantic life, institutions, children; a jaded view of sex;
a tired feeling that nothing will come up on the horizon to save
a lost character. The synthesized technique which gets so little
critical attention is burdensomely keyed into portraying *angst*
at its most enervated. It seems significant that both Anne Bancroft and Bibi Andersson, in roles that are worlds apart—a
stale John O'Hara captain of the fleet and a hard-working
blonde dumbshell—are exposed with similar morbidness by a
Pat and Mike team: Bergman and Nichols. (Another weird case
of two directors inflicting the same treatment: Godard and Antonioni with their perennial mug-vamps, Anna Karina and
Monica Vitti.)

Nevertheless, the critics go on with their old ploys on a movie
in which editing, camera moves, acting have been preconcen-
trated, mostly done "in the mind." It seems irrelevant to compare *In Cold Blood* with the best-seller and find 80 per cent or
more of it to be an exact duplicate in terms of cheapness. Or, in
the case of Anne Bancroft's female shark, middle-aged and
middle stream (you're never told what she'd be puttering at, if
not Benjy's manhood) to make out a case for her acting far
above the movie.

"Go to the bar and order yourself a drink." Giving directions
on clandestine love to a boy who suggests Mary's lamb, embarrassed by her every move, Bancroft acts like a traffic cop.
Except for a two-minute stretch in the Taft lounge where she
glows with a chilled humor, education, that the role demands,
her whole performance—steely and disengaged—is done by
camera set-ups.

It is a funny love affair, strange rather than ha ha. All the
piquancy has to do with (1) the difficult sketch-class poses, age-
revealing and impossible to act, that pin down Bancroft, (2)

the curious split and distance between the two supposed bed-mates, with the woman always being turned away, as though she were a disgrace.

With all its overtrained acting and nonsense (Perry's day-dream before a mirror, fantasying himself as a Vegas star), *In Cold Blood* is a somber, slablike, all-of-a-piece inclemency that bears little resemblance to the open, cheap-knit style of Capote's writing. All the puzzle is created by the Conrad Hall image, incredibly dense, a concretelike block of Kansas scenery, damp climate, that is almost impossible to enter. With the semi-virtues of a John Vachon photograph, the real curiosity is how so much pictorial movement and variety could be rerouted so that it is contained within a scene that is always fronted and classically static.

HOW I WON THE WAR 1968

How I Won the War, a neither admirable nor contemptible al-
truism about the villains who coin money making war films, has
enough material to stock several war films. Basically, it's the
war story of the fictitious Third Troop, Fourth Musketeers.
Among its luminous personnel are a sweating coward digging
himself into holes and hiding under pots and pans; a working-class mocker in steel rims played by the Beatles's John
Lennon; a mad clown who prates Falstaffian brain-dulling
lingo; and two zombies—a pink and a green man returned from
the dead.

The exploits of the boy leader, Michael Crawford, and his
dotty Musketeers, dragging a heavy roller across sand dunes,
building a cricket pitch, and so on, are hard to follow on screen
but funny to recall. The movie starts with a public-schoolboy
type in a yellow rubber raft, presumably on a night patrol
across the Rhine. It is one of the only humanistic moments: a
palpably left-alone scene with one little peppermint stick of a
man having believable trouble staying inside a raft which
thwarts his every attempt to stay aloft. The raft's action sug-
gets a bar of soap squirting out of a soapy hand. This is the one
scene where Crawford is allowed a margin of gallantry: he is a
scissors in this raft trying to remain upright. Everywhere else
he is a forlorn figure locked up in a unit of action: the little
boy trying to cut a snappy militaristic figure, trying to be a
dandy good guy to the men he commands.

Visually the movie is quite impressive, something like a confetti storm in which the spectator never gets to rest. The Moon
Mullins comic strip is more realistic than the average shot, a
scene on a desert that suggests an old used-car lot without cars.
The Musketeers—a gaggle of quirks and quacks always bitching
about their pontificating, but out-of-it, leader who gets each one

predictably killed—are antlike, scurrying around in this mediocre B-movie scene. Before the spectator can get his bearings, there is another disturbingly hollow scene: old newsreel shots, given density with inserts of reallife actors. Not too interesting as visual images, these actor-newsreel bits have a ferocious, scabby humor: a wife suddenly appearing on the battlefield to comfort her nearly dismembered husband, saying in a cold, platitudinous voice, "It's impossible to tell the million tragedies that happen in wartime." Meanwhile, her soldier spouse, in pain, murmurs, "They hurt, Flo, they hurt," and his wife breaks her stilted officialese with: "Run 'em under the tap luv." The whole situation, with a soldier bloody from waist down, contrasted to the wife's blitheness, is a real shock for its callousness.

The first question to ask of this not unfunny Surrealism is "Why is it so weird?" Save for the opening bit of old-fashioned knockabout comedy, apparently inserted to make the spectator feel normal before he gets confused, the movie employs enough technique (collage tricks, non-sequitur inserts, oblique satire, a sound track that keeps most of its jokes to itself) to take care of the five films that are crammed into its flashback-choked two hours.

The mucky sound track is the first major weirdness in this film. The movie is built on the complacent notion, held by young British cinéastes, that the most artistically meaningful voice is one so deeply colloquial that it just escapes understanding. In this particular movie, the voices seem filled with a slurring machine or an electric amplifier, with the ends of sentences being either swallowed or lifted.

One of its buzzing, electrocuted, nonstop sounds belongs to an ex-cavalry colonel, played in a possessed, Mad-Hatter vein by Michael Hordern. In one scene this Super Idiot, leaning forward in his tank, symbolizes victory like the figurehead on an old schooner. Conducting an insane court-martial, surveying the land from a desert tower, climbing from underneath an overturned jeep ("Damn, damn, damn"), his whole face seems bloodshot, always cocked toward the sky as though he were listening to some private demon that was feeding him ideas and lines. As his voice constantly jaws on about the wily Patton or the common soldier ("Tend to their feet, Goodbody, they're no good to you without feet"), it becomes fairly clear that he is putting down the genius of sand and tank, General Montgomery, as a snobbish fantasy-obsessed Officer Nut. But this parrotlike battering ram is a grating agony.

In one part of the fluxlike plot—a boring stretch kidding (?) the cultural butchers idea of *River Kwai*—Crawford says to a noncommittal Nazi: "You're the first person I've been able to talk to in this whole film." This Fauntleroy Jack Kennedy, whose voice spirals metal Cheerios into the atmosphere, talks bales of words. At the peak of heroism, killing off his patrol, sending up signals to bring down a barrage of bombs, he becomes a titillating figure, not through comic style, but because an apparatus of technique has been slipped between the character and his material. Everywhere, there is this Svengali jamming apparatus between soldiers and their war activities.

Actually, this is the film's key effect: the cross-references from the small activities of the troop to the hallowed image of large consequential Dunkirks. The misalliance makes strange wit out of a fat man's last words as he is about to be bayoneted in the chest: "Ah, 'ave a 'eart." A guy can't even die without being metamorphosized into and out of newsreel footage before he draws his last breath. Sometimes, Crawford's nerve-scratching voice circles above him, as though it were carried in a cartoon balloon, while his body unrelatedly goes about its business.

Secondly, the movie's weirdness comes from its inept image: the movie actually gets into the area of hallucinatory art through the malapropisms of people and locales. Just after the troop has been chopped up in a sortie against a Nazi patrol dump, the furious boy-leader lines them up for a bayonet drill to correct their courage. It's hard to forget this bungled composition: The Musketeers look like a cast of characters from a greasy spoon near the docks—a smart-aleck dishwasher, a fat and unkempt short-order cook, and an angrily anxious owner who thinks he can get more work by worrying his help to death. An ultrabright scene, everyone squinting: it is a demoralizing time of day—high noon after a brief defeat—to be taking part in a savagery drill.

Finally, along with the freak accents on a jazzed-up sound

track and the misanthropically crude scene, the movie gets its weirdness from cowardliness. It scatters its energy, never staying with any scene enough to exploit it.

Why is this not quite up to the loathesomeness that Lenny Bruce fed, funkwise, into his excrementlike social conscious humor? At its best, it has a crawling-along-the-earth cantankerousness and cruddiness, as though the war against fascism were being glimpsed by a cartooned earthworm from an outhouse on a fake hillbilly spread somewhere in the Carolinas.

But genuine funk is a pretty rare item, at least as exemplified, say, in Sam Fuller's vulgar, belittling directing style, W. C. Fields's two-reelers as a sleazy-souled barber or store owner, Jack Oakie's suggestion of pigskin hide encasing a sneaky conceit and cheapster's malevolence. It occurs where the insurgent artist views his subject matter from a position so far down on the ladder that his work is knee deep in muck, misery, misanthropy. Situating himself in the Bowery reaches of technique and exposition, the artist can take pot shots at the accepted notions of Style, Beauty, Gentility. The debased position allows a desperate film man to hold onto his wit and dignity while creating a richer surface through crudity than he could achieve through niceties, skill, taste.

Since the mid-1950's, funk was discernible in the TV shows of Sam Peckinpah, in a scummy Siegel remake of *The Killers* that far outclasses the Siodmak epic, in parts of Frank Tashlin, Burt Kennedy, and in the young French wizards—Godard-Truffaut-Malle—who apparently breathe funk but are never unpretentious enough to stay in it.

This movie is as far into funk as anyone has gone in 1967 in the major leagues. When Crawford slips into a kind of reverie, he achieves a human effect that is half funk: he gets the qualities in the old English version of the word (fear, cowardice, anxiety) but misses the part that comes in the Negro jazz term (slangy, sweaty, low-down) which his colleagues embody. An agony takes over Crawford's performance, as though he were moving beyond the wooden, cut-out cartoon figure that is supposed to be synonymous with satire in this film. There is one scene in which he seems to be flying through space, like a mad eagle, as he shows his men how to signal an airplane down.

The unmatched toothpick legs never touch the ground, his voice is like metal filings spraying the air. And then, when he cozies up to one of his men to bare his soul, the performance gets lunatic and hypnotic, losing itself in its Jack Kennedyish elegaic heartfulness.

However, the film is filled with estheticisms that pad it out and make it insipid: documentary shots, corny references to *Lawrence of Arabia*, slapstick that is within the reach of Jerry Lewis and not contaminated or unique. In its scabrous, unrefined attack on the Establishment, the movie suggests Lennie Bruce, with one glaring difference: it is limited in its tasteless jokes and material to the mentality of a bright schoolboy. Like *Help* and the Zero Mostel *A Funny Thing Happened on the Way to the Forum,* it suggests an overaged boyishness almost incapable of relating to the hard-nosed, dry, sardonic war films supposedly under attack here. There is little connection between these soft-cheeked near-baby Musketeers with petulant voices, and the underplayed leanness that makes up the background of *Air Force,* or *They Were Expendable.* To cover up the puerility of acting, wisecracking, and imagery, everything has to be partially hidden by racing past the jokes, which pile up like cordwood, swallowing any gag that threatens to make itself known as a tiresome gentility.

CLUTTER 1968, 1969

The movie scene: crawling with speciousness; one type of clutter examining, reporting, publicizing another. The dictionary defines clutter as a confused mass, untidy collection, crowd (a place) with a disorderly mass of things, litter. Just to go near the art theater district on Third Avenue is to be jostled by the definition, a cattle drive that includes the little pink plexiglass sign with $2.50 printed into it (if you're lucky; sometimes it's $3), and a character, tenacious as Epoxy resin, guarding the sanctuary with red velvet hose and an unswervable litany: "There will be no further seating for the present showing. Buy your tickets now; seating will begin at 7:50 for the 8 P.M. show." A customer comes out of *The Graduate* saying, "Finally, I've seen it," and you realize a hysteria has been built up by a thousand-headed ghoul named Advance Press.

This involves a jangle of affirmations and pronouncements by critics, raging controversies that follow and overlap one another (Bonnie-Titticutt-Jason-Graduate-Tell Me Lies-Fox), crazy lines—a critic's quote or a line from a movie ("I think you're the most attractive of all my parents' friends, Mrs. Robinson") stamped on every subway rider's brain, Sunday supplement interviews in sensation prose by Flatley Rex detailing Sunday morning with a Saturday night hero in the Royal Suite of the Plaza.

And this festering, knickknacky swarm doesn't stop when the lights go out. For example: *China Is Near,* a beehive film in which a dozen digitlike, turned-away people, mostly unlikable (they seem small even in the bed scenes) suggest a kind of ratty elegance within a humid, *Marienbad* structure of boredom, deeply dimensioned pieces of nothing, somber suavity. The plot, criss-cross or mixed doubles, centered around an innocuity running (who knows why) for local office, has been likened to Stendahl and genius. Some of it is fun, particularly two lower-class lovers with a cynical snap to them, but most of the time you just sit there and watch.

Each of the characters (a ninny professor who happens to have two aunts who are nuns, a teenaged brother who is a raging Maoist, a sister who is a beautiful fullback) represents a different segment of society. The professor, besides being a dead loss as an actor—immobile, cowardly, puddlelike—stands for the effete dregs of played-out aristocracy (a superior actor in this role: the James Fox architect in *The Servant*). His sister travels this film with incredible self-love, as though the other actors were Little Leaguers: she gets her ennui, distemper from Jeanne Moreau in the Antonioni role of a woman who is Lost because men have disintegrated. Then there's a Joe Lampton —*Room at the Top* type (he suggests a sneaky buck private, *faire savoir*, after impregnating two of the film's disgusted women). He chills it through the film and moves in on the professor as a political adviser.

In one scene, which shows Bellochio's talent for getting multiple angles on a locale, the director backs the Italian Fernandel into a village square where he's to give his first man-of-all-parties speech. Chilled by the lack of turnout for his debut, scared to address even the three straggling locals, infuriated by a kid who bicycles off with his speech notes, beaten down by villagers who attack him for cuffing the kid around, the professor is squirted in and out of a nice shuttling action filled with familiar ideas about little people, losers, and small-time politics. This is a readable scene, also an atypical one.

For the most part, this prize film is comprised of hard-to-relate skits, composed in a puzzling staccato manner, creating an ambiguous feeling of high modern skill in Renaissance-style scene sculpting. Scenes of a bird-shooting range (mindless sadism of the rich), cherubic boys clustered around an old bedridden monsignor (ravishing charm of child muggers), girls and boys together in dark rooms (lack of proper lighting). The sex scenes, rather than ideal love or great passion, suggest pleasurable passing of time, second-rate opportunism. Underneath is the insinuating esthetic idea that texture, technique, and subject should be dedicated to how lousy, discordant, an average day is when it isn't sharpened and cleaned by an orthodox script-writer.

The Fox (bleak outlands, two forbiddingly lonely women trying hopelessly to make a go of a chicken farm, an extremely willful hunter-soldier wants the stronger of the two girls) is always in a middle area between decorum and sensationalism: a rough-stuff movie dished up in the most insipid, uniform, up-tight manner.

The movie has the piddling, top-of-a-cookie-tin look of a painting over a motel bed. Nothing unstaged ever enters the chicken farm. No woodchuck, no birds, but a great army of tensed-up technicians trying to charge up a scene with the sense of sexual obsession. So a fox—quivering nose, piercing stare, head jutted out—performs admirably. He moves up to a chicken coop just like a little train, well behaved in the manner of Brandon de Wilde acting Shane's kid idolizer.

One of the problems is the landscape: a dry, coldless snow setting, in which everything has the feel of pieces of glass, with no sense of nature. Because of the lack of pliability in handling this snow scene, delay (not Dullea) becomes a major actor. The scene stays simple—calendar scenes of winter woodsiness—but it takes an eternity to look through those damn crystallized twigs at a gabled house sticking out of a woodland thicket.

Indoors, Lawrence's earthy, work-ridden story is transformed magically into a silent, ersatz psychodrama. In a quiet evening after pitching hay, chasing a cow, the movie gets hung up on a trolley wire, journeying between three faces lushed up with color. Sandy Dennis, doing her homework in the farm book, is quivering like a baby rabbit ("We would have come out even this month, if we hadn't lost those chickens to the fox"). An empty weight is in the room as her loneliness sinks home and the movie trundles over to the solid, self-sufficient partner, Anne Heywood, an actress who has an up-down fence-post quality, reading in a chair. After a short-long stop over her rigid and slack face, the movie crosses the room to Primeval Male, cleaning a rifle Step by Step. The movie is stolid, patient, but Dullea gets it to a plod by his mystical enunciation, penetrating features (he did the same stretching job in *David and Lisa,* another psychoticdrama).

The thing about *The Fox* is that it needs Clutter, i.e., distraction from its deadly adherence to a coarsened Lawrence theme (seething earth, the dark enveloping force of sex). The smart people in films—Satyajat Ray, Godard, Warhol, George Kuchar (now and then)—realize that the scene today is one of Clutter and the problem is finding the disarray technique to fit the discordancy.

The Museum of Modern Art, the Fort Knox of film footage, has recently had major retrospectives of the following closely related giants: Michel (salt of the French earth) Simon, the Charlie Chan conceptions of Sydney Toler, some third-rate Japanese pornographers, and Middle European animated films. Relating these four entities would be a trial; but actually the juxtaposition makes sense if the Museum is considered as a notions counter: bathing caps, steno pads, combs. Under Iris Barry's tutelage, the Museum's library had the feeling of a camphorized chamber; now the film department suggests the work of a Lon Chaney curator, a man of many faces, a Tinker's tinker. Unbeknownst to the savants above the E and F trains, the Museum has osmotically picked up the idea that film is clutter as much as it is a multi-driven vehicle that can be simplified to the point where it can suggest any philosophical content, stylistic acumen.

The element of debris, disconnection, has been in most finished films, but it's obliterated by Mr. Clean critics who need antiseptic design the way some people need catsup. Tons of criticism have been written about Hitchcock: the Catholicism, talent for directing viewers, cosmic homicides—a Lewtonish conception, in which environment, a shower curtain or telephone booth, is inclement and capable of unleashing the most violent destruction on a mild clerk or schoolmistress. More tons have been offered about his overrated knowledge of cheap thrillers, his synthesizing of diverse events into a pathlike visual event, compacting a whole Gulliver's adventure into a silent linear pattern that takes five minutes.

It beggars such uneven films to keep pressing in on them with more and more analyses, favoring the film as a one-man operation, pure genius. As late Hitchcock passes into history, his bashful cleverness ("I used the high angle; I didn't want to cut; I insisted that the audience . . .") becomes less apparent than the feeling of pulpishness, a mostly unbelievable woman's mag thriller. Spotted throughout are those much celebrated stretches, frittery and arty, where the director's hand is obvious: the berserk carrousel, the feet going this way and that into a Pullman encounter, the bloodthirsty crows on a jungle gym (OK, send the next bird out).

To put Hitchcock either up or down isn't the point; the point is sticking to the material as it is, rather than drooling over behind-the-camera feats of engineering. *Psycho* and *Strangers On a Train*, respected films in the Hitchcock library, are examples of good and bad clutter, though the first third of *Psycho* is as bare, stringent, minimal as a Jack Benny half hour on old TV.

Seeing *Psycho* today is disturbing for the amount of suppositional material. Why is taxidermy necessarily a ghoulish hobby? Are stuffed birds in a motel's back parlor dead giveaways of an aberrant mind? First, a passing motorist, then a wily detective, takes one glance at seven stuffed heads and becomes either queasy or intrigued by the psychological significance ("What kind of a warped personality is this?"). The great supposition is that the haunted house, California Gothic, is going to scare people. Having picked such a Casper the Ghost, turretted antique, a cliché before Charles Addams stamped it to death, his choice isn't justified by anything more daring, unexpected, against the grain than the Abbott-Costello rudimentary Eeeeek. Forget the faky mother-mummy down in the wine cellar, a-rocking with one hand on each knee, a stock old lady wig on a stock skull (the viewer is supposed to faint), the most contrived scene is the head-floating-backward of a stabbed detective falling downstairs. Hitchcock and his devoted auteurists have sewed and sold this time-expanded scene a dozen times.

Taking this "classic" apart, scene by scene, is pointless because the horror elements have dried up (with the exception of the shower scene) like mummy's skull in the cellar. The most striking material is the humdrum day-in-the-life-of a real estate receptionist: Godardlike, anonymous rooms, bare, uncomfortable. Except for the World War II armor-plated brassiere, the opening of a girl having only her lunch hour to be in bed with hardware swain is raunchy, elegant. The scenes later are even better: packing the bags (there's something wonderful about the drabness), and the folks from her office, off to lunch, passing in front of the embezzler's car: the little smile and wave, and then, nearly out of the camera's range, the doubletake.

The point is: why deal with these films nostalgically as solid products of genius? *Strangers* is medium-superior to *Psycho*, right through the murder in a pair of fallen spectacles: a ravishing wooded island with a pavilion, a balmy dusk air that can actually be felt. If "pretty" in a good sense can be used about film, it's usable here. There's nothing handsomer than the calm, geographic scything through Time, from the moment of the feet going through a railroad station to Robert Walker's head back-foot out promise of sex in an open-air carnival, the unbeatable elegance with which he rings the bell in a hammer-and-ball concession.

Nothing, even the pristine engineering of the bashful, uncomplaining Master, is sustained here (how many movies since *Musketeers of Pig Alley* have been sustained?). Walker's contaminated elegance, which suggests Nero Wolfe's classy, intricate hedonism, with omelettes in a brownstone, dissolves into momma's boy brocade. Alongside a pretty block of husband-wife bickering in a record shop, its unusual use of glass partitions, sexual confidence and bitchiness in a girl with glasses, there are literally acres of scenes in elegant homes and tennis stadiums which could be used to stuff pillows if there were that many pillows in the world.

One of the best studio actresses (Laura Elliott: a sullen-sexy small-town flirt with ordinary, nonstudio glamour) gives a few early sections extraordinary reality, eating up the sexual tensions created by a posh character who tails her around an amusement park, while she juggles two local louts. Then, like a homing pigeon, the movie goes back to the old Hollywood bakery, dragging out those supposedly indispensable ghastly items: Senator rye bread, daughter egg twist, and little Babka. Hitchcock has always been a switch-hitter, doubling a good actor with a bad one, usually having the latter triumph. It takes real perversity murdering off Elliott and settling for Ruth Roman, a rock lady in Grecian drapery, plus Pat Hitchcock, who, aside from her clamped-on permanent wave, carries an open-mouthed expression from one dull blocklike scene to another.

Charlie Bubbles is the first movie about a cool-sleek 1968 artistic success: an ennui-ridden, spoiled-rotten writer who can hardly breathe from the fatigue of being an acclaimed artist. It is for the most part an irritatingly stinting film, even though the photography's pleasant, the apple orchard color is cheery, and there are two fairly good female performances by Liza Minnelli, an extraordinarily willing no-veneer actress, a gnomic, quaint, slight girl with enormous eyes, and Billie Whitelaw as Bubbles's casual, leathery ex-wife.

It's also a single-minded film. Bubbles, in Albert Finney's puritanical, sucked-in ungiving performance, is not so much a man as a particular stage when life has lost its zing and there are no more visible goals on the horizon. It's a unique performance of a Bully who sullenly recedes: Finney keeping his acting technique below a dead flat surface, acting as a foil for the other actors, in the one-note role of a washed-up, limp prick. No matter how far back and under Finney plays, he is like a bull trying to hide. Every time the camera works around a stiff scene, the one outstanding fact is not so much the obnoxiousness of the role (even ordering some prime roast beef is an imposition; he makes a point, offensive manner and all, of flashing five-pound notes as tips, with the recipients being obsequiously grateful, never showing the slightest resentment) but the fact of Finney's bulk. His deliberate sulks not only spring him in front of scenes, but suggests a self-centered soreness.

Part of the fascination is that *Bubbles* is so singularized. It's beyond simplification into a Chaucerlike parable of Ennui, each section of the journey illustrating one or two explanatory sentences about the Writer's Life ("And on the road he met a friend from his youth"). The opening fiasco sequence sets Bubbles up as a puzzled Personality, appalled at the vacuity-complacency-greed in an upper-class restaurant (nowhere else does Finney score so heavily with his pancake make-up and posh clothing); the rest of the film continues as a wooden march through stock situations. There's an awareness that these situa-

tions (the fact that a guy, no matter how rich, still has to deal
with nagging intrusions: bullying servants, a wife who doesn't
think Bubbles the hot shot that the public does—in her eyes,
he's the guy who wrecked her life, a son who is contemptuous
and distant) are stock, but the film stands on the belief that any
given person, successful or not, is involved continuously in the
Banal.

Bubbles is beset by parasites of all types: inbetween men,
aspiring neophytes, crocodiles who work in cafeterias and at
gas pumps, snotty lower-class types who watch enviously, seething on the sidelines while Bubbles fills up his Rolls with pre-
mium gas or views a football match from a glass-enclosed booth.
There's the implicit fact that Finney's male seconds give him
little competition in acting or physical attractiveness in these
scenes. But more interesting is the weird notion of how much
obeisance is given a Famous Writer.

The chief effect is of a constipated actor hooked onto a trolley
line. The first half is comprised of programmed, rigid segments,
holding on to scenes which, to begin with, are of questionable if
not zero interest. The low point: Mrs. Noseworthy and her
relentless kvetching over the chore of having to prepare a cheese-
cracker snack for Finney. The only occasions where the paral-
ysis works are situations where the action would be normally
run down: the creepy, dazed, don't-bother-me mood of an ex-
pressway stop and its waitress at about postmidnight. Even here
the situation crumbles with the arrival of some hedonists out
of late Fellini. Who the hell are these lacquered zombies who
seemingly bring an assortment of vapors into the scene and also
work magic on the image, which begins to tilt and get giddy?
Everything's a mystery: where they came from, the insidiously
familiar way they begin addressing Bubbles, the dialogue from
L'Avventura by way of Outer Space.

After all this mannerism, the back door is opened near the
end and the work becomes a memorable fresh air film starring
Billie Whitelaw, as the sharp-tongued Mrs. Bubbles, no time for
anything except her son and animals. A straggling Julie London hairdo on a packed frame, she is unimaginable as a health-
food nut or a byway hideaway (what's that broad doing so far
out from the Action?). But she goes well with a living room,

and is very likable feeding livestock, a cigarette dangling from her lips, crouching down to chuck some grain, still dispensing acid around the funny-fishy Finney farm; barnyard animals all over the front yard, but perfect grass?

This last twenty minutes suggests a flower suddenly blooming out of a wooden box. Compared to the strongly typed symbolic parable style of every other actor, Miss Whitelaw is loose, relaxed, attractive inside a taut, bitter portrayal. The whole section blooms, due to her unpretentious act and the fact of the house, how it's conceived in movement, credibility, exact timing: the way that even the up-to-now wooden Finney is made easy by the fulsome-calm house, turned off from the I-love-Finney isolationism. It's one of the richest twenty minutes to be found in current film. There's good casting: the whole undertone of negativism in the boy's regard of his father (the parental wrangling over his upbringing, the dead-look-alike down to the short neck and broad face). The peak of this magical treatment is at the very end, with its Dylan Thomas exuberance and scenery. A film that starts as Big Finney seems to end up as Little Finney floating away over a devastatingly lovely countryscape in an aerostatic balloon.

A consistent minus in deep-dish foreign films has to do with a jog that occurs in mid-film (the hour of the woof), about the time Monica Unvital or Jeanne Morose is turning green with jadedness. It usually involves a peanut-butter orgy and a contaminated group of upper-class people who are supposed to stand for muck, sordidness, disillusionment. A police line-up turns up, people who look like they issued from a vacuum cleaner that serviced the set of a Theda Bara movie. Even before they're overdressed in vampire movie costumes, gone-to-seed Victorian elegance, these fusty ensembles apparently have been hired for the stale dumpling look of their skin and the effect of super dullness, as though they came from a Transylvanian employment office for decrepit domestic help.

A large section of *Hour of the Wolf* is devoted to this Instant Horror, a preachy chastisement to suggest that this decay can happen to anyone in the audience. Someone pushes a computer button and out pours another variation of these Fag Ends of life, a more solemn, stonelike, Northern version than the ones you find in *L'Avventura* (shallow and gossipy), *La Notte* (grossly commercial), or *Juliet of the Spirits* (fatty, with rancid makeup). *Hour of the Wolf* tries to solve the mystery of a half-mad, all-bad slick Baskinish symbolist, who disappears mysteriously while breaking apart on a craggy isle off the coast of old Frizzled. Almost from the start, an Arklike scene of a giant rowboat (a deathboat, as opposed to a lifeboat) creaking into and then out from shore, the feeling is old, old, old, as though the color (a grailer shade of angst), faces (syphilitic), and obsessional idea (the danger of pursuing art to its furthest extremity?) had been dug up from an abandoned mindshaft.

There's this self-centered Swede (Max Von Sydow) who stares morbidly between his cupped hands at a flickering candle, peeks furtively behind curtains to see if the dawn has arrived so that he can finally go to sleep, or studies his wrist watch as it ticks out sixty seconds. What's bothering smileless Max? His wife (acted with fine patience by Liv Ullmann) waits with the spectator for Max to Sydow, but he just glums it.

The painter, supposedly a combined Munch and Bosch, is obsessed by Night Creatures (big idea, *circa* 1832) who poke out of the landscape to bedevil his painting and peace of mind. One by one, they turn up, minus footsteps: an ancient aristocratic Isak Dinesen lady, meticulously dressed in the style of 1918, and a couple of pallid, bodyless Undertaker types.

One of the most disgusting relics of Bad Living is an executive's wife, totally useless with a dyed hair, eyebrowless face put together at a beauty parlor. Supposedly the essence of Beef Broth in its most sexually rapacious form, this woman produces a disgusting movie effect everytime she appears: bragging about the bruise near her crotch, all the while talking nonstop of the delicious bedtime excitements shared with a cold-faced husband (one of the Undertakers).

The banality of Max's visions should make him unhappy. His ghosts, the emissaries from his past, are like an empty day in New York's Forty-second Street bus terminal. Occasionally a spare *nebbish* with very thick lenses in his horn rims asks for a light, and what happens? Getting a sadistic pleasure out of letting people know about their intrusions, Max responds with a fantastic indignation, his bowling-pin face going very cold and hard.

Actually, before it gets involved with the castle creeps, the movie reveals Liv Ullmann as a unique perpetrator of humanistic depth and female presence. Like a sharp knife going through old cheese, she opens up the entire first third of this film: natural, perhaps even homely, shunted to the side, she portrays an accommodating frump. This whole off-actress treatment is remarkably different from her Elizabeth Vogeler in *Persona,* where she is decidedly intellectual, willful, and controlling. She is one of those rare passive Elegants in acting who can leave the screen to another actor and still score.

The Big Eat is another growing factor in films, an effect probably invented by Finney in his *Saturday Night.* In his case, it was a combination effect, involving a big chomp, heavy breathing, slashes of braggadocio, a side swivel, and baring of his teeth. This emphasized eating has been fined and slowed down in his latest work, but within the time span of four Finneyfilms, it has taken hold, cementing a new convention for giving an underside, the animalistic traits, to character. The same message-laden eat has appeared in *Pumpkin Eater* (James Mason steals it with his putrid, lecherous teeth and mouth work), *Accident* (a symphony in Bogarde-Baker nuances around the cooking and eating of an omelette), not to mention the current indigestion examples: Henry, a yellow sweater in *La Chinoise* who keeps cutting away to talk while buttering and jamming sixteen pieces of bread; in *Hour of the Wolf,* there is a crucial scene where Ullmann goes on in an inspired sadness about the household expenses (she's just read about her husband's infidelity), and Von Sydow inexcusably kills the scene with a wrong note of silent arrogance.

In other words, Specialized Eating has become a pocket for arty effects, but more importantly it is one of three new maneuvers which scriptwriters are using to get the movie into an undertone area and away from overt dialogue. This tangentialism—taking off at an angle from the movie's plot self—also includes athletics and pop music overloads. Benjamin the graduate, as he floats in his pool, or races in his red sports-car, is enmeshed in an endless grid of wire sounds, back and forth nasality, a dreamy blanket of Garfunkel simon or semen. *Hatari, Live for Life, Darling, Bonnie and Clyde*—in so many films, there is a scene of a mod type in jeep, car, airport lobby, with the celebrated music by Miles Davis or the Yardbirds stamping chicness on your temples.

Up the Junction is a love paean travelogue in which Suzy Kendall, free living and free loving, takes music-engulfed walks, looking like a blah-sweet version of Julie Christie. Whenever Kendall starts her philosophical, Marxian-toned sight-seeing, the image takes on the misty pretty color of Tulip Week in Rotterdam. Swans are seen through weeping willows, smiling eighty-year-old lovers stroll by. While she drifts in a molasses-like park scene, the music track is the dregs of sweet folk rock.

It is a conglomerate of up-shot stray scenes in which there are three inevitable presumptions: (1) a good British sound track consists of giggling, jeering, well-aren't-you-the-cheeky-one; (2) the coolest movie is one jammed with blotched skin, snarled hair, grease; (3) good acting is the automatic result of a deep, uncritical, tough, saccharine grubbiness.

The Wild Bunch has a virile ribbon image, often an aerial view, of border life in 1914 Texas, stretched across a mottled wide screen in which there are so many intense, frontal details —five kids marching in a parade with their arms linked, a line of bounty-hunters riding straight at the camera—that the spectator's store chest of visual information is constantly widened. Someone seems to have studied all the frontal postures and somber-sharp detailing in Civil War photographs, as well as the snap-the-whip, across-the-page compositions that Homer often used as a perfect substructure for the spread-out, pastoral, early 1900's. There is a lunatic intensity in exploiting this archaic photography, getting the inside effect of life in movement, having people in rows, the pride and uprightness of a pose, emphasizing dishevelment in peasant huts or the dry-dusty exit from a Mexican walled city.

From this pulverizing attempt at photographic beauty, the movie becomes a bloated composition. There is an unpleasant feeling of expense, of enormous amounts of money being spent, tons of footage being shot in order to get one slow-motion instant that will stamp home Peckinpah's obsessive theme: that man's propensity for cruelty and self-destruction is endless. This expanding and slowing gets unbelievable effects: a bridge blowing up with nine men on it, all sinking in a row, facing the camera. They drop at the same time and rise up again out of the water in unison, only to sink again, and, with ebbing force, bob gently up and down while floating downstream. Probably the best second ever filmed showing fumbling ineptitude in the face of ungraspable horror: a young sergeant's instant realization that a quarter of his troops are going to be crushed to death.

What is unique in *The Wild Bunch* is its fanatic dedication to the way children, soldiers, Mexicans looked in the small border towns during the closing years of the frontier. An electric thrill seems to go through the theater when Lucian Ballard's camera focuses on groups of kids: two pale blonde children, straight and sort of stiff, holding on to each other in the midst of a gun holocaust. There are others crouched down next to buildings, staring out and cringing. It is remarkable enough to focus on kids in a shoot-'em-up, but the Ballard-Peckinpah team, without condescending to the Amishlike children, gets this electricity with positions, the coloring of hair, hats. These rough Pershing uniforms have been in Westerns like Rossen's *Cordura*, but here there is a crazy fanaticism woven into the cloth and shapes.

With all its sensuous feel for textures, the engineering of events that take place from three different points of view, the movie is ridden with a flashy, Rubenslike virtuosity. Even the dry, fantastically unified, visual characterization of Robert Ryan's Deke Thornton doesn't escape the *éclat* of Peckinpah's hectic drive. Part of Peckinpah's love of gusto and bravura involves repeated scenes of raucous belly laughter—by kids watching a scorpion devoured by red ants, by a badly acted young sadist making a production of holding three prisoners in a bank, by paeans to camaraderie built through the laughter of five buddies—that are an outright case of bad judgment and poor observation.

Very close to the end a beautifully vehement exchange between two squarish, beyond-the-pale criminals creates the mood for the unbelievable ending. William Holden, his face clammed up and looking as battleworn as it should, says in defense of Robert Ryan, who has betrayed him: "He gave his word." Borgnine, with great contempt: "He gave his word to the *railroad.*" Holden replies: "It was his *word.*" And then Borgnine: "It's not your word that counts but *who* you give it to."

This mind-stopper is of the genre of Burt Lancaster's explanation in *The Gypsy Moths,* for his career as an exhibitionist sky diver: "A man can choose his way of dying as well as his way of living," or the young German student-turned-junkie in *More* who says: "I wanted the sun and nothing was going to stop me. If I had to die to discover life that was okay too."

With Ryan's remarkable deathlike portrait and some good spontaneous-combustion acting by other old Hollywood war-heroes, *Wild Bunch* is an old style action film filled with these modern non sequiturs that suggest an effort to find some deeper purpose or point for the travelogue that goes on elsewhere. They serve only to highlight the drifting content and the weird alternations in current films between an obsession with death and situations in which the people strain for some point over which they can do some willful, extended, fake laughter.

Easy Rider, a sparsely written cross-country movie with a Don Quixote and Sancho Panza on extravagant motorcycles, is marred by draggy, romantic material: chunks of time spent on glinting handlebars, hippies solemnly sprinkling the earth with seeds at sundown, ghastly Bachrach portraiture. Dennis Hopper's lyrical, quirky film is better than pretty good in its handling of death, both the actual event and in the way the lead acting, like Ryan-Holden's in *The Wild Bunch* and Shirley Knight's in *The Rain People,* carries a scent of death. The death scenes, much more heartbreaking, less programmed than Peckinpah's, come out of nowhere, involve an explosion of grief-stricken acting (Fonda and Hopper), and are snipped off. The finality and present-tense quality of the killings are remarkable: the beauty issues from the quiet, the damp green countryside, and a spectacular last shot zooming up from a curving road and burning cycle.

There's quite a portrait dead-center of *Easy Rider*: a young Southern lawyer, ex-athlete, town drunk, good-natured and funny. Practically a novel of information, this character's whole biography is wonderfully stitched from all directions (a lawyer's son with a shaky but established position in the town, with an unbiased scorn for his own mediocrity), sprung in short time without being obviously fed. Jack Nicholson's acting of "George" is done with dishevelment, squinty small-town gestures, and a sunniness that floods the performance.

More is the oldest of movie stories: down the sluice with a poor duck who has fallen into the hands of a heroin heroine, Mimsy Farmer. The film is a voyeurish, fondling showcase for two new beautifully tanned nonactors, a nice unpretentious boy and a blonde slim animal who barely accompanies her clothes through a whitewashed Antonioni island. It's encyclopedic on rich hip clothes.

A Place for Lovers, a De Sica concoction in which Faye Dunaway knows she's dying from the first reel and is unable to act one speck of disease, has zero credibility or interest, although scripted by a team of six writers. At any given moment, she is an icicle version of Mimsy Farmer posing for another fashion spread in *Harper's Bazaar.* Mastroianni's performance suggests a compassionate chauffeur or else a slightly overweight poodle following the mysterious lady around. One of the best laughs is watching Dunaway working on the subject of despair.

The ridiculous idea in *The Gypsy Moths* is that Deborah Kerr, an unhappy small-town wife, should run off with a parachute trickster. Like a frozen food, glummer and slower than Robert Stack, she has trouble crossing the street—and Lancaster wants her to travel with his parachute troupe. A singularly square movie for this period, more stolid than Frankenheimer's last coin waste, *The Fixer,* it still has the pretension of presenting the "real America." Every other shot is a preciously done insert that some assistant director achieved after the main shooting was over (a poison-pen portrait of the high school band warming up for July 4th) followed by a pointless Inge-type scene of a typical family wake featuring Lancaster's red-puffy face about to explode from acute decency. Gene Hackman and Scott Wilson just weather the cape dance and are the film's only half-assets.

The Rain People is a fine example of acting and writing that exploits modern dislocation, the mulling, glumness, and revery of people in tight places. One of the countless current films that are basically travelogues, this one is made up of Warhol-type monologues in telephone booths and motels along the turnpike. Actually, if Francis Coppola's film had something stronger than the pastel Lelouche image and a more intense identity in its grim, preoccupied Long Island heroine, it would be harrowing as well as touching, because James Caan and Shirley Knight must think about acting twenty-four hours a day, and are good at drawing the spectator inside the mournful textures and grotesque-sad moods of turnpike life. There are some excellent scenes in one of those masonite-monstrous motels and in the home of a 100 per cent real and idiotic Virginia family, with Shirley Knight doing the keyed-up New Yorker trying not to believe what's going on around her.

Paul Mazursky's *Bob & Carol & Ted & Alice* comedy treads skillfully on a questionable, overworked subject: the all-round crassness, eyesore appearance of anyone who lives around Beverly Hills. It's amazing that it keeps such a questionable cast (Natalie Wood, Robert Culp, etc.) absorbing despite the fact that every inch of the film is intentionally played in a quasi-abstract-clever area generally hailed as "satire." This is a very self-contained movie. Charles Lang's hot-hollow camera hawks the bodies and faces as closely as the one in *Faces,* but the put-down acting at every moment is a half-snobbish Elaine May mimicry of middle-class patois that is both an abstraction and a generalization. The script stays right on top of its subject, which isn't the wife-swapping scene or the sensitivity institutes, but gullibility: how easy it is to get sucked into the latest turn in fashionable mores, and the humiliation of resisting or going along. A crucial part of the tight structure is the patient, unpretentious playing through of a scene: each segment, like a Nichols-May bit, is a dialogue played long and shot in one take.

I sort of liked and admired Mazursky's handling: inside the dialogue is the gracious, savvy-filled shrewdness of a Burns-Martin second banana who knows how to set up his partner, keep the dialogue moving, and amiably swallow mistakes and crassness. Someone has to be a small genius to even make palatable such a Weird Bunch cast, less than a genius to use them in the first place, and a genius to rig their normally loud personalities with mile-long eyelashes, oxblood suntans, and underwear made of daisies sewn into shaving cream froth.

The most interesting scene: a psychiatrist, a cynical Buddha with a velvety cogent voice, goes through an hour with patient Dyan Cannon. Just the registering of her embarrassment, and geyserlike involvement on his face, soft as a cloud and enormously sensitive as well as half asleep, seem to soften and wipe out the loudness and instant-compromised modernity that threatens to sink the movie.

SHAME 1969

It's about 6:30 in the morning, and this pair, the woman all efficiency, trying to keep to a schedule, the husband always lagging behind, are loading lingonberries into a station wagon that has a funny brinelike crust on its discouraging surface. The mood that encases these two—the wife trying to make a go of a failing farm operation, the husband becoming more and more of an isolationist (first he doesn't want to get out of bed, then he wants to discuss his dream, finally he figures out that neither the radio nor the telephone needs to be fixed)—is of one tiny exacerbation scraping against another. It's a very nice scene: the scale is perfect; the fact that a dusty car, two crabby people, and an unflourishing farmyard are in perfect alignment is only part of the feeling of serenity. There are no camera gimmicks or script dramatics to distract from the small chafings between a husband (before he takes a big dip in this picture, Von Sydow is an attractive, crotchety guy without the cocky sternness that narrowed his previous work) and a tough-practical farm wife (Liv Ullmann, very sophisticated but achieving an un-self-consciousness that makes her more woman than a movie can bear).

Shame is a thematically grim movie about a nonpolitical couple, both violinists, who have been forced into farming by a civil war and the husband's bad heart. Stranded by their lack of commitment, as the war moves into the front yard, they sink first into a drunken, slothful existence, and then into the furthest reaches of despair and dishonor, until these quiet, decent, and sensitive people become caricatures of misery; Von Sydow is now a calculating murderer and his woman a numb beast of burden.

Shame is a complicated, crazily plotted film that loses most of its development in a slot between the time that the Rosenbergs are rounded up as suspected collaborators and a Millet-like scene with exasperated Ullmann and her spouse digging for potatoes and being real bitter ("When this is all over, we'll leave each other"). During this slot that you don't see, months in duration, the wife has become hopelessly miserable, estranged, and a compulsive drunk. The head man of the district (you guessed it: Gunnar Bjornstrand) is showering the couple with gasoline, special wine and cheese, his life savings and an heirloom ruby, and a speechless neighbor, who is on screen no more than thirty seconds, has metamorphosized from a kindly fisherman to a Resistance leader so powerful that in one crazy scene he has his men methodically break, slash, and blowtorch every inch of the farmstead searching for a wad of money that was in Von Sydow's pocket all the time. Even allowing for war working drastic changes on people, the two protagonists are never credible again: a man who couldn't kill a chicken to fill his pot becomes a shrewd killer who carries around a tommy gun and a knapsack full of stray knives; his wife, who started out in the movie as the most fetching body-face-spirit since Ann Dvorak, develops a droopy mouth, a Neanderthal forehead, and the piggy, sunk-in-mud features of a sow.

There's great tact and spareness in the way the Rosenbergs are initially presented: a still room at dawn, a woman with a beautiful volume to her body walks with her pajamas opened to the waist to the kettle, moving with an exciting, brisk, hard walk. Between this episode, where everything is quiet except the woman's energy, and the scene on the ferry as the Rosenbergs head for their customers, a serenely satisfying cadence sets up as two large, entertainingly intelligent bodies chafe against each other.

No one has concentrated so hard as Ingmar Bergman on the principle of push-pull as it is worked out by two people dependent on each other because of a lack of diversion or support from their surroundings. In *Persona* and *Hour of the Wolf* (a bomb), as well as in *Shame,* a fated duo is isolated on a craggy island, far away in the country. In *Silence,* a strangely sexy and physical movie with no male lead, a haggard fight for approval and love goes on between two sisters in a foreign hotel where no one speaks their language. In *Winter Light,* a snowbound rural district and a congregation that has its own problems are the purgatory for a stolid, uncommunicative minister and his plain, morbidly loyal mistress.

This setup, with two people inextricably bound together, both lovers and bitter enemies, at the same time each other's sustenance and downfall, is similar to the one that characterizes

Bergman as a moviemaker. His played-down naturalism has picked up grace and elegance in his latest films, but each one presents a bleak arena, with two Bergmans entwined in a battle that never resolves itself. There's so much lust for naturalism that it's puzzling how he keeps being seduced into a soupy, pretentious symbolism where characters become anonymous in a charred landscape and sink leadenly into the pathos of a Kathe Kollwitz "despair" drawing.

NEW YORK FILM FESTIVAL 1967

If any symbolical figure appeared at the film festival in New York, it was the emergence of the Flat Man, a central character structured like a vapor, a two-dimensional hat salesman, telephone-operator, or decrepit dirt-farmer who doesn't appear to come from any relevant Past, and, after aimless reels of time, there is no feeling that any Future is in sight.

The only one who could be remembered with any clarity, with any sense of physical impact coming from the screen, was a sportscar fanatic, a late adolescent (Jean-Pierre Léaud) who gives shampoos and delivers wigs throughout *Le Départ*. With his crimped manner, a darkly impassioned face, and intensely clear definition of some vigorous act that makes him suggest a pair of scissors gone angrily out of control, Léaud is somewhat less frenetic than he was in last season's *Masculin-Féminin*, where his innocence was more apparent than the exhibitionism that is all that's present in Léaud's other festival appearance, a sort of shadowy sidekick whose main occupation is entering and exiting in *Made in USA*.

Jerzy Skolimowski's *Barriera* is a gentle infant-asy of monumental contrivance, such as a scene in which students tumble onto their faces from a kneeling position on a table, having had their hands tied in a competition, the object being to mouth a matchbox which is held just tantalizingly out of reach by the outstretched hand of an anatomy-class plaster model.

On the order of *Mickey One*, this film is a Surrealistic maze about a man named He, astir in the new Poland. He, picked arbitrarily from the four students who are involved in the quest for the matchbox in the opening *tableau* semi-*vivant*, is almost too boring to describe. Sort of handsome in the Ricardo Montalban, dark, muscular style, with Vittorio Gassman's downpointing nose and chin, his indecipherable career is aborted by

225

a series of Bauhaus compositions that shunt him into corners and tie him into square knots—at one point a gauze-draped horse chases him into a bathtub.

There are street scenes on top of street scenes, like a club sandwich of masonry, in which crowds stream while street lights march backward across the screen in perfect alignment into space. Later on in this convoluted Odyssey, we enter a dead-white ballroom (the "dead" here is used advisedly) in which youthful He and She come face to face with "capitalist opportunism," a featured star in this festival. Skolimowski's idea of capitalist wreckage: no one on the dance floor, waiters seated like last year's autumn leaves at tables, the one other important detail being a few palm trees, suggesting the old Poland, or the old Coconut Grove in Hollywood in the era when a ballroom scene meant literally twenty minutes of uninterrupted laughter with Harold Lloyd wearing a magician's jacket and its zoo of hidden animals.

In most of the festival films, particularly the limp, pale grey ménage of *Puss & Kram*, where the theme is a smooth, muscleless gliding in and out of love, a definite disassembling of people and events takes place. Eva (Agneta Ekmanner), as a free-swinging sex cat, takes on lovers in a quick, deadpan, indiscriminate way that makes Julie Christie, the dip-lipped Diana of *Darling*, seem erotically stodgy. The peculiarity of Eva's most uneccentric body and her democratic style is that she is amazingly mellifluous, almost unobservable, and her languid nothings seem to take place in an amphitheater of dead space and dead time.

At the center of this new European entertainment—no pace, a desertlike evenness—is a threadbare, condescending treatment of the individuals: the character who is no deeper, no more developed, prepared, explained than the people in fashion advertisements. In the limpidness, the anemic charm of *Puss & Kram*, the haberdasher Max and his statuesque wife appear transplanted from *Elle* magazine. Repeatedly, the classic Richard Avedon fashion-shot appears (the kind of image that also opens and closes *Le Départ*). It shows a large photograph of the antelopelike wife, in bellbottom pajamas, legs akimbo, seated in white space. This blow-up appears above the movie's central bric-a-brac, a bed, and it consumes an enormous amount of silly footage.

First you look at this dark silhouette of the wife framed with a finely etched contour, then the movie image slides with cliché chic down the wall, onto the two cute heads barely perceptible beneath the sheets. Again, it's more white and a more deadpan sophistication of a type that seems to go back to Cary Grant–Carole Lombard–Topper humor: sunshiny, well heeled, contrived.

Too often, the movie character has been stripped of many of his functions: not so much the victim of a totalitarianism (the smileless boys boarding school in *Young Törless*) or a paternalistic Japan (Toshiro Mifune fighting the clan in *Rebellion*) as a puppet in the hands of his director. The actor, the incredibly passive Törless, a young Audrey Hepburn in military uniform simply bystanding in esthetic fashion, has been sacrificed to the self-interests of the director, while the modishly leaden scene moves around him.

For instance, the *Puss & Kram* scene is supposed to be carried by an interesting looking actor, Hakan Serner, a bowlegged star with a Popovlike face, whose Pinteresque mission is to defleece his school-day pal of house and hold. His puckish mimicry becomes pointless—trying to sustain slight sophistications whose purposes in the new movie syndrome are to belittle him and keep his world trivial. The wife's need for sunglasses before she can breakfast in bed sends him to retrieve the errant glasses: nothing must weigh down or slow up the general buoyancy of the situation. The trouble with this movie program is that, in the effort to keep out any complication that might gum up the works (the message about a decadent laissez-faire world), the Serner character is forced into moves that are insipid.

One of the elements scalping the New Actor is a simple-minded contrariness to the old story-telling film. An amazing complacency allows any arbitrariness as long as it reverses-mocks traditional expectations.

During the festival, there was a steady rain of names and erudition, calculated to score instantly with the In segment of the audience. This eclecticism—someone gets murdered on

Preminger Street, a character runs off in mocking ecstasy to catch a showing of *Hatari*, over the loud-speaker in a swimming pool comes a deadpan "Will Ruby Gentry please come to steam bath 67," two girls cavort with the giggling innocence of the Gish sisters in a scene that has the wintry desolation and spareness of a Dovschenko—is too blatant to be bothersome. What is unsatisfying is that this snickering appeal to the sycophantic spectator takes over the forefront of the movie which the actor used to have.

Actually there were peaks at the festival where the actors were given opportunity to Go. One of the great scenes in *The Battle of Algiers* is the besieging of an FLN hideout, a frantic scrambling in a wet clammy Arab house. It's a perfect scene of shock and terror constructed with a multiplicity of detail, a palpable tremor working through the inner court of a four-story building. But the real hammer in *Algiers* is its vengeful, ferocious women, who seem to go on their own: three Arabs, dressed as Europeans, planting bombs in a crowded *café* and dance hall, a fifteen-year-old bride whose incredibly thin-limbed body projects a flower's delicacy blended with suicidal courage.

Le Départ, a conventional New Wave film, balances a cheeky, flake-type actor against the French notion that outdoor telephone booths or tunnels are—bang!—nerve-centers of the modern psyche. Léaud's acting trademark is a passionate decision that peaks his frenzied exasperation, quizzical compulsiveness. His taunted, berserk, exhausted moods are not unlike Julie Harris's Frankie Adams in *A Member of the Wedding*, the same sense that everything around them is insipid, banal, and what they need, crave, is a release to some glamorous scene. With Léaud, the release never comes; he's a sort of Lilliputian given a streak of go-go energy, trying to keep from sinking in the middle-class sloth, a near paranoid who's dead if he ever slows down.

There is a surrender being played out in many European films, a decision to forgo any apparatus of pleasure (any groping in the acting that will make the role transitory and human) in order to show the deficiencies of modern man.

In *Made in USA*, there is a joke amongst the actors that each is to act below his normal talents. Thus the image is truly contrary: in a scene of total artifice, surfaces covered with an enamel version of nighttime Times Square color, the actors are pinned down in curious angularities and stiffnesses. Unusually small-sized even for French actors, all looking as though they were dressed by Ohrbach's (the Junior Dept.), the general impression is of the Ken and Barbie dolls, a cardboard lower-echelon Madison Avenue group maneuvered into cramped setting and held there.

A typical image presents a man named David Goodis, seated at a tiny table squashed between bed and window. His uncle lies bruised on the bed, spot of red paint on each cheek. Meanwhile the woman he loves sits in a bathtub, scrunched up, shell-shocked, singing plaintive Rock and Roll on the guitar. Choked with people and no movement at all, the scene is so disconnected that every word, person, decoration presents itself as a solitary unit. The over-all effect is a pastiche of fakery, a day in the life of a hotel room, Atlantic City.

Midway in *Far from Vietnam,* this same contrariness and condescension is repeated: a long dull dissertation by a French actor reviewing Herman Kahn's book *On Escalation.* Explaining the war to his wife, he is a man drowning in a no-technique film. The only relief he gets in this static situation is an occasional glimpse of his wife, her eyes glued to him, dripping melancholy, plus a heavy sense of art objects in his vicinity. This cultural surface—pontification, name-dropping, the appurtenances of High Art—is one of the chief dilemmas that is vaporizing the movie actor. The actor in effect is being flattened by erudition.

This is probably the hidden message of the festival: the notion that a surface rich in suggestions of high culture is becoming more the character in movies than life itself, whether the life comes through characterization or a vital use of the medium. It is as though the movies were acquiring the character of the place itself: Philharmonic Hall, with its overwhelming sense of worthy endeavor, posh program notes, a cheerful club-room atmosphere for critics, plus a special aroma of Money Being Spent.

NEW YORK FILM FESTIVAL 1968

There is nothing so funny in the recent New York Film Festival as the Romanyesque overland coach in *Lola Montes,* a blood-colored Pullman on wheels that belongs to Franz Liszt, and serves as a major trysting nest for the scandalous heroine. A love affair on wheels is a nice idea but this overdecorated vehicle is the hub for eight minor events which are nothing but crazy make-up, improbability, and an ordeal of graceless acting. Martine Carol, an hourglass made out of stale golden cupcakes, is a mock George Sand, locked on a chaise longue; her boyfriend has a goofy smile, silken curls, and stumbles about putting the finishing touches to "The Farewell Waltz." The real nuttiness is the feeling of hometown operetta around them. Lola's getaway wagon, which follows behind, is operated by a husband-wife servant team who run out from behind the wheels, carrying bird cages and carpetbags, shouting "spaghetti." Some other fake elements: a painted backdrop of the Italian countryside and one of those villas which once housed Ricardo Cortez, a domineering mother, and a raging river, the wildest in 1920's melodrama.

The oozelike structure about a Garboish woman of affairs played by a non-Garbo as stupid, not very classy, and two shades from pure ugly, is a perfect Festival film, steeped in attitudes. The theme, from *Naked Night,* through three festival films, has the director as a ringmaster, magician, lion-tamer, vulnerable to man's foibles but knowing everything about life. There is a grandiose attempt at cosmic embrace, pro-life and pro-love, with the requisite number of peculiar bosom shots: the breasts are pushed up and then bounced, always a couple of fleshy folds around the armpits. Any Ophuls movie is supposed to be fluid magic, but after the first five minutes of circus, it is like hauling an old corpse around and around in sawdust.

The truth about a film festival is that it is a parlor of myths,

a dilemma bound to overrun a place that is supposed to be exhibiting only the best blue-chip films. Some of the very clear
myths are (1) that Renoir is deadly accurate on "human pas-
sions," hard-working folk, and the plight of the poor, (2) that
there is a torrent of important films washing through Czecho-
slovakia, (3) that Ophuls made better films in Europe than in
Hollywood, (4) that American moviegoers want and need the
taunts directed into films by Franco-Italian mandarins and
mad-dog labelers.

What a queer sensation to be face-to-face with a causeless film
that can draw a "my God, I like it" remark. Mailer's *Beyond
the Law* has a zillion little irritations, but it has authentic scur-
rility and funk before it goes sour with Mailer's Irish brogue
monologue. *Faces* is a real break-through in movie acting, despite the wrong stamping of Americans as compulsive laughers;
it also goofs such motivations as a husband cheerfully clicking
his heels and greeting his wife after spending ten hours with a
high-priced whore, and a squad of elderly males, who are just
rancid hams with facey leers.

Bresson's *Mouchette,* by about three-hundred miles the most
touching and truly professional film in the festival, is about a
fourteen-year-old girl of the peasant class, living in a small
French village, the daughter of two alcoholics. The film has
apparently melted down to a short story, being adapted from a
Bernanos novel, but it moves on about five levels. It has to do
with the surpassing beauty of a girl who is in a state of excruciating physical discomfort. On another level, it is about difficulty, an almost pure analysis of its sides and, in this case, the
way it multiplies when luck is out. (Mouchette has some luck in
a bumper-car concession at the amusement park, but it doesn't
last long—only long enough to create the most poetic action
sequence in years.) Other levels deal with a particularly bitter
village and its inhabitants (the snare theme, Life chasing the
human being into extinction); the conception of people as being
so deeply rooted in their environment that they are animallike:
the simple effect of a form briefly lit by a truck's headlights.

Mouchette, played by Nadine Nordier, has a touching toughness, the crushing sense of not expecting anything from anybody, and a harrowing know-how about every niche of village

life. Unlike Frankie Darro, who got the same desperate shadow effects in *Riding High,* Nordier's singularity is tied to painful appearances: apathetic about her well-being, hair uncombed and probably lice-ridden, a large part of the painfulness has to do with large lumpy legs, stockings that won't stay up, big shoes. Despite all these humiliations, she is never cartoony and gets enormous somber dignity into her walking tours, combats with other girls, and a terrific moment when she climbs into bed, wet from a rainstorm, and then goes into some slovenly chores for the baby.

Some of the most important things movies can do are in this film. The barmaid, for instance: a queer and singular girl, as muscular as she is narrow, her character, which has tons of integrity and stubbornness, is just barely caught: through a crowd of locals, from an offangle, pinning up the top flap of her apron, drying the glasses. The role is backed into through gesture and spirit, rather than through direct portrayal. Then there is the great device of placing Mouchette's house on a truck route, and milking that device for the most awesome, mysterious wonders. Also, for a film that is unrelievedly raw, homely, and depressed, it seems a wild perversity to bloom for five minutes into sudden elation with Mouchette and a likably acted boy riding some dodgem cars at a fair. After so many misused amusement parks in films, it is remarkable to come across one that works.

In the category called Bloody Bores, the Festival offered *Capricious Summer, Hugo and Josefin,* and *Twenty-Four Hours in a Woman's Life.* Orson Welles's little orchid, *The Immortal Story,* missed by being only minutes long and having but four audible lines ("Take back your five guinea piece, old master." The next line—"In one way or another, Miss Virginey, this thing will be the death of him"—is repeated at least four times. What makes Eilshemus Levinsky so sure?)

Capricious Summer features three middle-aged crocks hanging around a 1920's bathhouse doing their thing. An ex-athlete gone to girth swaggers, brags, and plays dull largesse. An army officer is an irritating, strutting performer doing worldly cynicism. The third, a minister, works on timid innocuousness. A slender, owlish magician (acted in fey, fond-of-itself mime style

by director Jiri Menzel) comes to town with a threadbare tight-
rope act, and, after his blond assistant diddles the three dul-
lards, this rerun of dozed-off acting, Renoir color, and Bergman
soupy philosophy winds up with the notion that a circus invariably leaves whistle-stop town sadder and wiser than it was in
the first reel.

The most interesting work always occurred outside the self-
conscious languor acting that grips French and Italian films.
Jacqueline Sassard and her Lesbian owner in *Les Biches* sit on
this veneer act so hard that it becomes possible to decide how
much cosmetic art has been planted on an eyelid, or the number
of small elegances that transpire in getting one bite out of a
chicken leg. There is a strain of this nauseous elegant with-
drawal in the two dozen conceited stiffs who make up the young
Parisian middle class in Godard's *Two or Three Things I Know
About Her,* led by Marina Vlady, a project-dwelling housewife
who daylights as a prostitute when she isn't haughtily walking
through a dress shop, sniffing the air, discussing her inner life
with the audience. It's amazing how Raoul Coutard's camera
can transform this puerile conceit into a singingly crisp image.

In *The Red and the White,* a swift, fresh-air war movie about
Czarists, Red Russians, and a band of Magyars who get tangled
within the scythelike moves of both armies in a Hungarian border locale that has a grandiloquent sweep, there are a dozen
actors with amazing skin tone, sinewy health, and Brumel's
high-jumping agility in their work with horses. These actors
have an icy dignity—they never mug, make bids for the audience's attention, or try for the slow-motion preening that still
goes on in cowboy films. (Jack Palance in *Shane,* hanging over
his saddle iron, spitting tobacco juice, menacing poor townfolk,
relating to his horse as another part of his stylist's costume.)

As far as acting goes, though, *Faces* is a far more important
case. Lynn Carlin is near perfection, playing the deepest well
of unexplored emotions as the wife of a rubber-faced business
wow who seems like a detestable ham walk-on until he surprisingly lodges into the film's center for good. This Carlin style
starts as soap-opera face work, a camera intimately registering
the melancholy of an American woman, but it builds velocity
and possibilities for itself by working into the area that Warhol

has pioneered. It's amazing how far Carlin swings her role as a middle-class wife: she's so deep into the events that, after one night out or in with a gigolo swinger, she seems to have expanded the role out of sight by the time her husband returns from a bored-with-job whore.

Faces is a Loser Club movie, the theme being about people straying into brief sexual relations, or wanting to stray and not being able. The strength of the movie is the depth to which it dives into a particular situation: four middle-aged women, uncomfortable with themselves, awkwardly trying to be swingers, entertaining a blond hustler who does some sexy dancing around the living room. The movie—no rush and plenty of time—sits and stares at each. It stares at a pair of blazing eyeballs in a woman who is scared, out-of-practice. It's very good on a woman nearing sixty, greedy, and nearly out of her mind at the possibility of making it with a young cat: she palpitates with suicidal abandon and blatant lust. There's a sweating excitement in the work with Carlin, a decorous young wife full of twitches, stiff postures suddenly dropped, and prissy lips that never stop working into nervous moods. One of the movie's unspoken themes is the disparity between this unworldly woman and her husband, an oily actor (John Marley) who suffocates the movie with he-man sophistication. The top moment is a profile shot catching this actress at the end of a marathon, teasing evening of too many cigarettes, lousy drinks, and faded chances. The movie ricochets from a drunken semicomic dance to the coldest close-up of Carlin's frazzled side of the face, an innocent mouth that exudes the feeling of a long night's journey into deafening defeat.

NEW YORK FILM FESTIVAL 1968,
Afterthoughts

"Manny, how are you holding up? How's your Festivalitis?
Oh well, Lola Montes *will do it to the best of us. ('What film did*
you like best?') Definitely The Nun. *I liked the whole projec-*
tion of the period. But my favorite director is Jancso; he's a
great stylist. ('Didn't you like anything about that German film,
Signs of Life?') *Good God no. When the Germans deal with*
minutiae, they leave me."

—Film critic

"What a corny coincidence that both the husband and wife
manage to get laid in the same night. I just can't stomach
that kind of unbelievable coincidence in a film which pretends
to be raw realism."

—Director of a film department

"It's just a shitty film. These North American sincerists call
me up all the time. I caught your film: simply fantastic or ter-
rific. But I know it was nothing but a shitty film, just shit. I
didn't delude myself for a minute. I didn't like the French en-
tries, the Bach thing was a bore, Mouchette *was a piece of shit,*
the German film was rather nice in a crude sort of way. Couldn't
seem to get an image, could he?"

—Canadian film photographer

People talk a lot about the star glamour, action, straight-ahead
drive that the old Paramount film used to have, but one thing it
didn't have is even a fraction of the talk that goes on outside of
theaters today. This drone, which starts the moment the *Times*
informs you that *Pretty Poison* is a bang-up job à la Hitchcock

and doesn't stop until sleep rubs out an important comment about Jacqueline Sassard ("She looks slim, but I'm sure that when she has her first kid her ass will spread"), goes on everywhere, all the time, until life is one long, steep ramp leading upward to a classy double bill at the Elgin Theater. This hum, which could occur driving down the West Side Highway, over a phone to a friend in Brooklyn, in a roadside college bar where Janis Joplin and Aretha Franklin are soul-shouters just barely audible over "Jean Vigo was a master at street scenes complicated with a lot of cross-currents," is compulsive, decisive, scrofulous, flapping about, and completely engulfing once it gets under way.

One of the desperate facts about being part of movies today is that every thirtieth word might be "Truffaut-Moreau-Godard," a depressing, chewed-over sound, and that a heavy segment of any day is consumed by an obsessive, nervous talking about film. This is often a joyless sound that couldn't inspire anybody, but it suggests that modern moviegoers are trying to possess the film or at least give it a form or a momentousness which it doesn't have.

Godard's *Weekend* is the handsome, maddeningly long pilgrimage of a jaded, fascinating, wrinkle-faced woman (Mireille Darc), which gets more and more barbaric while the actress shows a sexy, haunting talent for withdrawing, going blank when she hasn't anything to say. It is a soul-shouter movie which often devours the violence it wants through a spoiled rotten, rich-man's technique, a toylike presentation of highway cannibalism, sexual expertise, capitalism at its hate-consumed dead end. Sometimes the web of words builds into a good funny speech and there is a growling display-room color, a vehement moving from one grotesque, humorous texture and setup to another.

There is a scene in a gas station, after a sports car smashes up against a tractor, that has a dizzy, blunt, Mel Frank momentum. Odd, wonderful stray faces are flashed on screen, and the actress's unconvincing rhetoric somehow becomes menacing and real as she prods herself, trying to charge herself up into more and more vituperation. It builds into a jelly-apple shrillness, with a last terrific shot of stray onlookers banded together in a we-are-the-French-nation camaraderie, soul brotherhood. Through her last words, "You crumby Jew bastards," the idea gets implanted that these onlookers and the victim herself can only get together when they find a common enemy: a possibly Jewish couple in another sports car who won't give the girl shouter a lift.

For its Cubistic pace and garishly cruel throwaway dialogue, this scene in a gas station has a wild, daring, hit-and-miss excitement. The rich girl, whose boyfriend is killed, screams at the farmer driving the tractor: "You filthy unwashed peasant, you killed the man I loved and ruined my car. He was handsome and he was rich and now he's dead and you're stupid and ugly and you don't even care. You hate us because we screw in Saint Moritz. You probably don't even know how to screw. You just get screwed by the union. You probably don't even own the tractor. [She kicks the tires.] Cheap tires? My car was beautiful. It had a Chrysler motor. I got it because I screwed the son of General Motors."

It's a film which loves its body odor. A husband and wife sit on the side of the road. She says, "I'm fed up," climbs down into a ditch to take a nap. Husband lights a cigarette. Tramp comes along, asks for a light. Husband says: "Haven't got one." Tramp spots the wife in the ditch, says, "Hey, that's a bird down there. Is that your bird?" Husband doesn't answer, just looks bored. So the tramp climbs down into the ditch and rapes the wife. The treatment, with the motionless camera, far back and across the road, is offhanded, antiformal, so slight and slack that the spectator feels, "Well, OK, what's next?"

What's next is a scene with two garbage collectors who give the couple a lift. The garbage men, a white and a black, lean against the truck, eating submarine sandwiches. The ravenously hungry husband asks for a bite, and the Negro gives him a small section, saying: "If this sandwich were the American budget, what I gave you represents the portion the U.S. gave to the Congo this year." Movies like *Weekend* show the spectator how to run off at the mouth and keep a sense of self-importance at the same time.

In yet another scene, there is this delighting in far-fetched spuriousness. Mireille Darc takes a bath, and, while the camera watches her washing her neck, her husband, not seen on screen, tells a story about a hippopotamus: "The hippo goes to the master of the animals. 'Please let me live in the water.' The master says, 'No, you'll eat up all the fish.' The hippo answers, 'If you'll let me live in the water, I promise that when I shit, I'll spread it out with my tail and you'll see that there are no fish bones in it.'" This story (most of it is Darc in the bathtub, plus cuts to previous material) has charm and piquancy, but in the recounting there is the uneasy feeling of a director moving unresisted material that he knows backward and forward from one end of a film to another without snarl or conflict.

Czech films, Underground films, Hollywood films. Now people who take films seriously study skin flicks, TV commercials, scopitone. In the days of Wrath or Raft, there were just Hollywood films, "B" or "A," Arthur Rank, and a few art directors like Renoir. The sheer bulk of what is known as film, plus the equal cheers for so many different types of film, has loosened everyone's bowels. Everyone's in the cat-bird seat casting out rambling comments.

A smarmy, navel-rubbing movie like *Zita* shows this instant aging process with its pretentious and precocious facility by a crew of movie-world teeny boppers. The film's point is that the circle of life goes on in a delectable, heartfelt slow motion, as this French Debbie Reynolds, whose beloved aunt is dying, finds earthly love at the same moment that her aunt passes into the hereafter. The main presumption is that skill permits any amount of goo to run into a film: a blue-ribbon ram on a tear through Paris streets, a little red toy auto taken as a memento, lovers coyly eating peach preserves out of a jar by the spoonful.

Among the visual gimmicks is an embarrassing bedroom scene, a wispy prancing *pas de deux* in slow motion as the two lovers undress. Imagine Bogart, in a haze of spring blossom color, pantomiming ecstasy as he drifts around the bedpost, tearing off his shirt, a flower opening to the sun. Or standing with such fey charm in the middle of a highway at dawn, playing a bass fiddle.

Signs of Life (three Nazi soldiers on a cushy detail, on an island near Crete, pass the time making fireworks, dozing, eating in the yard at a small card table) has been the subject of a typical noisy dismembering: "A modern Don Quixote, apathetic and inhibited, is at last stung into rebellion against society, and reveals the first senseless signs of his humanity only in insanity." Very ephemeral in its charms, *Signs* has some of the casual goodhearted zaniness that Gassman injects into *The Easy Life*: playing up meandering activity over dialogue, getting all the times of day, the feeling of friendship in its inactive-silent aspects. The meals at the table are perfect: dramaless, engrossed in eating, an unemphasized graceful Greek wife who comes across as a war bride who doesn't know the language or the people she's living with. The hub of this sly, dry, truly comic movie is a cranky-bitching soldier, a butcher of insects, so serious working away in the corner or on the beach trying to devise Rube Goldberg traps to devastate the "cookalockers."

The Nun is a young girl in a Chardin pose doing needlepoint. A maid comes in with a message: "Your mother will see you." The camera, an undistinguished onlooker, doesn't move, and the perfumy scene doesn't develop until there is a cut to another stagy setup with people in chalk-marked confrontations.

Les Biches, Secret Ceremony, and *Negatives* are psychologically oriented movies about fetishes in which the subtlety consists of playing perversion very close to normality, unlike Huston's *Golden Eye* movie, which goes sour because of the "oh-look-at-that" attitude about soldiers riding bare ass or playing with a Baby Ruth wrapper.

With a constant lacquered barrenness, from its stylized acting to its setting, Saint Tropez in December, *Les Biches* is an exploitation-doesn't-pay film. Two women meet in the middle of a bridge where the younger one, "Why," earns a living doing chalk drawings of does on the sidewalk. Frédérique (Stéphane Audran), a droll and spicy sybarite, circles around Why, flamboyantly throws her a large sum of money, and, after moving indoors and putting one too many sugars in her coffee, seduces her. In this seduction scene, Jacqueline Sassard has just bathed and is standing around, a pretty girl with a strange neuter manner and the walk of a dull penguin, her head always down, constantly in need of a good nose-blowing. The whole scene plays as though it were inside a mattress: Audran slowly rearranges Sassard's shirt, and, in the corniest of hushed close-ups, the camera frames itself around her hands as they start to unzip the girl's blue denims.

The movie depends on Audran's willingness to lay it on in a pure baloney performance. One of her slow, succulent moments takes place in her stadium-sized kitchen where the frazzled cook is whipping up some veal and brussel sprouts, the favorite dish of two dull-acted pansies who live off Frédérique. Looking as though someone rubbed berry dye on her face, using a slow cat-like walk, making one small name, Why, sound like three bars of an organ piece, she addresses the cook: "Vio-let-ta! Ça va? Ici Mademoiselle Wh-y-ee."

Tropics, a fictional documentary about a Brazilian dust-bowl family on the road, is a lukewarm muddy river. There seems to be a film over the film: no blacks or whites, nothing emphasized, a limp-vague father moving through villages bereft of script and money, even the air and trucks evidently needing a Geritol pick-me-up. ("You know, I didn't really mind it. I couldn't bear the first half, but in the second half, I got interested in those crabs they were pulling out of the mud. I thought it gave a true projection of what it means to be poor. You know what I mean: standing out in the mud all day long, reaching down for those ugly things.")

Hugo and Josefin is life as seen through the eyes of people in a Kodak camera ad. There is the sense of a hummingbird or apple orchard just around the next bend in this clean-fresh-buttery movie. ("It could be called something like a preadolescent *Elvira Madigan,* impossible to resist.") Their Breck-shiny hair, photographed through lichen, pine trees, and spotless windowpanes, has an equal importance with Hugo's little tooled Tyrolean suspenders and Josefin's beautifully pressed micro-smocks (there is an obsessional effort to get the gray flannel pinafore above her tiny white drawers). It's the epitome of a Blonde Is Beautiful and Best film, a proper bourgeois mentality and relentless wholesomeness that should further madden the already maddened Stokely Carmichael.

NEW YORK FILM FESTIVAL 1969

In the type of multisensation circus that is the New York Film Festival, it is difficult to pin down the precise intellectual tone and incredible grace of Eric Rohmer's *Ma Nuit Chez Maud*. What makes it so special is that it's involved with a whole stratum of European culture that's totally ignored in films: the intellectual Catholic living in the provinces. Constructed on the encounters of a single person in a new town, its pleasure comes from specificity: of time (Christmas), locale (a bustling job-prosperous town of narrow streets), geography (a wintry, sparse landscape), cast (an unimposing man leading a deftly ordered life meets a bristlingly alert charmer who seizes opportunities and is a hard loser when they dissolve; these two are brought together by an interesting old friend whose specialty is conversational fencing). The most important specific is that the movie is centered on the private intellectual and emotional areas of the very civilized, educated, believable French professional class, and, moving along through small, unpointed, often unconnected events, it gets to the component parts of this class's life. The tone of their conversation, their bookstores, food markets, how they might meet in a bar or go on outings is sensitively phrased, spaced out, observed. Such consistently undramatic material is extraordinary in films today and needs tempered lightness to bring it off. And, actually, Rohmer's film, in its last third, begins to run down, as its good Catholic finally effects a date with a girl who meets all his qualifications.

One obvious fact about this *auteur*-minded festival is that it contained only one rich, satisfying, hard-to-accomplish performance: Jean-Louis Trintignant's indirect, intelligent acting, which fleshes out Rohmer's cerebral, problematic script. An older version of the shy, rather lonely, poignantly vulnerable student in *The Easy Life,* Trintignant keeps the movie elastic, droll, and

dryly exciting through a mastery of slightness: he's slightly
prissy about his Catholicism, slightly awkward defending himself against accusations of Jansenism, slightly graceful as he
dashes across a snow-covered street in pursuit of a pretty blonde
he's been sizing up in Mass as a future wife. It's a fascinating
idea for a movie—a young man's undramatic settling into a new
town and job, structured around a long philosophical discussion
in the rooms of a sexy, taunting divorcee—and, though it is
immaculately written, it depends on taut smudges of elegant
acting to keep it afloat.

While criticism gets hung up on old problems of taste, right
and wrong, history in the making, the New York Festival at its
simplest is an unweeded garden of mixed delights and endurance
tests. Most of the interesting work—the BBC anatomy of Sternberg's unfinished *Claudius, Le Gai Savoir, Ma Nuit Chez Maud*,
and Bresson's transposing of a murky, believable Dostoevsky
story into an afternoon piece for clavichord—were far from
traditional movies. The BBC *The Epic That Never Was* is ap-
petizingly special for the collage effect, but it's no movie. Godard's uncompromising stab at the story film is one of the few
occasions when English subtitles under French-speaking voices
are a positive design element.

What is good about Bresson's *Une Femme Douce* is the mulishness: the direct, resolute, obsessional artist always driving
after the idea of exalted suspension and ascetic rigor in small,
quiet phenomena. The movie works despite the spooky queerness
of its three inhibited, sleepwalking actors and the silly verbatim use of Dostoevsky's lines, which are rescued from total
silliness in the film by a blatant throwaway quality. Bresson,
trying for a kind of Cubistic misalliance, doesn't care if the lines
are understood or whether they fit in with the image. As story-
telling, the movie is a brain-twister in which few sentences con-
nect to the image they accompany. A young bride jumps up and
down on her new bed, and her husband, the ultimate in prissi-
ness and mundaneness, says, "I threw cold water on her ecstasy." Also: "I knew she had behaved honorably, there was no
question about it." This blank, icy man has just seen his wife
passionately necking in a roadster.

Through movies about hand-task-oriented social outcasts—a

poacher setting his traps, an imprisoned man weaving ropes and making hooks for his escape, an apprentice pickpocket learning the trade—Bresson's vocabulary has been honed over the theme of humility as nobility. He likes a face to be as free from reflection as an animal's: his sensitive-faced outsiders do what they do without the face making any comment on the action. Before speaking, eyes methodically drop in nervous, hopeless abjectness. People turn away from the camera, assume prayerful or meditated poses, pass one another as though on a private procession.

On one level, the film is a geometric ballet of doors opening and closing, people exiting and entering, husband or wife turning down the bed covers, of objects or people moving into and out of range of the stationary camera, a young wife's dazzlingly white fresh face against the sharp, crotchety profile of her black-haired husband, TV sets turned on and off, bathtubs filled and emptied. Despite the stylized repetitions of gesture, the rigidly held camera angle at stomach height, the uninflected voices speaking desperate, passionate lines, *Une Femme Douce* is an eerie crystalline work, a serious affirmation within a story of suicide.

The Epic That Never Was is a British TV documentary about the making of an unfinished movie called *Claudius*. Narrated by a strangely stiff, schoolboyish Dirk Bogarde, the movie gets sparkle and dimension from intercutting candid interviews with a few completed segments from the elephantine Korda production that mysteriously smashed up after a month. A lot of the sparkle comes from smart-aleck remarks by the writer, Robert Graves, and the costar, Emlyn Williams. There are pathetic-exciting shots around the abandoned Dedham studios, and, along with the funny, uncut rushes of *Claudius,* the flubs, nervous wise-cracks, false starts, Charles Laughton's strong, emotional turmoil turns up like a ghostly giant in anachronistic crowd scenes. At moments, this BBC document reaches a poetic peak above its witty gossip: somehow the material becomes layered, recapturing a moment in time, through the mind of a costume-designer still puzzled at this date by Sternberg's giantism ("I want sixty naked vestal virgins dressed in white gauze on the stage by to-morrow morning"). Or the oblivious, quivering voice of heart-faced Merle Oberon: "Korda wanted to make the film to make me a real big star, to really make me shine." (She has the same naïve-vain expression thirty years earlier when she answers Caligula's "Wouldn't you like to marry my Uncle Claudius, Messalina?" with a helpless "My family has other plans for me.")

In Godard's *Le Gai Savoir*, which looks for the most part like a funny, daring, remarkably lighted, neon-colored rehearsal on an empty stage, two bright-faced Parisians, aged twenty, get together each night between midnight and dawn, to examine the meaning of words and their relationship to the phenomena they describe. Practically all of the movie is structured on one static frontal image in boundaryless black depth, the edges of the two seated figures picked out by a powerful floodlight. This mysteriously inky-hot lighting is hypnotic, slowly joining usually unseen nooks and crannies in the sullen Léaud-Berto faces with some sense of the young Leftists' purpose and youthful energy. To describe its content (silhouetted faces alternating with Tom and Jerry cartoons, newsreel footage of Paris students rioting, illustrations, ads flashed on the screen with words or parts of words scrawled over them, flashes of colored photography of city streets that are as deep as the rest of the film is flat) fails to convey the exhilarating goofiness. As always, Godard's sound track is distinctive: sporadic, unsettling, and, as with the visual material, apt to issue from any source. Does anyone else use sound as a totally filmic weapon?

Pierre and Paul is an eccentric film with a headlong self-involved propulsion. Wry and affectionate, it never managed to get inside the young working couple, a stocky, self-made builder and a nicely acted slender typist. The subtheme, the extent of the inroads into Paris life of plastic modernity, is sort of amusing and skillful in its details. Bergman's *The Ritual* is a self-indulgent film with one good actor, and some good writing about people defiling each other. The good actor is a Richard Basehart type with funny embedded-in-fat eyes and a crisper style than Thulin and Bjornstrand. The movie probably evolved when a David Susskind Swede made a phone call: "Mr. Bergman, would you be interested in writing an original play for TV? There'll be no censors and no cutting to save time. You'll have complete control. Would you be interested in that kind of a project?"

Susan Sontag's *Duet for Cannibals* looks and feels like

skimmed milk. An airless, room-locked, unusually adroit draw-ing-room comedy. A young man with the style and dress of an avant-garde painter is employed to catalogue the life work of a political refugee. There is nothing convincing about his task, his employer's career, or the reason he and his girl are swallowed up by the powerful personalities of the two urbane, pompous vampires in an ultrabourgeois house. The combination of a gut-less spirit and sadomasochistic games (I kill you, you kill me, and then we all get up and walk out the door) kills the film midway, when a suicide, with unbearable playfulness, hides herself and her lover behind a windshield that she covers with shaving soap. What is amazing is how little juice there is in the inventions and characters, yet this gray coagulation keeps going forward in a half-entertaining way.

Sifting through a Festival experience, a madness, 100 hours sitting in a dark chamber, brings back a half-dozen vulgar, ter-rific, enervated images that are anything from piercingly poetic to whorish. Norman Rockwell's vignettes of adolescent rural life, full of obsessively researched and accentuated-beyond-realism detail (buttons a little larger than life, suspenders filled with folksy charm), were never more fastidious than the nostalgic redo of the early 1930's in *Adalen '31*. It is the craziest picture of people out of work and on strike: an intensely lyrical evoca-tion of slender boys in caps and trousers, flowering meadows, delicately patterned wallpaper and summer heat. Two big scenes in *Bob & Carol*, played on a slow-curving Spanish stairway, have squirts of hard, modern patois ("Why didn't you call me first?" "I couldn't call and ask you, 'Bob, can I have an af-fair?'") calculatingly poised together, while a vulgar camera reveals old hard-core Hollywood physiques in long-forgotten Edith Head costumes.

EXPERIMENTAL FILMS 1968

The theaters of the Underground—often five or six docile customers in an improbable place that looks like a bombed-out air
shelter or the downstairs ladies room at the old Paramount—offer a weirdly satisfying experience. For two dollars, the spectator
gets five bedraggled two-reelers, and, after a sojourn with incompetence, chaos, nouveau-culture taste, he leaves this land's-
end theater feeling unaccountably spry.

In the cliquish, subdued atmosphere of the New Cinema Play-
house or Tambellini's Gate, there is more than an attempt to
dump the whole history of films. One glance at the pock-marked
terrain and the placid spectator suggests a new concept of
honesty and beauty based on beggarly conditions. Tambellini's
paradise, the Gate, on Second Avenue, starts as an entrance to
an old apartment house, moves through a 1920's marble hallway,
and engulfs the customer in a black chamber. God help him. The
big sensation here is the ancient unreliable floor, which, like the
ceiling in this blitzed miniature cathedral, is indescribable.
Sometimes, the shredded carpeting, with its patches of masking
tape, feels as spongy and sandy as the beach at Waikiki. Actually, it is an old room of murky origins, painted flat black, no
two dimensions the same. There is a bombed-out area in the front
half, which houses the screen, and a number of wooden constructions that have been started by a nonunion carpenter and then
thrown up as a bad job.

A respectable uncle of the Gate Theater, the New Cinema is
located dead center in the basement of the Wurlitzer Building.
This likable chamber has filigree woodwork, flat dove-gray walls,
and a legitimate cashier's window that belongs in front of
Carnegie Hall. The theater, only somewhat larger than the Gate,
sits behind the cashier's booth, and has these piquant walls,
which epitomize the ancient Stonehenge character of the Underground. Alongside the seats are little arches scalloped along the
wall, each one with its own recessed ledge on which the customers

sit, when they're not asleep in the aisle or sitting with trademark lassitude in the seats.

The Undergrounders with the quickest talent—Warhol's virile close-close-up, George Kuchar's homely family humor with pixyish use of a roly-poly flirt, Bruce Baillie's *Castro Street* —are involved in what seems like a sentimentality but is much better than that. The apparent sentimentality: the idea that a shrunken, impoverished film is necessarily purer, more honest than a highly budgeted studio film. Actually, the Kuchar-Warhol is so impoverished that it gives a spectator the kind of disenchantment, sordidness, feverish wastage that no other movie even suggests. The films of late Bergman-Godard-Penn, like a private elevated paradise in lovely waltz-time, are based on ideals in acting, camera work, and story technique that have become absurdly removed from the spectator's experience.

Right now, the Head Chef is a bland pastry with bangs whose newest film, *Four Stars*, is almost a *Ulysses* of non sequiturs dished up with the most galling largesse. Warhol's latest is a sort of jaded valentine in twenty-eight flavors, in which he salaams, butters up, betrays, and fondles the three female exhibitionists he favors: a 1967 Theda Bara, whose chief feature is a deep kohl line; a nymphet, who is boyishly slender, short-haired, gaminlike; and, finally, the female Falstaff of his company: a grotesque who suggests the underworld of drugs and dissipated, humiliated flesh.

With its rich gemlike image and its elegance, this sinister movie is dedicated to exposing people as far from their life functions as possible. From its opening shot of Nico chanting (a primitive sound in which the notes are sucked in and rasped out), the audience is disengaged. The actors are continually in nonacts: they sit in bathtubs with no thought of bathing, couples are in bed boring themselves to death, endless application of cosmetics for no apparent purpose, a hungerless face eats an apple, a slender body rolls his Chinos down and up.

Devoting about twenty minutes of droning improvisations to each of its "stars," (Ultra Violet, Viva, International Velvet), the movie offers a violently physical image. It's as though the whole of Genet's perverted world were funneling into the shot,

from every inch of the frame, by way of the rawest close-up
technique and those Drool colors—sherbet, bonbons, marzipan,
icing—now fashionable in Leo Castelli's, Capezio's,
Schrafft's.

This image is basically the *Harper's Bazaar* photo set in
motion, most of the motion coming from superimposed sounds
and scenes. For example, in one rapid-jawing segment, a female
Lenny Bruce comes on in a silvery boutique, doing a stand-up
monologue sitting down. Wearing knee-high silver boots, a blond
wig (a big bouffant job, every lock like a banana), fondling and
twirling gadgets made of tiny mirrors arranged in mosaics, this
human poison-pen letter is seen and heard in triplicate. Her big
joke about a twelve-year-old and his erection keeps returning,
so that, like the horse race in Kubrick's *The Killing*, every line
returns three or four times. Despite the hopped-up monologue,
the cliché-lurid-lamé-on-lamé setup, the scene is weirdly cozy.

One real problem today is the fecund quality of Warhol's
image. There are dragging sections: a gang of lymph nodes
wrapping themselves in bands of yard goods. Even this scene
picks up incredible vegetation of vitality when a hirsute honey-
bun describes his rape by an adorable Puerto Rican "Golden
Gloves type" and his three uncles named Sammy. This dread-
naught extrovert, detailing his quadruple "sex" ("It was disgusting. . . . I just lay there and let it happen") is wearing a
red satin mantilla, the scene is like a pajama party, with everyone lying around the floor. An outrageous ham actor steams
with life, due to Warhol's parlay of indolence, who cares, fun,
and a largesse eye which seems to lap shots, sounds, into a
unique multiplied vivacity.

Ribald, inexplicable, *Hold Me While I'm Naked* (Kuchar) is
a hit-miss funny film, because, like the Gate Theater, it seems
a mockery of the detailed movie courses now taught in every
university. For the Kuchars, Edison has just invented the movie
camera, and the industry is getting ready for its infancy. Even
the various themes that come back like a belch in Underground
film—the big party or orgy, lyricism in the bathroom, the body
beautiful or ugly, genre work around the film-maker's home,
exotic clutter—are all present in any Kuchar two-reeler.

In a lunkish comedy about two marriages gone flat, the cornerstone of humor is anything that can be exaggerated, bush-wacked, so that it is fashionably out of kilter, gruesome. The most toothsome of its actors—a grotesque bratwurst played by Bob Cowan—has such funny factors as straight-cut long hair parted in the middle, skinny legs, a pillow beneath his shirt. His comedy, a sluggish, witless version of a type of goon comedy kids sometimes use in their play acting, is built around a bent-kneed walk that suggests his body is a heavy flour sack.

The sad thing about George Kuchar's soured talent is not so much the confusion, the skidding around in old movies, Jewish Mama humor, do-it-yourself Rabelais, but the curious assumption that the audience—particularly the In Society segment —are enthralled with the very smell of his rambunctious, gal-umphing Bronx personality.

CANADIAN UNDERGROUND 1969

The best film at "Canadian Artists '68" is a study of a room not unlike the basement room at the Art Gallery of Toronto, where the films were privately shown. A bare and spare room with the simple construction of a Shaker-built outhouse, the gallery room had an austere charm, a continuing dignity, even after twenty films had been seen. Exactly like the interiors of schoolrooms in Winslow Homer, it has a magical plain gray color and an equally magical pattern of woodwork on the side walls, four-inch boards running horizontally from floor to ceiling, divided by four-inch studs spaced two feet on center. The back wall is brick, but it has the same transfixing green-tinged gray paint plus that eye-level line of coat hooks that American architecture should never have given up.

Michael Snow's *Wavelength,* a pure, tough forty-five minutes that may become the *Birth of a Nation* in Underground films, is a straightforward document of a room in which a dozen businesses have lived and gone bankrupt. For all of the film's sophistication (and it is overpowering for its time-space-sound inventions), it is a singularly unpadded, uncomplicated, deadly realistic way to film three walls, a ceiling, and a floor. Maybe if all moviemakers worked as directly and simply, leaving out the literary and commercial hangovers from the days of Cecil De Mille, other film content than this one white room would possess a startling freshness.

Probably the most rigorously composed movie in existence, Snow's film is a continuous zoom toward the lineup of windows and the complex of signs, tops of trucks, second-story windows outside the loft. So integrated, taut, fully realized, not like an idea-suggestion someone could pick up and use, in one aspect, the minimal project picks up the *Blow Up* theme. An unexplained murder occurs, the camera dissolves itself into a moody, turbulent photograph that is obsessively present but not immediately discernible. This photograph is the target for the relentless, oncoming zoom, which is an abstract corollary of photographer Hemmings's concentrated gazing at the print mutations on the *Blow Up* murder photos. There is a marked similarity in the choice of photographs in both films.

Good as the darkroom episodes are in Antonioni's hit, Snow's working out of the idea is more abstract, and, by being so, gets to the uncomfortable bones of the theme: the overpowering, indestructible reality of the physical world alongside the wispiness of the human presence. This kind of paradox is hardly original, but Snow brings off the horrible largeness of the idea by doing it austerely, in the right cold, objective tone and with unusual balances between the unpretentious acceptance of room objects and severe abstractions of time-space techniques.

The zoom, always at eye level, is almost imperceptible and goes from the widest view of the field to a particular point between the windows, ending up inside the sea photograph. The journey—accompanied by exactly syncopated natural sounds from street and people plus an electronic sound, which comes up to an unbearable point when the camera is six feet away from the wall and then depreciates—is broken into four equal time-space intervals by human entries. There is nothing fey about these incidents: they are quick, realistic, and lightweight. The film opens with the first human event, a cabinet being moved into the loft, while an alert, rotund woman directs two movers, and ends with a young girl making a telephone call. She says, "Could you come over right away, I think there's been a murder." These events happen as the camera determinedly presses forward, slowly ingesting every possible fact of place and light, and, like Fate, sees every wall-person-light detail as equally important.

If a room could speak about itself, this would be the way it would go. The movement of the camera is almost nonmotion, or a room's movement. The people—very small, never filling the room, their feet making slipping sounds—are seen as light, impermanent guests. The color-light, which is so multiple and unpredictably changing, is really ravishing. One stretch of the journey has the field in reversed negative colored with sepia and burnt-sienna tones. The street, which has been a changing, shadowy backdrop, goes in an instant explosion to pure tone when all the complementary color is removed. The middle section is an assault of abstracted color, but the compositional elements, the tall rectangular windows, are still those of the room. It's like flushes of color in the consciousness of a room: a green shudder, a sort of visceral perception of the walls and windows.

The best quality is that the rigorous, high-level diary of a room is so itself, so unlike anything a moviegoer might imagine. Suddenly, with these exciting but soothingly balmy color-light variations in a worn interior, what had seemed a tabby-cat movement, the Underground film, takes on the profundity and sophistication, austere dignity and inventive wit of a major art. It is hard to believe that a film could be more taut or intelligent.

The actors who star in the Canadian films—desultory, lacking in intensity, numbed and ominous—never win awards in the category of either the beautiful or the damned. There is no passion about the casting. It is usually the guy next door, a girl friend, or the family pet who are willing to work free and have an inert boldness in front of a camera. The funniest is the sort of likable kid who does nothing in *On Nothing Days*. With a colossal mindlessness, a body in which no part strikes a harmony with another, and too embarrassed to breathe, he shuffles around downtown like a coat sleeve looking for an arm to stick in itself. The first time you see him he's in bed debating with himself (Guess I'll get up. What's there to get up for? You don't have to get up, you know.) and examining his fingernails. Forty minutes later, after he's bummed around town, ridden the subway, had a fantasy about the girl across the aisle, he comes home, lights a cigarette, sits on the windowsill, and this adolescent-frustration movie ends.

This is a draggy, heavy-footed movie: the air is heavy and hanging, he walks as though pulling up molasses with each step, and the scenes never come to anything. A spectator going through such a day would be ready for suicide.

The horror film of the Festival, *Slow Run*, is about free love amongst the enlightened in some tenement of New York. A young man's misadventures in a Manhattan that has never been photographed in more depressing tones, a continuing sluggish gray with interior scenes that are mordantly airless and street life in which the people are slow, stoned, and silly. This is a film about a girl undressing and a folk-rock group type with bangs over his eyes, sort of delicate and vague, who sits collapsed in a stuffed chair or stands naked in a shower soaping himself with a zonked-out expression on his face. Between these two repeated incidents there is some mysterious *schlepping* around the living room, some going-nowhere playfulness in bed. All this determinedly minor material is ridden over by a willfully pretentious narration, forty unclear words a second, that keeps pounding home the theme that this movie is a run-down version of Joyce's *Ulysses*. In effect, this ode to freedom and youth is a profoundly grim and depressing film.

Right now, the two polarities of the independent scene are the Static Field film (*Wavelength*; Mekas's stunning study of swelling tides and shooting sailboats in the French seaport of Cassis; Andy Warhol's films, which, for all their overlapping, are basically static field; and some of Bruce Baillie's "haiku") and Nudity. *Soapy Run* has all the signposts in this latter film: (1) the touching is scant and sort of paternal, considering the amount of nudity and the hot-blooded bragging of the narration, (2) the eroticism is played out singularly with the man completely dressed, gazing with a blank face, (3) the moony-faced nudes treat themselves like illustrations in a science lecture, unveiling as though they were performing a social service, (4) the film heads for the bathtub as though it were the altar of love, and, when there, the activities consist of plastering each other with soap suds.

Joyce Weiland had three entries: the first, *Cat Food*, studies the eating habits of a luxuriously furred cat devouring separately five fish just arrived from the market. The viewpoint is always as though the camera were held at the edge of a table while the cat operates on top against a black backdrop. It is filled with supreme succulent color, sometimes recalling Manet in the silvery glints of the fish scales, and, as in the *Rat Life* picture, getting the deep, ovular splendor of a Caravaggio. The second entry, *1933*, is a slight exercise which alternates the numerals of that year when Miss Weiland was born with a speeded-up street scene shot from a window. The third and most ambitious, *Rat Life and Diet in North America*, proves that she's been looking long and affectionately at animal life and is a sort of whimsical Evelyn Nesbit, never corny and creating with an intense femaleness.

A band of revolutionary gerbils escape their cat jailors and journey up the Hudson, where they hide out at a millionaire's estate and perfect their tactics as guerrilla fighters. It has some hard-to-forget, singular images: One, captioned ''Skag Mitchell was the first to escape,'' shows a grimly bare section of floorboards with the tiny gerbil hovering against the wall furtively waiting for the moment to make his escape. Another, with incredible color shots of fruit, rolls piled on paper doilies, cut-glass goblets, a lavish spread on which the hungry rodents eat their full, is overpowering for its recall of Spanish still life, and the animals are pretty charming. The third is the earliest shot in the film, the actor rats jumping up and down against a screen while the huge cats guard them with fixed attention. Just the glinting texture of grass against pitch black night and her use of black burgundy gem color in the cherry festival sequence suggest that Miss Weiland is more than a diary-like recorder of domestic enthusiasms.

R34, the name of a cadmium red dirigible which appears in a cartoony-loud color painting by Greg Curnoe, is the name of a movie documenting the life of this Ontario painter. The documentary reeks with the idea of this artist, a cool and industrious Gideon of Scotland Yard (no neuroses, just a lot of industry), as a good-guy-husband-worker. Always in a steady metronome-pace production, Curnoe *schlepps* the garbage back and forth, sits at a drafting table cutting-assembling-pasting little collages from a welter of commercial labels, magazine ads, bits of type, colored paper (he seems to command his pile of elements like a Red Army ant). The one quality the film shows is that there's hardly any wavering, missteps, backtracing in his production.

One of the questions provoked by *R34* is why are these moments —three shots of a blonde combing her hair, Curnoe grazing the top of a mannikin's wooden bald head with his palm, wetting his moustache with a glass of milk, repeated shots of his and his wife's smiles filling the screen—considered salient in the life of a creative person? These lackluster, haphazard moments are obviously intended to counter the heroic garbage that goes into a *Lust for Life* painter's biog. Chambers's selection doesn't come any closer to the creative process than shots of Kirk Douglas feverishly fighting inner voices and the mistral of Provence. There is one fascinating stretch: Curnoe applying opaque lilac with an absorbed certitude to a serpentine, hard-edged picture.

The great acting of the festival is done by a white loft room, some rodents up the Hudson, and a forest of small industry-made "sculptures" that make up a personal, eccentric pair of films by Gary Lee-Nova. Hinges, toggle bolts, gauges, dials, bolts, an all-yellow map of the United States drawn in 3-D, a cartoon drawing of the Bomb's mushroom cloud, roadway signs, railroad and shipyard iron fixtures, a lot of pipes, cable patterns, spools, capstans. The thing is that Lee-Nova's is a discriminating, coherent choice of Pop, utilities, hardware: a cartooned cloud, a toggle, and a huge, flat giant next to a roadside stand are equalized in scale, all become kin, like the way Léger paints scaffolding, clouds, and workers so that each has the same weight and texture.

MICHAEL SNOW 1969

The cool kick of Michael Snow's *Wavelength* was in seeing so many new actors—light and space, walls, soaring windows, and an amazing number of color-shadow variations that live and die in the window panes—made into major esthetic components of movie experience. In Snow's *Standard Time,* a waist-high camera shuttles back and forth, goes up and down, picking up small, elegantly lighted square effects around a living room very like its owner: ordered but not prissy. A joyous-spiritual little film, it contains both Snow's singular stoicism and the germinal ideas of his other films, each one like a thesis, proposing a particular relationship between image, time, and space. The traits include rigorous editing, attention to waning light, fleeting human appearances (which suggest a forbidding, animistic statement about life: that the individual is a short-lived, negligible phenomenon and that it is the stability of the inanimate that keeps life from flying away), a rich-dry color so serene as to be almost holy, and a driving beat that is like updated Bach.

Standard Time is an astute, charming exercise compared to the other Snows, which are always steered into purposefully intolerable stretches: tough, gripped snarls of motion which have to be broken through to reach a restful, suave, deltalike conclusion. In his sternest film, titled with a ◄—► sign for back-and-forth motion, a specially rigged camera swings right, left, left, right, before a homely, sterile classroom wall, then accelerates into an unbearable blur (the same frenzied scramble, as though the whole creative process was going berserk, that occurs three quarters through "Abbey Road"). In *One Second in Montreal,* ten stray photographs, culled from the library, all of them of little drab parks connected to public buildings, are turned into a movie that has a special serenity and is pungent with a feeling of city, snow, unexcitement, the mediocrity of public buildings and parks (no fresh air). Despite the dirgelike sonority, I question the length of time that Snow holds on each park to create a majestically slotted ribbon composition.

When the electronic sound in *Wavelength* reaches an ear-cracking shriek, the one-shot movie, a forty-five-minute zoom aimed at four splendid window rectangles, burns hot white, like the filaments in a light bulb. This middle section is composed of violent changes of color in which the screen shudders from intensities of green, magenta, sienna: a virtuoso series of negative and positive impressions in which complementary colors are drained out so that the room, undergoing spasms, flickers from shrill brilliant green to pure red to a drunken gorgeous red-violet. Despite the grueling passage, which always comes three-quarters through a four-part construction, his two major statement films, *Wavelength* and ←→ are liftingly intellectual. Besides his Jeffersonian mien, Snow's films are filled with the same precision, elegance, and on-the-nose alertness that went into Jefferson's slightest communiqué to a tailor or grocer.

His film career, a progression from austere painterly to a more austere sculptural style has peaked into this queer "double-arrow" film that causes a spectator to experience all the grueling action and gut effort of a basketball game. Just listing the ingredients doesn't sound like a real night out at the films. This neat, finely tuned, hypersensitive film examines the outside and inside of a banal prefab classroom, stares at an asymmetrical space so undistinguished that it's hard to believe the whole movie is confined to it, and has this neck-jerking camera gimmick which hits a wooden stop arm at each end of its swing. Basically it's a perpetual motion film which ingeniously builds a sculptural effect by insisting on time-motion to the point where the camera's swinging arcs and white wall field assume the hardness, the dimensions of a concrete beam.

In such a hard, drilling work, the wooden clap sounds are a terrific invention, and, as much as any single element, create the sculpture. Seeming to thrust the image outward off the screen, these clap effects are timed like a metronome, sometimes occurring with torrential frequency.

The human intrusions in *Wavelength* and *Standard Time* are graceful, poignant, sensitively observed: a fair-sized turtle walks on a line through the camera's legs straight toward the right-angled corner of a studio bed; at another point, a cat does an arching, almost slow-motion leap onto the bed; then a woman walks briskly by with a towel over her shoulder on her way to the bathroom. There's no eclecticism to these events, which show a good touch for the tactile quality of 1969 loft existence. Formularized and stiffened, the humanity in the double-arrow movie is a bit dried up. Things are done on cue: a man and woman self-consciously play catch, a cop cases the joint, a mock lecture is given to three students, a gawking and hodgepodge group is seen uncomfortably standing around.

The movies are utterly clear, but they get their special multimedia character from Snow's using all his talents as painter-sculptor-composer-animator. Obviously a brainy inventor who is already a seminal figure and growing more influential by the day, there is something terribly different about this Canadian in the New York sharp scene. Incapable of a callow, clumsy, schmaltzy move, he's a real curiosity, but mostly for the forthright, decent brain power that keeps these films on a perfect abstract path, almost always away from preciosity.

JEAN-LUC GODARD 1968

Each Godard film is of itself widely varied in persona as well as quality. Printed on the blackboard of one of his Formicalike later films, hardly to be noticed, is a list of African animals: giraffe, lion, hippo. At the end of this director's career, there will probably be a hundred films, each one a bizarrely different species, with its own excruciatingly singular skeleton, tendons, plumage. His stubborn, insistent, agile, encyclopedic, glib, and arch personality floods the films, but, chameleonlike, it is brown, green, or mudlark gray, as in *Les Carabiniers*, depending on the film's content. Already he has a zoo that includes a pink parakeet (*A Woman Is a Woman*), diamond-black snake (*Contempt*), whooping crane (*Band of Outsiders*), jack rabbit (*Carabiniers*), and a mock Monogram turtle (*Breathless*).

Unlike Cézanne, who used a three-eighths-inch square stroke and a nervously exacting line around every apple he painted, the form and manner of execution changes totally with each film. Braining it out before the project starts, most of the invention, the basic intellectual puzzle, is pretty well set in his mind before the omnipresent Coutard gets the camera in position. He is the new species creator, related directly to Robert Morris in sculpture, in that there is an abhorrence of lethargy and being pinned down in a work, alongside a strong devotion to Medium. Travel light, start clean, and don't look back, is the *code du corps*.

Each of his pictures presents a puzzle of parts, a unique combination of elements to prove a preconceived theory. Some of his truculently formulated beasts are:

A Woman Is a Woman ("I wanted to make a neorealistic musical, which is already a contradiction") is a monotonously scratching, capering version of a hack Arthur Freed musical, perhaps the most soporific, conceited, sluggish movie of all time. The crazy thing about this movie is the unrehearsed *cinéma verité* feeding on littleness, love of the Real slamming against the Reel, the kind of studio-made pizzazz that went into *My Sister Eileen*. The elements include deliberately artificial Times Square color, humorless visual puns, each scene pulled out like taffy, the action told so slowly it paralyzes you, awful mugging that is always fondling itself while the bodies are dormant.

My Life to Live. The fall, brief rise, and death of a Joan of Sartre, a prostitute determined to be her own woman. The format is a condensed Dreiserian novel: twelve near-uniform segments with chapter headings, the visual matter used to illustrate the captions and narrator's comments. This is an extreme documentary, the most biting of his films, with sharp and drastic breaks in the continuity, grim but highly sensitive newsreel photography, a sound track taped in real bars and hotels as the film was being shot and then left untouched. The unobtrusive acting inches along in little, scuttling steps, always in one direction, achieving a parched, memory-ridden beauty. A film of extraordinary purity.

Les Carabiniers. A rambling, picaresque-piquant war film, seen through the exalted, close-to-earth vision of a Dovschenko. As a bitter against-war tract, the film is a gruesome contradiction, played as deadpan slapstick with two murderously stupid rustics for its heroes. Since war is a grand mistake that sweeps across borders, the movie leans heavily on mistakes, vulgarity, around-the-globe and around-the-calendar hikes.

Each new movie is primarily an essay about form in relation to an idea: a very deliberate choice of certain formal elements to expostulate a critique on young French Maoists; a documentary report on prostitution, poetic style; or a gray, somber, sophisticated portrait of an existential hero of confused commitments. *La Chinoise*, for instance, is incredibly formalized, a doctrinaire syntax to go with a doctrinaire group of modular kids. The movie's not only in one classroomlike room, but the actors are in an uptight acting arena in the manner of fervid teachers in front of a blackboard, and the camera and the actors never move except in a straight left-right motion.

However, there is a huge gap between the purported intention of the films and their actuality. And it's the undeveloped space between intent and end product that gives them their nutty, Dr. Kronkite character. In front, the movie is the most ponderous undertaking: in *Le Petit Soldat*, an assessment of the political climate after the Algerian war is the theme, but the actual film time is taken up with a dull day in Geneva: one driver ineptly trying to get in front of another, a photographer shooting rolls of film, a mock torture scene. Certainly Anna Karina and her usual inept, little-girl exhibitionism is a Grand Canyon away from the point of *My Life to Live,* which is to document the short career of a spunky, self-educating Heart of Gold able to go through a phase of prostitution without losing decency or chipping her soul. There is so little sex in the movie that she could be pure High School, 1950 version, acting cute with her lollipop Louise Brooks hair, if the narrator didn't tell us she was a risk-all prostitute. There is something so far fetched about Anne Wiazemski, in *La Chinoise,* solid lassitude inside a girl's fastidiousness and politely controlled snobbery, living communally, murdering coldly, plotting a bombing of the Louvre.

The overlapping constants of his cerebral, slapdash movie can be summarized in the following seven points:

(1) Talkiness. His scripts are padded, coruscated with Chatter in all its forms, from lecture hall to afterdinner talk. His actors become passive billboards for a mammoth supply of ideas, literary references, favorite stories. That he is a man of verbal concepts should never be forgotten; his visual image is an illustration of an intellectual idea, and often his lists, categories, rules, statistics, quotes from famous authors come across with pictorial impact.

(2) Boredom. This facetious poet of anything-goes is the first director to reverse conventional film language in order to surround the spectator with long stretches of aggressive, complicated nothingness. There is a contrary insistence on outrageous lengths, lassitude-ridden material, psycheless acting, the most banal decor, a gesture that is from left field.

(3) Ping-pong motion. The heartbeat of his vocabulary is the pace and positioning of a slow Ping-pong match. Marital couples compose themselves and their wrangling into a symmetrical ding-dong. One of his pet systems has a couple seated opposite one another, between them a dead lamp, ornate teapot, or a train window opening on a travelogue French countryside. Why should the most intellectual director employ such a primary one-two, one-two rhythm? His is basically an art of equal emphasis: it's against crescendos and climaxes. Violence becomes a boring,

casual, quickly-forgotten occasion. *La Chinoise,* his most controlled film, is also his most equalized, and behind all of its scenic plays is the regular, slicing motion of a pendulum in a narrow area.

(4) The Holden Caulfield hero. Inside every character is a little boy precocious who resembles one of Salinger's articulate, narcissistic dropouts.

(5) Mock. Rather than being a mocker, a real satirist, Thackeray or Anthony Trollope, he makes mock versions of war, a Maoist cell, a husband-wife fight, strip acts. He even makes mock profound conversation, and, in those Greek statue shots in *Contempt,* he is doing a mock-up of beautiful photography. Mockery suggests an attitude of being against; invariably this director is in a middle position, finding it a more flexible, workable situation not to take sides. The role of pseudospecialist allows his movies to go where they will go, with no feeling of clampers on the material.

(6) Moralizing. An urban Thomas Hardy, he sees the world as a spiky place, the terrible danger of brassiere ads, the fierce menaces of Coca Cola and Richard Widmark, the corruption implicit in praising a Ferrari when in the character's heart-of-hearts it's Maserati all the way. Just as Tess, the once-laid milkmaid, is a landscape-consumed figure, the idiot children in *Band of Outsiders*—waferlike, incubated snits—are beset by, and get their meaning from, the darkling air around them. The moralizing is always a tone that sneaks in despite the ambivalence that keeps his surface brittle and facetious.

(7) Dissociation. Or magnification of the molehill as against the mountain, or vice versa. He's a thing director, though he doesn't imbue articles with soul in Polanski's manner. Mostly he goes in the opposite direction, free-wheeling across the scene. He dissociates talk from character (a tough secret agent in a freak-boring-weird discussion of conscience), actor from character (Bardot is often flattened, made into a poster figure rather than the spunky-shrewd wife in *Contempt*), action from situation (two primitives in a Dogpatch kitchen holding life-size underwear ads against their bodies), and photography from scene (a mile-long bed scene, the cheapest record-cover color on a Petty-posed, baby's-flesh nude.)

It is easy to underestimate his passion for monotony, sym-metry, and a one-and-one-equals-two simplicity. Probably his most influential scene was hardly noticed when *Breathless* appeared in 1959. While audiences were attracted to a likable, agile hood, American bitch, and the hippity-hop pace of a 1930's gangster film, the key scene was a flat, uninflected interview at Orly airport with a just-arrived celebrity author. The whole movie seemed to sit down and This Thing took place: a ducklike amateur, fiercely inadequate to the big questions, slowly and methodically trades questions and answers with the guest expert. His new movies, ten years later, rest almost totally on this one-to-one simplicity.

This flat scene, appearing at points where other films blast out in plot-solving action, has been subtly cooling off, abstracting itself, with the words becoming like little trolley-car pictures passing back and forth across a flattened, neuterized scene. This monotony idea, which is repeated in so many crucial areas, in sculpture (Bollinger), painting (Noland), dance (Rainer), or underground film (Warhol), has practically washed his film away from all of its eclectic old movie moorings.

At the *Breathless* station, fourteen features and ten shorts ago, he had not yet perfected his idea of the actor as a mere improvising face which pops in and out of a carnival curtain while the director throws verbal baseballs at it. This is a strange elaboration of the ping-pong effect, which had the ball bouncing erratically back and forth, first one face talking, then the other, while the top of the screen appeared to curl over in the sagging atmosphere. During the next years, he perfected this abstractionism into a shooting gallery effect, first one face moving into range, then another, while the bodies diminish into strings and their owners recede behind the words.

But this ping-pong technique has impelled a minimalizing that gives a pungent tactility to his worst (*Made in USA*) and best (*My Life to Live*) films. When Anne Wiazemski, *La Chinoise*, is talking about serious things (and a lot of the audience to sleep), plucking at her lip, showing her two middle teeth, the image is pure, spare, reduced, and rather wondrous.

Boredom and its adjuncts—lack of inflection, torpor, mistake-embracing permissiveness—get his movie to its real home: pure abstraction. When he is just right, his boredom creates kinds of character and image that reverberate with a clanking effect in one's mind and gets across that morbid nullity which is so much at the heart of his work. In the last analysis, it is just the amount of deadness that gives the film a glistening humor: Véronique and her partner, seated in cardboard Victorian elegance at opposite ends of the table, a fancy tea service between them. The whole scene picks up the lovable gimmick of children's books, the stand-up illustration that goes into three dimensions as you open the page, and then dissolves into flatness as you close it again. Looking blankly across the table, she says "et cetera" and Guillaume repeats the word with the same deadpan inflection, so that each syllable carries a little, sticking, Elmer's glue sound.

Behind the good (*Band of Outsiders*), bad (*Woman Is a Woman*), and beautiful-bad (*Carabiniers* is visually ravishing at any moment, but nearly splits your skull) is the specter of an ersatz, lopsidedly inflated adolescent, always opposed to the existing order, primitivistic either in his thinking or in terms of conscience and feelings. In all the film's expressions is the feeling of a little boy drifter, a very poetic and talented self-indulgent Tom Sawyer, who can be a brainy snot throwing doctrinaire slogans or coyly handling books so that the hip spectator can just barely make out the title. Every one of his actors, with the exception of Michel Piccoli in *Contempt*, has been shifting his performance around this Salinger adolescent as a grown-up: few of these people—Seberg (tinny, schoolmarmish), Belmondo (outlandishly coy and unfinished; squiggly little grimaces with his mouth), Bardot (coarse, spunky shrewdness), Brialy (old-fashioned egotism, stolidly sissified), Jack Palance (fiercely elegant, better silent), Sami Frey (whiplike), Macha Meril (fairly human pug-noise), Jean Pee Loud (vigorous rodent), Brasseur (chunky, mock methodical), Michel Sémianko (nicely unpushy; high school clarinetist type), Fritz Lang (businesslike self-effacement and warmth)—seem less than obnoxious or escape the flattening technique of a director always present as a shadow over each actor. Actually his actors are halves, and it is only our awareness of the director's dramatic presence behind the camera that gives the character a bogus completion.

Ordinarily the character is queer, sawed off, two-dimensional, running the gamut from brainless brutish in *Carabiniers* to the shallow, disgustingly cute Belmondo-Brialy-Karina triangle that worries about getting a stripper pregnant in *Woman Is a Woman*. There's one last variant of this type, the politically sensitive boys in *Masculin-Feminin*; also the narrowly smug clique in *La Chinoise,* who are loaded with sophistication and act as self-contained units (or eunuchs). Obviously these new, stark, cool characters have a closer kinship with the director than Nana, a prostitute who is hung up on personal freedom. Secret, Ban, and Fresh, his new product, come off the screen strong willed, determined, passionately committed, and they give his movie a new decision and affirmation that can make a spectator feel flabby and drifting by comparison. With its shallow space, shadowlessly antiseptic surfaces, and photography that shoots from the waist up as though the camera were resting on the counter, *La Chinoise* is like a modern diner employing a summer waitress (Wiazemski), busboy (Léaud), a skulled scullery maid (Berto), and a toast boy (Sémianko, who dispenses intelligence despite a sitting-still position and a scene that sinks him up to his blue eyeballs in words).

Had he done nothing else, Godard should be remembered for having invented an army of graceful, clumsy, feeble oddballs. With foot-loose acting in the most sketchily written roles, these figures come across like Chin Chillar in Dick Tracy or Andy Capp, defined to their teeth, exposed in space from the awkward feet to their crazy heads (which are always punched up with some caricaturing element: mostly hats and wigs, occasionally an obscenely large eyeball).

One of these, Arthur (*Band of Outsiders*), memorable for his woolen stocking cap pulled down over most of his malignant Jim Thorpe face to his nose, is an argyle-sweatered sweetheart to forget. As the chosen beau in a triangle, he implacably keeps his eyes, like a hungry airedale, glued to the curb, while Claude Brasseur acts him with the unyielding sneakiness of a furtive fireplug.

Another, as poetic in a different but equally crazy way, is a bunchy, layered concoction of vamp make-up and thrift-shop clothes acted as a latter-day Gish sister by Catherine Ribeiro in

Les Carabiniers. Cleopatra is a primping, prancing, real primitive, the mistress of a dinky one-room house that shifts around a dirt plot and a mailbox that spits letters the way old movie calendars once dripped leaves.

Lemmy Caution (Eddie Constantine, in *Alphaville*), known as Richard Johnson to his enemies, a bullfrog whose face has been corrugated by a defective waffle iron, has the flexibility of an undistinguished low-income "project" building. His role consists of walking through hallways, rooms, and up and down staircases, either pinching his nonexistent lips or blinking against the torrential onslaught of lights.

Compared to the soft-shoe nonchalance of a Hawks war hero as played by Cary Grant, the moronic warriors, Michel-Ange and Ulysse in *Carabiniers,* are heavy, stillborn bricks falling off a building. Why does a celebrated artist devote so much time to inane time-wasting cockiness, the showboating of a character so limited he's close to a wisp? Karina's little fawn, eyes blinking and hair shaking, limbs used like stilts, hasn't anything of reality or good acting, but she has a robust, complacent ego that presumes her one-note acting is tireless. A collegiate little girl, a partisan captured in the forest in *Carabiniers,* has this same unchallenged *chutzpah.* There's an inner sureness that he's going to score, no matter what he does, that is repellent in Albert Juross's dumpling Michel-Ange. The director is like a street vender who has a suitcase of windup dolls, which he sends out to do their little, cranked-up turns.

One of his personal gambits is the cocky fun that he gets into these scuttling figures: his fake Bogarts and Mary Pickfords shoot, slide, and trot in a bizarre carbonated fashion on a semi-abstract screen constructed like a pinball machine. It's a trademark of his landscape work that he cuts against the newsreel image by formalizing the shot: a diagrammatic line of action, a syncopated stop-go sound track, someone yapping tick-o-tick, tick-o-tick. A funny, waistless chick in cute cotton pants embraces her nude breasts in a defiant X formation and marches outdoors and indoors like a football referee stepping off the yards; a car chase shot backward in rigid, linear patterns; Bardot pacing diagonals on a roof, using her arms like the guy who signals an airplane down to a carrier (did he do this because

the villa roof is the size and shape of a ship's landing field?).
Cleopatra, waltzing out into a dusty yard, does a couple of big-
footed pirouettes and, with a melodramatic shove, sends an aging
lover packing in a Sennett Essex.

He gets the most singular acting response, probably with a
magical dishwater command like "That's OK for now." The response he gets is supreme slackness, seemingly without worry or
prethought about the role, and a sublime confidence in the director's unerring genius. The result is a mindless drifting, in
which reactions come mystifyingly late. Brasseur's desultory,
undistinguished dance style in *Band of Outsiders* is peculiar in
that it is so self-absorbed, out of sync with his two partners;
occasionally something beautifully sinuous suggests itself
amongst his mock absorptions.

Since the role is almost invariably a reference to an image or
actor out of film history, the clothes, basically unpretentious
and everyday, are supplemented with misaligned *outré* items:
an unnecessarily heavy overcoat and prol cap from *Potemkin,*
a trench coat and Sam Spade lid from Dashiell Hammett. The
gestures also seem tacked on. A blob-faced actor (Juross in
Carabiniers) dressed in dirty swaddling clothes fatuously and
hammily pats his hair into place. Kovacs and Véronique at pensive moments, one every two minutes, pass a thumb in slow
motion across their lips, a gesture that is a flagrant pun on
mouth tricks, from Bogart through Steve McQueen. Instead of
being unobtrusive, these tics are applied like thudding punctua-
tion.

He just doesn't care whether any of these actions carry convic-
tion. There is no antiwar scene more strained and irritating
than a kid soldier methodically terrorizing a female hostage by
raising and lowering her skirt, delicately, with the tip of his
rifle. Meant as a real raking-under of the military, it's a slow,
crude, visual metaphor for rape, ending in a house being burned.
The oddness about the scene is that the havoc is played so deadpan: a lot of emphasis on the dopey way he orders her to "un-
button," the Rembrandt self-portrait on the wall underlined.
Instead of the atmosphere of outrage, the sentiment is reversed
and the scene played as though the next-door neighbor had come
in and demanded a cup of sugar. This severe dissociation of tone

from content spreads the scene with grotesquerie, a fantastic comic-strip feeling coming off the screen, discordant bits of ungodliness like Juross's glazed leer, the fact that the skirt is raised at a point dead-center on her person. He is a master of the brusque and angular. He'll play along with Juross's booby incompetence because it brings him an antiheroic oafish bayonet-pointing line of action. This kind of jabbing, off-balance virulence is at the very heart of his brilliantly diseased message.

Godard's legacy to film history already includes a school of estranged clown fish, intellectual ineffectuals, a vivid communication of mucking about, a good eye for damp villas in the suburbs, an ability to turn any actress into a doll, part of the decor, some great still shots that have an irascible energy, an endless supply of lists. I think that I shall never see scenes with more sleep-provoking powers, or hear so many big words that tell me nothing, or be an audience to film-writing which gets to the heart of an obvious idea and hangs in there, or be so edified by the sound and sight of decent, noble words spoken with utter piety. In short, no other film-maker has so consistently made me feel like a stupid ass.

LA CHINOISE AND BELLE DE JOUR 1968

La Chinoise concerns a summer shared by four to seven youths intoxicated with Maoist Communism: a humorlessly vague, declamatory crew made up of Jean Pierre Léaud (taut, overtrained, exhibitionistic), Anne Wiazemsky (girl intellectual), Juliette Berto (girl ineffectual with a year of prostitution behind her) and a sensitive tapeworm with steel rims, always dunking his bread and butter in coffee. Reclusive, never penetrating or being penetrated by the outside world, they study, debate, never seem to converse but try to out-fervor one another, while the camera images suggest a scissoring motion, shuttling back and forth, giving equal billing to the doors and shutters, rough-brushed with red-blue-yellow, and large blackboards covered with measured handwriting.

What has to be made clear is that this is an infuriating but cagy film. Why? There is such a wide swath of rhetoric, dogmatic rights and wrongs, employed or deployed through replicas of the pop media, pamphleteering, TV interviews, slogans, and protest march placards, as well as in the mechanical recitations of the adolescents, escapees from a local nursery school.

What is maddening is not the facile manipulation of modern communication devices, but the hollow shaft between the hot-shot imagery and cunning rhetorical jam-up. Scene after scene has a gaping hole, as well as, admittedly, a kind of piquancy: the hollowness seems to result from a number of curious policies: (1) limiting actors to one trait, like Wiazemsky's single-minded zeal, plus one maddening repeated tic, lip-pulling, shifting the eyes dreamily, fingering the hair, (2) pre-editing scenes into anagrams, talking news-photos, pettily pedantic debates, (3) flashing the screen with a Pepto Dismal of modern painting devices (Marvel Comics heroes), which seems as peculiarly out of date as the supposedly hip clothes.

Given the stunted bloom on their faces, the parrot talk, as though they're reading a news report, and the With It air, these Marx-Lenin jabberers come across with enormous dairy-fresh impact. Living surprisingly cleanly on a Paris top floor, always fresh new 1957 prol clothes to wear (palish yellow and red cardigans and pull-overs), these kids seem to be pushing out with intolerable talentless mugging. Véronique (played with hard-to-say blandness by Ann Wham) stands smack in front of the screen and does Nothing. Pushing her innocuousness into a virulence, she and her buddies turn the Cubistic Mary Poppins set into a nursery, a French primary school called Notre Gang. Scenes are set up like a first-grade primer: Dick and Jane drink tea, Dick-Jane-Jasper-Max do morning exercises on the veranda, the kids take an afternoon nap, looking like happy little mummies, no reaction, like zombies.

It is hard to get this sealed-off Communist cell as a shrewd portrait of youth protesters: Berkeley-Tokyo-Paris. While seeming to patronize these foolishly idealistic fishlike girls, green-garrulous boys, the film actually sees itself as being part of the movement to shake up the Establishment. Bomb the Sorbonne, bomb the Louvre, "Donnez-moi un bombe" incanted endlessly. The film is summed up in the pathetically slack-faced amateur presence of the second-girl lead, an aimless player who acts out a series of talking newsphotos. In one, she is a Vietnamese peasant cringing with terror as cardboard bombers buzz around her like gnats. In another, she's a Viet Cong soldier with a plastic machine gun, behind a barricade of firecracker-red books. Each one of these bits of play-acting is rawly, offensively puerile. The use of amateurs who play their ineptness to death is a deliberate, effectively gutsy move, but, nonetheless, it can make your skin crawl.

Unlike the sliding-door effect of *Chinoise, Les Carabiniers* has a surprisingly wet, fluid mossiness: its people seem beautifully wan, primeval, murky, little woodchucks camouflaged by nature. Forget the allegory about war: this is a topsy-turvy series of pastoral gambols, with so many throwbacks to Sennett, etc., that it suggests a Movie-Lover's Diary. The movie takes place on an interesting piece of real estate—it's flimsier than dilapidated —a cropless farm in Southern Question Mark. Four mysteriously demented ragamuffins exchange their brother-daughter-mother roles like demented kids, bundled up and waddling on this dusty D. W. Griffith plot. (Those girls are some tomatoes, like the Gish sisters, skipping around the back yard. The mother (?) is named Cleopatra and thus wears Egyptian-gypsy make-up). The two male clods get conned into an anonymous war, which ranges around the two hemispheres. Much of the battlefield looks like the Marseilles suburbs, but is referred to as Santa Cruz.

Michel-Ange and Ulysse have a hard time getting into the area of human beings. One of them is skinny but is covered with old rags, old Potemkin costumes, so that even he looks bloated, limp, and lymph, unable to act in any way except sort of cruising through events. They move through this war amazingly un-cognizant. The supposedly comic hubcap, Michael Jello, is a little rubber duck, a banal actor who keeps pushing a curds-and-whey, soppy milk effect. Raking his hair across his forehead à la Buster Langdon, using his limbs like club feet, this actor embodies the stupidity, sadism, and salt of the earth in one compressed shape.

One of the most haunting passages is that of Mike pawing, in Neanderthal fashion, two immobile customers before finding his seat in the Cinéma Méxique. (What's that neon sign about? Your eyes travel up and down for ten seconds trying to locate the hidden political association or anagramlike reference in it.) Buffeted about, climbed over, they never twitch (the effect is the same as the evil-face Kirilov marching over his sleep-paralyzed pals in the *Chinoise* bedroom). More extraordinarily, they don't move, as Michael, now up on the stage, slowly and stupidly and wondrously runs his hands over the screened image of a naked woman, and jumps up and down trying to see over the bathtub rim.

A thing you notice as the movie goes by is that this mid-film passage is the first in which there is a sense of buildings and streets being four-square to the earth. It comes after a swell of off-kilter scenes, lilting girls, and tilting soldiers. This mysteri-ously poetic effect is of a whole movie funneling into a stillborn chamber where a slow somnambulist pace takes over. It should be said about now that *Carabiniers* (French for "Shoot 'Em Naked") is beautiful, the nicest bleak photography since *Wretched Orchard* or *Bleak Blouse*. Rather than being ominous or warlike, this worn-torn allegory is likable and terrestrial:

frozen rivers, empty squares with van Gogh trees, the feeling of boy scouts on a Saturday morning hike, the men uncover their enemies, partisans, like kids would uncover slugs in the undergrowth.

The beautiful people in *Belle de Jour,* a queerly pseudo-Hollywood film, include a wife, pale blond from head to foot, her beefy male-model husband, an urbane Iagoish friend on the sidelines who cynically nudges the wife out of purity and the husband into cuckoldry. A singular trait in this cooly deadpan comedy is the sinister equilibrium in the alignment of these figures with their furniture and possessions.

In *Belle de Jour,* the viewer is apparently directed towards perverse eroticism of the standard types and a modernized *Bovary* story: a pair of patent-leather pumps (Cathérine Deneuve) takes a two-to-five job as a prostitute, supposedly because she wants to try some new moves but feels either shy or uninclined to try them with her Boy Scout doctor husband. This sunlit story, pampered wife driven into prostitution during the hours usually reserved for piano lessons and housework, is filmed with a linear concision, Daliesque clarity, and, like that painter's works, it works well within conventions forty or fifty years old. In the case of the pornography, the conventions are Victorian and earlier: a woman walking the corridor of a grand chateau, naked except for black transparent veils and a lily-of-the-valley wreath, heading for a necrophiliac encounter with a Count (an aged, stretched-out Jean-Pierre Aumont). The count has her lie down in a coffin, and begins an incantation about his deceased daughter before climaxing below the casket. This little pageant, as well as many others, is so well rehearsed and costume-oriented that there is little sexual bite.

"There's one wonderful *maison* that has such marvelous *ésprit de corps,*" enthuses Michel Piccoli, the Iago, murmuring in syphilitic sibilants about Madame Anais's fancy brothel. Truth to be, it's a very stuffy, furniture-cramped apartment, but Cathérine Deadnerve, who plays the wife, flourishes as Carmen-Bite-Me-Daddy until she runs into a possessive jealous client, an international dope-pusher with provincial brass-knuckles teeth. This never-ending thin ingénue is fantastic, the only element of 1968 post-*Blow Up* hip. Sulking, a lot of lip and gnashing, he seems to be on the wrong movie set, pushing through the rooms, trying to find his place in the film.

For such a clear, carefully styled film, *Belle* is a consistently jarring film, one put-on after another. Starting with the mezzo-tint color, a kind of sallow sunlight which throws every shot off kilter, off the realistic, the movie keeps knocking askew each character-actor-situation, going off a little or a lot into the *outré*. What seems like a Who Knows cut, a broadly caricatured death, a standardized fetish, a dreadful gag about geisha credit cards, a lead actress who gets happy at the strangest moments, turns out to be one deadpan twist after another.

The clientele and the staff at the whorehouse, on the surface, seem like mismatches and questionable movie solutions. Seve-rine's two cowhores, Anais's ninnies, are like two sides of the same dismal, unappetizing working-class woman: hard and soft, straight hairdo and Ann-Margaret tease. With each Joker Card client, these two merge and fade out, creating a solid background for Deneuve's golden-girl figurine effect. Unlike these two, who are simply reversed from the expected Mercouri effect, dropped back without causing any excitement at all, the men are an end-less run of assorted sordid weirdos.

The inch-from-convention bedroom innocuities of Séverine and Pierre Serisy have to be a pun on all Hollywood movies: Spencer Tracy and Joan Bennett in neat, expensively sheeted twin beds, the man always wearing white rayon pajamas with blue piping, a pair of white slippers alongside, in between the beds a little table with lamp, clock, and a cup of hot Bovril. There's no blood: when young handsome Meatface asks his wife if he can get in her bed, she says *Non* (Scram, buster, go fuck someone else).

How does one get passionate about a perfection piece like *Belle?*

A few things I left out so far are:

(1) A recitation scene in *Carabiniers*, with a partisan blonde reciting Mayakovsky's poem before the riffraff, the same way she would be doing an oral exam in Russian 1A. Without enu-merating the queernesses of this blasé blonde May Queen in a car coat and old slacks, she picks up the film's hollownesses. When her friend gets knocked down, she runs for shelter in the most

amateurish, no-ferocity manner. The effect that the movie is trying for: to fill her with a frenzied saintliness, like a witch about
to be burned.

(2) The swift, expedient, doesn't-make-it carpentering, which
still has a great deal of shambling charm. The first set starts
out as a small farmhouse with an assortment of chicken coops,
a bathtub, tall fences. While this dazzling Gothic single-room
house, foundationless, shifts around the plot (the better to photograph you, my dear) the movie also finds a new focal point, a
mailbox at shoulder height which is the only manmade item for
desolate miles. The two left-behinds skip to it and home again,
the mailbox drips postcards.

(3) It wouldn't be legit to describe the contaminated spirit
in *Belle de Jour* as being similar to the raunchy, down-and-out
decadent expression normally on the face of a Rolling Stone. In
fact, the movie's studied canterlike pace, its nicely staid-static
images, the complete lack of emotion or drama in its star, or its
photography, are actually the furthest reverse of Mick Jagger's
cruddy, carefully nurtured degeneracy. But this *Eau de Clean*
movie, its actors doused in deodorants and after-shave lotions,
harbors decadence. Also its casting suggests the *Fleurs du Mal*
put-downs that are inherent in a Rolling Stone production.

(4) Deneuve is so objectlike: even as a beauty she is lacking. From head to foot, she's like a porcelain dummy, probably
the most evocative shot of her mechanical-doll act shows her
walking along the edge of a tennis court, forcing herself to be
jaunty, walking with a forced stiff-legged jauntiness. Deneuve
keeps achieving a curiously intriguing detachment, as though
she's on drugs. What's so infuriating about her is actually her
contribution: that she's content to be all surface. Her very un-
rebelliousness, the fact that she stays in place, a contained element among other contained elements, is a large part of what
makes this film so precisioned and polite.

(5) Compared to the nice dappled, three-dimensional impressions of *Les Carabiniers*, *La Chinoise* has a suspicious sideways
movement: the actors and/or cameraman can't retreat or advance one inch. Watching it is like being forced into an insidious,
abnormal work that, sliding sideways, crab fashion, bars progress to its inhabitants, keeps turning the actors whirligig fashion
without revealing anything about them.

LUIS
BUNUEL 1969

His glee in life is a movie of raped virgins and fallen saints, conceived by a literary old-world director detached from his actors but infatuated with his cock-eyed primitive cynicism. It's this combination of detachment and the infatuated-with-bitterness viewpoint, added to a flat-footed technique, that produces the piercingly cold images of *The Exterminating Angel.*

Buñuel reveals a kinship to other moderns: to Godard (the basic feeling that the audience needs educating, and he is just the one to do it), Bresson (they share an absorbed interest in the peasantry and the role of religion in rural life), and the Renoir of *Toni* and *The Lower Depths* (what it is like to be poor). Often he seems to be duplicating Renoir, decades later. The same choked, peeling, dank courtyard through which Louis Jouvet walked in *Lower Depths,* like a halt-footed, bowlegged, giant rooster, is recreated in *Nazarin* long after Renoir's version of Gorky's tale. In *Nazarin,* the setting is characteristically comicalized with three cruddy whores fighting with caricatured abandon over a set of buttons, suggesting stock-company Carmens or Yvette Guilberts painted by a cross-eyed Toulouse-Lautrec. The Spanish workers who try to fix up the estate in *Viridiana* are brothers to the men who live at Marie's boardinghouse in *Toni.* They fit into their village milieu with the same vitality, as natural as animals. Renoir's Spaniards, less wacky by far than Buñuel's, are always in the grip of a human passion, either happy or grief-stricken as lovers, when they're not giving the feeling of hard, conscientious workers.

But more than any other modern, Luis Buñuel is a pariah, locked off by himself, stitching a sort of dank, bitter grotesquerie into a backhandedly charming movie that has an overpowering, haunting involvement with Catholicism. Just as Westbrook Pegler, in his newspaper columns, overpowered his incessant barbs and rancor with a deep love for classy journalism, Buñuel's anti-church movie just seems to give off the wonder and sweetness of being a member of the fold. His slow-cut scene, which stresses a

275

pet Gabrielle Figueroa shot of two sentimental characters standing on a hill with the twilight backlighting them, distressingly
suggests the passion plays put on year after year by R.C. par-
ishes the world over: the scenery suggesting the least talented
of Murillo's street scenes, the same costumes worn by the same
insurance agent who pridefully and possessively takes his role
each Lenten season. These cold movies—the way the shot is
framed and the airless edges, flaccid lighting—are redolent of
religious calendars and the small booklets on the life of Saint
Catherine for sale in the back of the church.

From early in his career—a powerful skin shot, in which a
widow washes her feet while a brash punk, Jaibo (*Los Olvidados*), languorously leans against the doorway and takes in the
act—his characters have suffered a nightmarish lack of privacy
in all their domestic setups, with no refuge from gossip, prying
eyes, nosiness. No secret can be cherished, no man or woman
is allowed to singularize himself for long. The rancor and malice
of the neighbors act to break down their resolves. In *The Exterminating Angel*, his most personal film, the characters exist in
an agony of exposure. All his population, even the fashionable
professional class in *Belle de Jour* or the powerfully rich in
Exterminating Angel, bear the poor man's feeling of being a
prey for anyone who wants to harass him.

In these *danse-macabre* films, it's shocking to see a character
alone, or one, like Cathérine Deneuve in *Belle*, who seems to respect the institution of doors (a wonderfully unexotic hallway
and sequence of embarrassed, fearful moves, suggesting the horror of applying for an unwanted job). One of the funniest
gimmicks in *Nazarin* is the stream of odd occupations and types
that flows through Padré Nazario's open window, either to look
for money, curse him ("You better clear out, Father"), snoop
around, ask him snidely personal questions, bring him tortillas,
and eventually burn his room down to get rid of a whore's
stinking perfume (of all the arson in films, this perfume-destroy-
ing motive is the silliest).

Buñuel's central characters—a happy-go-lucky priest on the
bum, a saintly figure on a platform in the desert—have a yearning to separate themselves, to live a more exalted life than those
around them. They're fervently idealistic and adore making

sacrifices of worldly comfort, while their pals, kinfolk, and enemies conspire to bring them to heel. It's an expected denouement
that a girl sighs, lets down her bunned-up hair, and surrenders
herself to the mob, "Here I am."

Most of the stories—they're about fall guys; it's Buñuel's
theory that if you try to be good, watch out: if a person wants to
spread cheer, wealth, or virtue, the whole community views him
as a sore hangnail they have to amputate—have to do with
complicity, the fact that everyone is the devil whispering "Do
it" in a pal's ear. A sort of preposterously dry comedy goes on
in each shot, having to do with the quick way evil little plots
are hatched: people fall into league with one another as often as
cowboys jump on and off horses in an Allied Artists' Western.
Working for his dinner, Padré Nazario gets a chance to put four
shovels of dirt into his wheelbarrow before his colaborers murderously gang up on him for horning in and undercutting their
wage rate. Most of the movie seems to be retelling old anecdotes,
but all these sudden conspiracies, partnerships, and deals give
the moral-cynical-mocking episodes a ridiculous surprise and
wildness. Every Buñuel film has one elegant actor moving at a
different pace from the others, and, in *Viridiana*, it's a wonderful maid acted by a stately-modest Spanish Jane Greer (this is
an overdue plug for Jane Greer). She lubricates a tedious movie
that needs all the mobility it can get by repeatedly dealing herself into the nearest available plot.

Each movie is a long march through small connected events
(dragged out distressingly to the last moment: just getting the
movie down the wall from a candle to a crucifix takes more time
than an old silent comedy), but it is the sinister fact of a Buñuel
movie that no one is going anywhere and there is never any release at the end of the film. It's one snare after another, so that
the people get wrapped around themselves in claustrophobic
whirlpool patterns.

When it's good—as in *Robinson Crusoe*, where he magically
harmonized with a normally outrageous overactor, Dan O'Her-
lihy—a Buñuel movie has a heady, haunting effect, like an
exquisitely enjoyed meal, the weather of a foreign country,
something private and inexpressible: a favorite pornographic
book. The musky quality comes from a variety of sources, from

the all-round oldness of his lighting and buildings, to the old-fashioned literary quality that flows over each episode: Rabal fishing through his inherited heirlooms, coming across a pearl cross that has a switchblade hidden inside. There's a lot of the dirty old man, a rotting lasciviousness in all Buñuel films. In *Un Chien Andalou*, a man and a woman are having a go at each other. He produces an army of ants out of a deep hand wound, whereupon she retaliates by growing a luxurious patch of hair on her armpit.

Los Olvidados, a turgidly heavy tract on hideous childhood, hasn't enough of the above Daliism (he unfortunately gave up the Dali-type line work early on and didn't revive it until *Belle de Jour*), but it has a heavy aromatic quality, due to Figueroa's tiresomely velvety photography, an occasionally biting image like the one of two performing dogs with some raunchy band music going on, and another scene where he goes light on the standard leftist tract work: Pedro's dream of raw meat. Within a wretched Mexican city of slums, hovels, and street fights, reigns an unforgettably repugnant, corrupt-to-the-core bully—with an irritatingly sparse moustache and languid mannerisms—named Jaibo. Like all Buñuel's villains (Pinto in *Nazarin*, the eyeless beggar in *Viridiana*), he flag-waves his evil, terrorizing children, in particular a spunky twelve-year-old whom he frames with a theft after laying the kid's mother.

Viridiana is a lush, pretentious Jane Eyre story given a heavy illustrational style and sentimental, parasitic characters that are not like Charlotte Brontë at all. The theme, the silliness of virtue, is implanted with a heavy hand, through conventional types like Sylvia Pinal's Snow White, a pure-minded virgin who tries to create a camp for beggars and ends up being raped by two of her more loathesome boarders. She and the syphilitics and unwed mothers, who cut her down when the chance comes, seem slow and drugged as though they were compulsory creations. These are explosions of truly independent work: the ferociously poetic dance done by a transvestite beggar, and a perversely experimental stretch where Buñuel varies a church-art impression of beggars praying in the fields with hard factual shots of construction work going on around the outside of the mansion.

Buñuel has always been a man of fits and starts, and his later career veers back and forth, from the preoccupation with so-called iconoclasm that seems very aware of the Yankee movie-goers (a dextrous, competent movie like *Simon of the Desert*, which is all surface), to more poetic work. *Belle de Jour* is one of his more straightforward films, giving play to his tight, narrow, provincial preoccupation with bondage, subservience. *Exterminating Angel*, a looser, less pretty film than *Belle*, seems the first occasion on which he doesn't attach himself to some convention.

In *Exterminating Angel*, an after-opera party finds itself unable to move out of the sitting room in a Frick Museumlike residence. Very tense, puzzling, sinister, and yet extraordinarily stodgy, this is the least anecdotal Buñuel and the most redolent of the Barrier effect that seems to murmur through his films. Once it is anchored inside the spellbound chamber, the movie becomes increasingly desperate, festering, pock-marked with strange crowdedness, bedding conditions, and particularly with powerful images—a Goyaesque scene of people in soiled, crumpled evening clothes, huddled around a fire built of smashed violins and eighteenth-century furniture, in the center of an elegant sitting room, and gnawing on mutton bones. A young bellowing bear, who makes a sound like a foghorn scraped against a blackboard, careens around the front hall, climbs a pillar, and swings on a chandelier with hard-to-identify menace. What powers these scenes is a new, more modern, Buñuel esthetic. The moral lesson is no longer encircled, and the tone is no longer so obvious: instead of criticizing outward conditions, it points inward. Excoriation is the point, but, as in all Buñuel at his best, the movie goes in a linear, imaginative direction, picking bits of subject matter that have been in his movies before but now seem encrusted with doubt, suspicion, and what amounts to creative self-torture. The same material poked out of other movies as far back as *El* when the jealous, envy-ridden husband zigzags up an elegant stairway knocking his cane in a tormented way against the stairs and balustrade.

One slant into his limitations is through his cutting, which, in each event, is delayed to the last possible moment but produces the only actual movement in the film. In *Nazarin*, he does as much as he can within the frame, but there isn't much action within any single shot (inept actors talking), and the frame itself becomes an enclosure within which he pays obeisance to a familiar "liberalism" and certain story-telling conventions favored in church art. Until his show of independence in *Exterminating Angel* and Gallic works (*Belle de Jour, Robinson Crusoe, Diary of a Chambermaid*), where he gives rein to an elegance and handsomeness that had been suppressed in consciously "unpretentious, profound" work (*Viridiana*, etc.) that made him a great favorite in America, he is irritatingly submissive to a moral narrative style. Buñuel translates his material through a leaden pedanticism that hides the narrow, provincial quality of his talent with underlined sentimental evidences of depravity, cruelty that shouldn't dismay any traditionalists in the church.

In a sort of entertaining old-Buñuel film, strong images occur only as a kind of explosion from the orthodox, sedentary way he moves through slime and crime. This kind of orgasmic burst of poetic styling after socioreligious conventionalism happens in *Nazarin*, when a limpid goody type, who might be Betty Compson playing Peter Pan, reacts erotically to the intermural fight between two whores. This imaginatively choreographed hallucination, from a weird eyelid fluttering to an orgiastic backbend on the bar floor, has a crushing dynamism compared to Buñuel's stodgier, normal style with sex: a seduction in an attic crowded with broken furniture. Buñuel typically overexplains the halting, sluggish mystery of this *Viridiana* scene, with its dirty old man feeling of not really being with it, by capping it with a mattress shot of a cat leaping on a rat. The symbol is as pedantically stitched in as the limply overstated facial work between Rabal and the maid.

The tremendous reputation that has accrued from exoticism and religious-toned "primitivism" mimics the safe route Buñuel has taken as a celebrity, from working in Franco Spain through a long span as an easily identified leftist. His bizarre films, airless and dank, a lot of perverse, festering plants in them, give the feeling of a hothouse. The best way to suggest this hothouse is to describe his handling of some of his actors; the princely Hotspurish Rabal, the puzzlingly inexpressive

Pinal, whose mystery, like that of the miscast Deneuve in *Belle de Jour*, comes from a clogged effect of a passive surface, a blond beauty who moves like a grandmother. These main characters (there's a good, more hesitant one playing the transvestite uncle in the *Viridiana* opening) are blander, cleaner, more straight up and down than the excessively picturesque bit players: Father Nazario's cell mates, the beggars in *Viridiana*. Buñuel, who always seems in a dark closet of privacy, like a nobleman sitting back and watching his vassals climb all over each other, hardly directs these conceived-in-sentimentality actors who don't punch so much as crawl and fester.

However, the fancy people holed up in the music room of *The Exterminating Angel*—professional society types; the women, crushed in boned evening gowns; the men, a little too old, paunchy Don Juans in opera clothes; the very outfits that would be most insufferable if you were forced to keep them on for two months—literally give off a steam of sweat, ill temper, physical disgust, a remarkable intensity of discomfort that hasn't been seen before in movies. The standard leftism is nowhere apparent in these shots where Buñuel doesn't try to gloss his vision and imagination, where he exposes himself in relation to Franco Spain, the Church, whomever he worked for. He seems to admit his stylistic limitations, the past compromises, in powerful images where often three look-alikes are in a strange shot, grousing at each other, sort of escaping cognition. The people lined up in the doorway, staring out as though across a great expanse of empty, messed-up existence, while all types of garbage is piled up outside their escapeless room, suggest that the director has finally departed the obvious, weary, message-laden work that made him more of a commercial-minded director than anyone suggested.

INDEX OF FILM TITLES

INDEX OF NAMES

DATE DUE

DEMCO 38-297